JILLIAN HARRIS   TORI WESSZER

FRAICHE FO♥D
FULLER HEARTS

Wholesome Everyday Recipes
Made with Love

PENGUIN

an imprint of Penguin Canada, a division of Penguin Random House Canada Limited

Canada • USA • UK • Ireland • Australia • New Zealand • India • South Africa • China

First published 2023

Copyright © 2023 Jillian Harris and Tori Wesszer

www.penguinrandomhouse.ca

Library and Archives Canada Cataloguing in Publication

Title: Fraiche food, fuller hearts : wholesome everyday recipes made with love /Jillian Harris and Tori Wesszer.
Names: Harris, Jillian, author. | Wesszer, Tori, author.
Description: Includes index.
Identifiers: Canadiana (print) 20220407495 | Canadiana (ebook) 20220407509 |
ISBN 9780735240780 (hardcover) | ISBN 9780735240797 (EPUB)
Subjects: LCSH: Pescatarian cooking. | LCSH: Vegetarian cooking. |
LCSH: Vegan cooking. |LCGFT: Cookbooks.
Classification: LCC TX837 .H376 2023 | DDC 641.5/636—dc23

Cover and interior design by Kelly Hill
Food and Prop Styling by Jillian Harris, Tori Wesszer, Team Jilly, and Team Fraîche
Photography by Rachelle Beatty

Printed in China

10   9   8   7   6   5   4   3   2   1

Penguin
Random House
PENGUIN CANADA

WE'D LIKE TO RESPECTFULLY ACKNOWLEDGE that we live, work, and cook on the traditional, unceded territory of the Okanagan Syilx People. We recognize, honour, and respect the presence of Indigenous people, past, present, and future.

Our heritage includes a mix of Ukrainian, German, French, and English. Marrying into Hungarian, Italian, and Irish has given us exposure and insight into a variety of cultures and cuisines, which you will find reflected in many of the recipes we share. A legacy of family gatherings centred on good food is something that was proudly passed down to both of us. This cookbook also includes many recipes that have been inspired by cultures other than our own. We recognize that food is an important part of people's identities and should be treated with respect. In creating this cookbook, we have appreciated the opportunity to deepen our learning of the traditions, history, and regional ingredients behind some of our favourite cultural cuisines. We hope you love our versions of these recipes, and we encourage you to explore the authentic recipes and beautiful cultures that inspired them.

To our incredible moms, Peggy and Patsy,
who have been a never-ending source of love, inspiration,
support, and giggles. You have taught us how to be strong,
kind, creative, and fearless women. We are forever grateful.
Thank you for giving us the gift of a childhood filled with
endless adventures together and loving memories.
The world needs more women like you.

Contents

Introduction

It has been four years since our first cookbook, *Fraiche Food, Full Hearts*, hit the shelves. It feels like yesterday! One look at the sweet family pictures we captured in the book is evidence of how quickly time passes. At that time, Jillian was pregnant with Annie and constantly on the road travelling for work and Tori was juggling life with two young kids while moving four (yes, four) times over the course of writing the cookbook. It was messy and chaotic, a process filled with love and tears, but oh what a feeling to open our very first copy.

As the two gals (we are cousins but grew up like sisters) in our family who play hostess the most to our crew, our debut into the world of cookbooks was centred on entertaining and family gatherings, which seemed completely fitting. *Fraiche Food, Full Hearts*, our first labour of love and dedicated to our legend of a grandma, was all that and more. Our own dog-eared, food-splattered copies are still proudly displayed in each of our kitchens, and our hearts still do a pitter-patter each time we pass a copy for sale in a bookstore. We hope that *pinch me* moment never goes away.

When we talked about what we wanted to accomplish in this second cookbook, giving you the gift of time rose to the top of the priority list. When we create recipes, we picture the busy lives we know many of you have, whether you are parents, professionals, or students trying to fit it all in. With this in mind, these recipes were created to be as simple as possible without compromising the result. Could three steps be combined into one? Was that impossible-to-find fancy ingredient truly necessary? Is there any way to reuse leftovers from one recipe to create another and reduce the amount of food waste and time spent in the kitchen?

Fraiche Food, Fuller Hearts is filled with everyday recipes that leverage fresh, readily available whole foods. We made the recipes plant-forward with adaptations for 100 percent vegan versions wherever possible. Recipes were designed to be family-friendly and perfect for weekday or casual weekend meals. We also included a robust section of homemade staples such as a simple freezer-friendly Applesauce (page 313) that will leave your house smelling amazing, an easy Sheet-Pan Tomato Sauce (page 314), and your very own Vegan Ranch Dressing (page 327).

Cooking for a family can sometimes feel like mission impossible. We get it. In this book, we've included tips for modifying recipes to fit different dietary needs along with suggestions for easy ways to make recipes more kid-friendly. We've created these recipes to be delicious, satisfying, and anything but bland. Note that the level of heat in our recipes tends to land at the lower end of the scale to make everyone at the dinner table happy (assuming that is even possible!). If you prefer a spicier dish, we encourage you to dial it up to taste!

We are forever grateful to family, friends, and other beautiful humans who either helped us create some of these recipes or allowed us to include their recipes to share with you. Throughout the book, you'll read about these wonderful folks and the impact they have had on our food journey.

Just like in our first cookbook, we did our best to make this cookbook as plant-forward as possible. Our food philosophy remains the same and embraces the idea that there is no downside to eating more plants. The environment, and your body, will thank you. If you are new to plant-based eating or are just trying to include more plant-forward options, this book is a great place to start. Most recipes can be adapted to include a plant-based protein where it isn't the default, but note there are rare exceptions, such as Chicken Paprikash with Nokedli (page 171) and Patsy's Fried Fish (page 190).

Within these pages, we've created over 135 plant-forward recipes to fill your kitchens and hearts. Our hope is that your cookbooks end up looking like ours over the years, with your favourite pages worn and wrinkled, earning their places in your regular recipe rotation. With the world moving at lightning speed, the value and comfort that a home-cooked meal brings cannot be overrated.

What a true honour it is for us to have the chance to create another cookbook for you! Thank you so very much for bringing it into your home. We truly hope that every bite and sip brings you and your loved ones joy. After all, food is love.

Note from Jillian

When Tori and I were approached to write our first cookbook, I was thrilled and so honoured, but a part of me was reluctant to take on the project. Although I have always dreamed of being an author and having my very own cookbook, I was juggling so much at that time. I had just had Leo, was travelling between two cities for work, was filming not *one* but *two* TV shows, plus we were renovating our home and I was running my business over at JillianHarris.com. I was *maxed* out, and that beautiful work/life balance was pretty much non-existent. But I didn't want to pass on the opportunity, so Tori and I took on the challenge of writing *Fraiche Food, Full Hearts*.

Looking back now, I am so grateful we made that decision. The book was such a labour of love, filled with so many amazing memories, and has truly become an heirloom in our family. *Fraiche Food, Full Hearts* made its way into thousands of homes and brought joy into the kitchens of many, including our own. A copy never leaves my kitchen counter—I still look at it in complete awe. All of our favourite family recipes are between the covers, including our Boomba's famous beet rolls. *What a dream!*

So much time, energy, love, sweat, tears, testing (and retesting) went into each and every single recipe. In fact, when we *finally* completed *Fraiche Food, Full Hearts*, I remember looking at Tori and saying, "Okay, that was fun, but let's never do it again!"

Yet here I am, writing a note to introduce our second cookbook! I feel that writing a cookbook is similar to childbirth. You kind of forget about what you went through the first time around and then suddenly, you're right back into it after vowing to never do it again. Months of growing, groaning, aching, and (almost!) breaking. But then it's all over! You *finally* get to hold that baby in your arms and bring it home! You forget the aches and pains and remember only the beauty of it all. Then you start thinking about making another, and history repeats itself. That's pretty much what happened here. That is my relationship with cookbooks!

With this second book, I was worried we wouldn't be able to muster up enough new recipes. And more importantly, how would I find the time? Since the first book was published, Justin and I welcomed a second baby into our family, sweet Annie (who I was pregnant with while writing our first book). With two kids and two rambunctious dogs in tow, Justin and I bought a farm, started two new businesses, and, like everyone else in this world, have been trying our best to navigate a global pandemic. Not to mention, our beloved Boomba had passed away since the last cookbook. (We dedicated it to her, though she never got to see a copy.) Little did we know, everything that was transpiring in our lives would give us the inspiration we needed for our second cookbook.

Both Tori and I were desperately holding on to our Boomba's legacy and reflecting on those "good ol' days" so much. I started thinking about how I could bring that same magic into our very busy lives now. I wanted to create something that would allow our Boomba's legacy to live on. I started thinking about conversations we had in the past, where she would talk about her farm and how much she loved it, and now Justin and I have *our* very own farm. We had our own little piece of magic *just* like hers. She would be in her glory if she saw it and how we spend our time there: around the campfire, cozying up inside by the woodstove, and making sweet memories.

I knew there was a way we could bring that old-fashioned nostalgic home cooking—this time with fresh, local (and even homegrown!) food—into our bustling lives in a way that was quick and easy. Those recipes that instantly transport you back to your childhood, when things seemed a little simpler, don't have to remain locked in the past.

Tori and I started to brainstorm what we wanted this cookbook to be. In fact, our first brainstorming session was at our farm, on a chilly spring day, in our winter jackets around a campfire. Our first book was all about celebrations—the big family gatherings that we now missed so much. The pandemic had changed that and so much more. We started talking about our everyday favourites, and some of our old-fashioned classic recipes inspired by the quick and easy '80s hacks our moms and granny used to throw together in a pinch, and the globally inspired recipes that we love and are eager to share with you!

Tori and I hit the ground running, and over the months of recipe testing and shooting the photography, I still had fears that this cookbook wouldn't be as special as the first. But as I sit here today looking at the more than 100 recipes we have created and re-created for you over the past two years, I am *floored* by how it all came together. I am so excited, and I'm proud of every recipe in the book.

We hope that this cookbook allows you to find joy in those everyday moments. *Fraiche Food, Fuller Hearts* is for everyone, no matter your household size or dietary restrictions. It is about sharing our love of cooking, about easy adaptations and hacks to make your life simpler, and about leaving more time for you to pamper yourself and spend time with the ones you love.

Thank you for being a part of our family and for following along on our journey. Now let's get cooking!

xo

Jilly

Note from Tori

My mom recently asked me if I ever get sick of cooking. I pondered a moment, and realized that no, I really don't. Even on my days "off" you will find me in the kitchen. Creating food and feeding others is my happy place. It always has been.

On any given day in our house, you'll find the music cranked with me and my husband Charles grooving to old country classics or Etta James, cooking or baking away, experimenting, testing, and sipping wine or coffee, depending on the hour. As a child, many evenings were spent catering my parent's parties, baking our family's holiday goodies along with extras for friends and neighbours, or packing lunches for road trips to make sure everyone was fed. In university, I was the gal baking my friends massive pans of banana bread in their dorm kitchens or getting creative with my little toaster oven in my tiny dorm room (I snuck it in, such a rebel) and wandering around grocery stores for hours like others do at museums.

I have always been game for a good adventure, and I jumped at my first chance to travel, alone, to France, where my eyes were opened to a different way of cooking and eating. It was love at first bite: the markets filled with fresh, vibrant ingredients, the habit of buying only what you needed for that day or that meal, and the passion surrounding food were life-changing to witness. I noticed this same approach to cooking and eating in other countries as well, giving me reason to reflect on what I wanted to bring to the world of food back home in Canada. This beautiful way of living, cooking, and eating now serves as my own compass. I realize now that it is a very similar food philosophy that our sweet Boomba embraced with so much love, and one that we had drifted away from. Feeding others was her greatest joy, a gift that she graciously passed on to me through years of rolling beet rolls and making homemade pierogies with those beautifully wrinkled hands.

Fast-forward to now. As a mom of two boys, my goal is for our home to be "that house": the one where you go to hang out any day of the week and where fresh homemade food is always on hand with an "open fridge" policy. Food is my love language. If I could feed the world, I would do so in a heartbeat. Knowing that this isn't possible, the next best thing is creating a cookbook filled with recipes that will give you that same "food hug" that I wish I could hand-deliver to each of you!

Since writing our first cookbook, much has changed in the world. Comfort, for me and others, has risen to the top of my personal priority list. And what better way to bring comfort than through food? With a cookbook all about entertaining under our belts, writing another to help you create comforting food in the kitchen felt like a natural next step.

Much like Jillian, I too had my reservations about jumping into another cookbook. At the same time that I was scheduled to write this book, our team was also creating the foundation for our online meal plan, Fraîche Table, churning out over 1500 new recipes in the same year. All this on top of our typical two-a-week recipe cadence on FraicheLiving.com. My brain hurt. Did we possibly have enough new ideas and recipes to fill a whole new cookbook? The answer, I'm happy to say, was yes.

While the world of nutrition seems to change daily, my own food philosophy hasn't changed much in the past twenty years. As a dietitian, I continue to be humbled seeing just how much trends have changed over the decades, swinging from the low-fat/high-carb movement of the '90s to the keto revolution of this decade. I have long since settled into a space where, when it comes to food, balance, moderation, and quality reign supreme, and it can all fit. Healthy eating shouldn't feel extreme. If there is one thing we have learned, it is that life is short and precious. Food is to be both enjoyed and nourishing, and I firmly believe that it doesn't have to be one or the other. Have your cake and eat it too! (I recommend our Peaches and Cream Layer Cake on page 265.) I hope that our cookbook nourishes you and your families in every single way possible and gives you all the food hugs we could all use right now.

xo

Tori

About This Book

Fraiche Food, Fuller Hearts was designed for everyday cooking, filled with easy-to-make plant-forward weekday meals and casual weekend fare. We are two busy working moms with young families, and this cookbook is a true reflection of how we eat and feed our loved ones, emphasizing fresh whole foods and family-friendly dishes. We even included a few kid-friendly drinks! Inside you'll find over 135 recipes organized in these familiar categories:

Breakfasts: Family-friendly breakfasts including Carrot Cake Breakfast Cookies (page 35), French Toast Sticks (page 43), and Jilly's Breakfast Sandwiches (page 39).

Baking and Bread: We simplified the joy of baking with cozy, easy-to-follow recipes such as a no-fuss No-Knead Bread (page 79), Magic Dough (page 67—one dough, so many ways to use it!), and a Beer Bread (page 64).

Appetizers: Nibbles that are great on their own, served before or alongside a main dish. Many make a great light lunch, or a snack to curb hunger when it strikes, or are perfect for popping into a lunchbox. The recipes range from Creamy Buffalo Chick'n Dip (page 91), Sweet and Spicy Vegan Lettuce Wraps (page 125), Loaded Hummus (with variations; page 113), and Pita Crisps (page 117).

Salads and Soups: Enjoy nourishing and delicious salads like our Grilled Romaine Salad with Roasted Tomatoes (page 136) and Spring Garden Salad (page 140). Cozy soups such as our Lentil Soup (page 151) and Broccoli Cheeze Soup (page 152) are sure-fire hits.

Main Dishes: Vibrant and hearty main dishes are the star of the table. We included our family's classic dishes that have been passed down through generations, such as Patsy's Fried Fish (page 190), along with fun veggie-packed dishes such as our Tortilla Pie (page 203), and Butternut Squash Gyros (page 167).

Veggies and Sides: The side dishes are arguably the most important part of the meal, which is why we put so much love into creating satisfying recipes, including Salt and Vinegar Potatoes (page 237), Sweet and Spicy Green Beans (page 221), and our favourite, Lazy Cabbage Rolls (page 222).

Desserts: We had so much fun creating a collection of mouthwatering desserts that we know you will love! Try our Baked Apples with Oat Crumble (page 254) for a cozy treat, whip up a batch of Blender Blondies (page 250) right in your blender, or try our Peaches and Cream Layer Cake (page 265) for a total showstopper!

Drinks: Whether you are looking for a coffee with a twist, celebrating a special occasion, or just wrapping up a long day, our drink recipes have got you covered. Start your day off with a Banana Coconut Latte (page 301) or clink your glasses with a pitcher of our Okanagan Sangria (page 292).

Staples: If you enjoy making your own staples, try our one-step Sheet-Pan Tomato Sauce (page 314) that doubles as a pizza sauce, make a batch of simple Chia Jam (page 310) to elevate your next breakfast of pancakes, or try our Quick Pickled Red Onions (page 320) that we promise you will have on repeat.

At the beginning of each recipe, we give dietary and freezer-friendly indicators when applicable:

Vegan: The recipe does not contain any animal products such as meat, eggs, fish, dairy, or honey.

Vegetarian: The recipe does not contain any meat, chicken, or fish, but may contain dairy products or eggs.

Dairy-free: The recipe does not contain dairy products.

Gluten-free: The recipe does not contain gluten. Be sure to read labels to make sure you are using certified gluten-free ingredients.

Nut-free: The recipe does not include any tree nuts.

Freezer-friendly: The recipe can be stored in a resealable container and frozen for up to one month or as indicated in the recipe.

Most recipes have a dietary adaptation option. We did our best to provide options to modify the recipes wherever possible, including options to adapt almost all of our plant-forward recipes for 100 percent vegan versions. We recognize that not everyone eats the same and that food intolerances, preferences, and allergies are not always simple to navigate (speaking from experience here!). And let's not even get started on picky toddlers. Spice levels of dishes, where applicable, can be adjusted according to your taste; we provide a range for these recipes.

Eat More Plants

Plants are the root of healthy eating—pun intended! One of the simplest yet most impactful pieces of nutrition advice that has stood the test of time: fill half your plate with vegetables and fruit. And with the trend toward plant-based diets, there has never been a more exciting time in history to eat more plants.

Plant foods in their whole forms are nutrition powerhouses, loaded with fibre, water, vitamins, minerals, and phytonutrients. When these foods form the backbone of your diet, you're already winning. Remember that it doesn't have to be all or nothing. While going vegan may be the path for some people, we encourage those of you who aren't in that camp to think of plant-based eating as more of a sliding scale. Try leaning into it, have fun, and see where it takes you! Consider starting with a more familiar dish, such as our Walnut Veggie "Ragu" with Rigatoni (page 208) or Baked Crispy Cauliflower Sandwiches (page 165). Or if something sweet tickles your fancy, give our Blender Blondies (page 250) a try.

Wherever you're at in your food journey, one thing is for sure: it must be convenient. Stocking your kitchen with plant-based staples that can be transformed into quick meals or ready-to-eat snacks is key. Our Kitchen and Pantry Staples guide (page 20) provides a solid list of such staples that we lean on during our busy weeks. Recipes such as our Classic Chickpea Hummus (page 110) with Pita Crisps (page 117) or a sweet snack like our Birdie Bars (page 60) are ideal for making ahead and having on hand to crush hunger in a pinch.

Knowing that food isn't one-size-fits-all, we include options to flex recipes wherever possible to meet a variety of dietary needs, from vegan to gluten-free. We hope these simple modifications help you enjoy our recipes with ease so that you can spend more time eating with those you love and less time stressing in the kitchen!

Fraiche Food, Less Waste

Reducing food waste is a priority for us. An astronomical amount of food gets thrown out each year, and a lot of that is household waste—2.3 million tonnes of it in Canada according to the National Zero Waste Council. What an opportunity to make a change! There are a number of ways you can reduce your own food waste to help save the environment, not to mention your wallet.

We included an A-to-Z Fruit and Veggie Freezer Guide (page 335) to give you ideas for reducing food waste in your own kitchen. Creative ways to use up food scraps can be found in recipes such as Carrot-Top Pesto (page 305) and Broccoli Cheeze Soup (page 152), which uses all parts of the broccoli. In keeping with this mission, we have included two sample meal-planned weeks (page 332) complete with suggested recipes that work well together to help take the stress off your plates (literally and figuratively).

We also suggest ways to repurpose leftovers to reduce food waste and time spent in the kitchen. For instance, leftovers of our Baked Apples with Oat Crumble (page 254) can be blended with milk and ice to create an incredible apple pie smoothie, and in the unlikely case that there is leftover Mushroom Risotto (page 189), it can be turned into the most amazing Mushroom Arancini (page 99).

Meal Planning Tips

Meal planning doesn't have to be complicated or stressful. Taking a half-hour to map out the plan for the upcoming week will save so much time, stress, and money. Reducing extra trips to the grocery store and prepping a few key ingredients ahead can free up hours in your week. Here are a handful of tips for you to follow to make your life easier, at least as far as cooking goes! As a place to start, we have put together a two-week meal plan using our recipes (page 332).

Prep Day. One day a week, try making one or two meals for lunches for the week that keep well, one or two meals for breakfast, and freezing any fresh ingredients that won't keep for more than a few days (not all are freezer-friendly). To make healthy eating convenient, make up a container of cut-up fresh vegetables for veggies and dip, and make a salad with hearty ingredients that will last a few days.

Keep Basics on Hand. If you've forgotten to meal-plan, or don't have time (it happens!), try buying the following:

- two proteins (such as tofu, beans, chicken, fish)
- three starches (such as quinoa, rice, pasta, potatoes)
- four vegetables (such as spinach, carrots, sweet peppers, zucchini)

These ingredients will give you the ammunition you need to create a variety of dishes throughout the week, like stir-fries, soups, pasta dishes, and salads. Frozen vegetables are just as nutritious as fresh and help make healthy eating convenient.

Batch Cooking and Freezing. Investing a few hours in batch cooking freezer-friendly meals can be an absolute lifesaver. Make a double batch of Sheet-Pan Tomato Sauce (page 314), Applesauce (page 313), or Fruit Crumble Muffins (page 57) and freeze extras for those busy days ahead. Make it fun by including the family or inviting a friend to cook along with you, multiplying the recipe (and the joy) to make cooking even easier.

Keep a Well-Stocked Pantry. A lot of meals can be made in a pinch just from pantry staples. Canned chickpeas can be transformed into delicious creamy Classic Chickpea Hummus (page 110), canned lentils make a satisfying Lentil Soup (page 151), and oats, nuts, and seeds can be baked into hearty Top Secret Granola (page 54).

Rotate the Same Menu. While you may feel pressure to always cook something new, there is nothing wrong with keeping a solid rotation of the same meals that you know your family loves! We include two sample meal-planned weeks using our recipes (page 332) to give you inspiration, but we suggest creating your own and mixing things up only when you want to. So everyone stays involved, ask those that you are cooking for to help choose the recipes!

Use a List App for Groceries. Many phone apps allow multiple people to use the same list, which is a beautiful thing when it comes to planning for grocery shopping. Everyone on the list can add to it as they wish, and the list updates in real time as the person doing the shopping ticks items off it. We've found this to be a big time saver!

Repurpose Leftovers. Getting creative with leftovers is a game changer in the kitchen. Many leftovers can be transformed into a brand-new dish, reducing food waste and saving you time. You can easily make a soup out of leftover Steamed Cauliflower and Cheeze Sauce (page 217) or Peaches and Creamed Corn (page 233) by simply adding some stock and a splash of milk before heating and blending. Leftover Pull-Apart Garlic Bread Biscuits (page 87) can be toasted for a delicious breakfast sandwich the next day or cut up and baked for a unique crouton for topping a hot bowl of soup like our Autumn Rice Soup (page 148).

Publish the Plan. Write it down! Writing down your menu plan helps keep you organized, and having it front and centre in your kitchen or dining area will give everyone line of sight to the menu for the week ahead.

Kitchen and Pantry Staples

A well-stocked pantry and kitchen will make a world of difference to your cooking game. While these are merely suggestions, they will most likely help make your life easier (at least in the kitchen!). Here are some of the ingredients and tools that we recommend you keep on hand. We pride ourselves in using ingredients that are easy to find at mainstream supermarkets or at local culture-specific grocery stores, but the internet can be counted on if all else fails.

FATS
Extra-virgin olive oil
Avocado oil
Sesame oil
Vegetable oil
Vegan butter (sticks)
Virgin coconut oil

NUTS, SEEDS, AND BUTTERS
Raw cashews
Whole raw almonds
Sliced raw almonds
Raw pecans
Walnuts
Chia seeds
Ground flaxseed
Hemp seeds
Pumpkin seeds
Sesame seeds
Almond butter
Peanut butter (natural)
Tahini

SPICES
(Purchase spices in small amounts to keep them as fresh as possible.)
Allspice (ground)
Black pepper
Cayenne pepper
Chili powder
Cinnamon (ground and sticks)
Cumin (ground)
Curry powder
Dried oregano
Garam masala
Garlic powder
Ginger (ground and fresh)
Nutmeg (ground)
Onion powder
Paprika (sweet)
Salt (sea salt, table salt, fleur de sel, Himalayan black salt aka kala namak)
Turmeric

CANNED AND BOTTLED GOODS
Vegetarian stock concentrates (we like the Better Than Bouillon Vegetarian No Beef and No Chicken soup bases)
Vegetable stock
Beans (black beans, chickpeas)
Full-fat coconut milk and coconut cream
Corn kernels
Diced tomatoes
Tomato paste
Hot sauce
Soy sauce (low-sodium recommended)
Vinegar (white vinegar, apple cider vinegar, white wine vinegar, red wine vinegar, unseasoned rice vinegar)

REFRIGERATED ITEMS
Almond milk (unsweetened)
Oat milk (unsweetened)
Fresh cilantro
Fresh flat-leaf parsley
Fresh dill
Fresh basil
Fresh rosemary
Fresh thyme
Fresh sage
Extra-firm and firm tofu
Mayonnaise (vegan)
Dijon mustard
Yellow mustard
Dill pickles
Capers
Cheese or vegan cheese (cheddar, mozzarella, feta)

FROZEN ITEMS
Frozen corn
Frozen peas
Frozen chopped spinach
Ice cream (dairy-free if desired)
Coconut whipped topping
Puff pastry
Phyllo pastry

MENU

MONDAY   TUESDAY

WEDNESDAY   THURSDAY

DRY GOODS

Nutritional yeast
Active dry yeast
Pasta
Green lentils
Quinoa
Old-fashioned oats
Flour (unbleached all-purpose
    and whole wheat)
1:1 gluten-free flour blend
    (if gluten-free required)
Baking powder
Baking soda
Rice
Cocoa powder
Coconut (unsweetened shredded)
Coconut ribbons (from the bulk
    store)
Cornstarch
Panko
Raisins (we use sultana)
Soy curls
Nuts and seeds (variety)

FRUITS AND VEGETABLES

Bananas
Apples
Lemons
Limes
Onions (yellow, red, green)
Garlic
Potatoes (russet, baby)
Carrots
Celery
Kale
Spinach
Tomatoes

SWEETENERS

Pure maple syrup
Brown rice syrup
Pure liquid honey
Medjool dates
Sugar (white cane, brown,
    coconut)

WINE

(Only use wine you would actually
drink. We used Sandhill wines in
our recipes, but use a different
brand if those are not available
in your area.)
Dry red wine
Dry white wine

BAKING TOOLS

Rolling pin
Parchment paper
Aluminum foil
Paper muffin liners
13 × 9-inch (3.5 L) ceramic or
    glass baking dish
8-inch (2 L) baking pan (square
    and round)
9-inch (2.5 L) baking dish
Pie plate
Quiche dish
Loaf pan
18 × 13-inch (45 × 33 cm) large
    baking sheets (half-sheet pan)
Muffin tin
Hand-held electric mixer or stand
    mixer
Spring-release cookie scoops in
    various sizes
Rubber spatula
Kitchen scale

COOKING TOOLS

Wooden spoons
Wire whisk
Soup ladle
Chef's knife (the best you can
    afford): a 6-inch (15 cm) is our
    preference
Paring knife
Bread knife

Vegetable peeler
Garlic press
Heavy-bottomed pots
Cast-iron frying pan
Nonstick frying pan
High-speed blender
Immersion blender
Food processor (and a mini
    version)
Citrus juicer
Microplane zester
Colander and mesh sieve
Potato ricer
Waffle maker
Ice-cream maker
Nokedli maker (Hungarian noodle
    maker)
Instant-read thermometer
Cocktail shaker

A NOTE ON TEMPERATURES AND MEASUREMENTS

All recipes have been tested in
a gas oven using Fahrenheit
temperatures with Celsius con-
versions. Ovens vary, so for best
results, use our visual descrip-
tions as the first indicator of
doneness instead of relying on
the times given in the recipe.

Breakfasts

Breakfast Burritos

Vegan option • Vegetarian • Gluten-free option • Nut-free option • Freezer-friendly

Serves 4 to 6

Prep time: 30 minutes

Cook time: 15 minutes

Veggie Tofu Scramble

⅓ cup (75 mL) unsweetened non-dairy milk

1 teaspoon (5 mL) apple cider vinegar

2 tablespoons (30 mL) nutritional yeast

1 tablespoon (15 mL) cornstarch

½ to 1 teaspoon (2 to 5 mL) Himalayan black salt

¼ teaspoon (1 mL) ground turmeric

1 tablespoon (15 mL) butter or vegan butter

1 cup (250 mL) finely chopped yellow onion

1 clove garlic, minced

1 package (12 ounces/350 g) firm or extra-firm tofu, drained

4 to 6 large flour tortillas, warmed

Fillings (optional)

1 batch Veggie Ground (page 309)

Sliced avocado

Grated cheddar cheese or vegan cheddar

Sour cream or vegan sour cream

Roughly chopped fresh cilantro

Pico de Gallo (page 329) or salsa

Spicy Mayo, Sriracha or chipotle variation (page 328)

Grab-and-go breakfasts have been complete lifesavers for our busy families, so wrapping delicious fillings up in a tortilla is always a win. We recommend using flour tortillas for this recipe, because they are larger and more pliable than corn tortillas. Homemade flour tortillas are popular in northern Mexico, which is better suited for growing wheat rather than corn. Ideal for wrapping food (and for carrying), flour tortillas are fundamental to making quesadillas, chimichangas, and burritos. Which brings us to these delicious burritos.

These Breakfast Burritos are the very best thing to batch cook on a weekend for the week ahead. Freeze them individually wrapped in resealable containers for a heat-and-go breakfast; just leave out the toppings that don't heat well (such as avocado and sour cream).

We used tofu instead of eggs, and this recipe's method for cooking the tofu yields a soft, egg-like texture. Himalayan black salt, also known as kala namak, is a kiln-fired rock salt with a pungent, sulphurous smell that gives the tofu an eggy flavour. It can be found at most health food stores or online. To add some extra greens to your breakfast burrito, throw a couple of handfuls of spinach into the hot tofu and stir until wilted.

1. MAKE THE VEGGIE TOFU SCRAMBLE: In a large mason jar (or similar container with a lid), combine the milk, apple cider vinegar, nutritional yeast, cornstarch, black salt, and turmeric. Seal the jar and shake until blended. Set aside.

2. Melt the butter in a large nonstick frying pan over medium heat. Add the onions and cook, stirring occasionally, until soft and translucent, 3 to 4 minutes. Add the garlic and cook, stirring constantly, until fragrant but not browned, 1 to 2 minutes. Crumble the tofu into the pan, stir to combine, and cook for another 1 to 2 minutes to heat the tofu through.

3. Pour the milk mixture into the pan and stir to combine. Cook, stirring occasionally, for 2 to 3 minutes or until heated through and the liquid has evaporated.

Recipe continues

4. ASSEMBLE THE BURRITOS: Lay a tortilla on a work surface. Place a scoop of **Veggie Tofu Scramble** in the centre of the tortilla. Add the desired fillings to the centre of the tortilla, being careful not to overfill. Fold the edge closest to you just over the filling, fold in both sides, and then roll it up. Repeat with the remaining burritos.

5. Enjoy immediately or wrap each burrito individually in plastic wrap or foil and store in the fridge for up to 4 days or in the freezer for up to 1 month. To reheat the burritos, either microwave (remove foil or plastic wrap first if used) or place in a 350°F (180°C) oven until heated through.

Vegan: Use vegan butter, vegan sour cream, and vegan cheese.

Gluten-free: Use gluten-free tortillas.

Nut-free: Use oat milk or other nut-free milk. Omit the Veggie Ground or use a store-bought nut-free veggie ground sausage.

Good Morning Smoothie

Vegan option • Vegetarian • Gluten-free option • Nut-free option

Serves 2

Prep time: 5 minutes

1 cup (250 mL) frozen fruit (peaches, pineapple, mango, pears, green grapes, apples, oranges)

1 frozen banana

½ cup (125 mL) coconut water

1 cup (250 mL) unsweetened non-dairy milk

1 teaspoon (5 mL) pure vanilla extract

1 tablespoon (15 mL) hemp hearts

1 tablespoon (15 mL) chia seeds

Optional Smoothie Add-Ins

Natural nut butter

Old-fashioned rolled oats

Coconut oil

Ground flaxseed

Soft or silken tofu

Fresh or frozen uncooked cauliflower florets

Sliced zucchini

Everyone needs a good smoothie recipe in their back pocket, and this is ours. It earned its name because it has everything you need to set you up for a good morning—at least in the nutrition department. It's loaded with healthy fats, vitamin-rich fruit, and plant omegas. What we love about this smoothie is you can play around with the frozen fruit depending on what you have on hand. To earn extra points, freeze any leftover smoothie in an ice-pop mould and layer with granola and yogurt or vegan yogurt if desired. Kids young and old will feel like complete rebels eating these showstopper pops for breakfast. We love this hack for helping reduce waste in the kitchen!

If you don't have coconut water on hand, use non-dairy milk or water instead. Feel free to add a scoop of your favourite protein powder for the adults. See page 28 for our favourite smoothie combinations.

1. In a high-speed blender, combine the frozen fruit, banana, coconut water, milk, vanilla, hemp hearts, chia seeds, and any add-ins if desired. Blend on high speed until smooth.

Tip: Don't toss that leftover fruit! Before it goes bad, chop into small pieces and freeze on a baking sheet. Store it in large resealable plastic or reusable freezer bags in the freezer, sorting the fruit based on colour or type as desired. Pit, peel, chop, and freeze ripe avocados the same way to pop into your smoothies for an extra kick of healthy fats in the morning!

Recipe continues

SMOOTHIE COMBINATIONS

Add your pick of the following combos to the base smoothie recipe (see previous page) to create some of our favourite smoothies.

Tropical Beach: For the frozen fruit, use 1 cup (250 mL) frozen pineapple chunks + ½ cup (125 mL) coconut yogurt + splash of pineapple juice

Jill's Green Power: For the frozen fruit, use 1 cup (250 mL) frozen fruit of choice + 2 cups (500 mL) spinach or kale + ¼ avocado, pitted and peeled

Peanut Butter and Jelly: For the frozen fruit, use 1 cup (250 mL) frozen strawberries + 2 tablespoons (30 mL) natural peanut butter

Blueberry Crisp: For the frozen fruit, use 1 cup (250 mL) frozen blueberries + ⅓ cup (75 mL) old-fashioned rolled oats + 2 tablespoons (30 mL) hemp hearts + ¼ teaspoon (1 mL) cinnamon

Orange Creamsicle: For the frozen fruit, use 1 cup (250 mL) frozen orange segments + 2 tablespoons (30 mL) hemp hearts + ½ cup (125 mL) vanilla yogurt or non-dairy vanilla yogurt + splash of orange juice

Vegan: Use non-dairy vanilla yogurt for the Orange Creamsicle Smoothie combination.

Gluten-free: Use certified gluten-free rolled oats or skip add-in in the Blueberry Crisp combination.

Nut-free: Use a nut-free non-dairy milk. Skip the nut butter add-in. Use a seed butter instead of peanut butter in the Peanut Butter and Jelly combination.

Big Breakfast Bake

Vegetarian option • Dairy-free option • Gluten-free option • Nut-free

---

Serves 6 to 8

Prep time: 20 minutes

Cook time: 40 minutes

¼ cup (60 mL) extra-virgin olive oil, divided

1 pound (450 g) baby potatoes, cooked and halved (about 2 cups/500 mL)

7 ounces (200 g) turkey breakfast sausages or veggie breakfast sausages, sliced

2 cups (500 mL) diced yellow onion

1 cup (250 mL) sliced cremini or white mushrooms

1 red, yellow, or orange sweet pepper, diced

4 cups (1 L) lightly packed baby spinach

Salt and pepper

12 eggs

½ cup (125 mL) table (18%) cream

½ cup (125 mL) crumbled feta cheese or vegan feta cheese, divided

2 cups (500 mL) grated cheddar cheese or vegan cheddar cheese, divided

Garnishes

3 green onions (white and light green parts only), sliced

¼ cup (60 mL) chopped fresh flat-leaf parsley or other fresh herb such as dill or cilantro

1 avocado, pitted, peeled, and sliced

Everyone needs a one-pan breakfast dish up their sleeve, and this is ours. This veggie-packed breakfast bake can be prepped ahead to bake the next day to feed a small crowd or for a week of busy mornings. We love that it can double as a quick grab-and-go breakfast before rushing out the door. The fillings can be varied depending on what you have on hand—just try to keep the overall quantity roughly the same as the recipe. This nourishing breakfast is great served with thick slices of toasted No-Knead Bread (page 79) on the side.

1. Preheat the oven to 350°F (180°C) and lightly grease a 13 × 9-inch (3.5 L) baking dish.

2. Heat 2 tablespoons (30 mL) of the olive oil in a large frying pan over medium heat. Add the potatoes and sausages and cook, stirring occasionally, until golden brown and the sausages are cooked through, about 5 minutes. Transfer the mixture to the prepared baking dish and spread evenly.

3. In the same frying pan (no need to wipe it clean), heat the remaining 2 tablespoons (30 mL) olive oil over medium heat. Add the onions and cook, stirring occasionally, until soft and transparent, 3 to 4 minutes. Add the mushrooms and cook, stirring occasionally, until softened, 3 to 4 minutes. Add the sweet peppers and cook, stirring occasionally, for another 2 to 3 minutes. Add the spinach and cook until just wilted. Season with salt and pepper. Transfer the veggies to the prepared baking dish and spread evenly over the potato and sausage mixture.

4. In a medium bowl, whisk together the eggs and cream. Season with salt and pepper. Stir in ¼ cup (60 mL) of the feta and 1 cup (250 mL) of the cheddar, then pour the mixture evenly into the baking dish. Scatter the remaining 1 cup (250 mL) cheddar and the remaining ¼ cup (60 mL) feta over the egg mixture. Bake until the middle is set and lightly browned around the edges, about 40 minutes.

5. Garnish with the green onions, parsley, and avocado if desired. Serve with toasted No-Knead Bread if desired. Store (without garnishes), covered, in the fridge for up to 3 days.

Vegetarian: Use veggie breakfast sausages.

Dairy-free: Skip the cream and use vegan cheese.

Gluten-free: Use gluten-free breakfast sausages.

Carrot Cake Breakfast Cookies

Vegan • Gluten-free option • Nut-free option • Freezer-friendly

Makes about 25 cookies

Prep time: 20 minutes

Cook time: 18 minutes

2 cups (500 mL) finely grated peeled carrot

1 cup (250 mL) grated peeled apple

¾ cup (175 mL) pure maple syrup

½ cup (125 mL) natural almond butter

½ cup (125 mL) ground flaxseed

½ cup (125 mL) water

½ cup (125 mL) coconut oil or vegan butter, melted

2 teaspoons (10 mL) pure vanilla extract

2 cups (500 mL) old-fashioned rolled oats

1 cup (250 mL) whole wheat flour

1 cup (250 mL) unsweetened shredded coconut

1 cup (250 mL) sultana raisins

1 cup (250 mL) chopped raw pecans

½ cup (125 mL) hemp hearts

2 teaspoons (10 mL) cinnamon

1 teaspoon (5 mL) ground allspice

1 teaspoon (5 mL) baking powder

¼ teaspoon (1 mL) nutmeg

¼ teaspoon (1 mL) salt

We can't think of a better way to kick-start a day than with a cookie (our childhood dreams coming true). These hearty and nutritious power cookies are packed with fibre, apples, carrots, and nuts and just happen to be vegan, giving you the right kind of energy to start your day. This recipe makes a large batch of cookies that you can store in the freezer for those rushed mornings or moments when you need a quick healthy snack. Follow the nut-free substitutions to make them lunchbox-friendly.

1. Position the oven racks in the upper and lower thirds of the oven and preheat to 350°F (180°C). Line 2 baking sheets with parchment paper.

2. In a medium bowl, stir together the carrots, apple, maple syrup, almond butter, flaxseed, water, melted coconut oil, and vanilla until combined.

3. In a large bowl, stir together the oats, whole wheat flour, shredded coconut, raisins, pecans, hemp hearts, cinnamon, allspice, baking powder, nutmeg, and salt.

4. Pour the carrot mixture into the oat mixture. Mix with a spoon or rubber spatula until well combined.

5. Using a small ice cream scoop or large spoon, scoop about twenty-five ¼ cup (60 mL) mounds of cookie dough onto the prepared baking sheets, leaving about 1 inch (2.5 cm) between them. Using your fingers, gently press down on the cookies to flatten them to ½-inch (1 cm) thickness. Bake until golden brown on the bottom, about 18 minutes, rotating the pans halfway through. Transfer the cookies to a rack and cool completely. Store in a resealable container in the fridge for up to 1 week or in the freezer for up to 1 month.

Gluten-free: Use a 1:1 gluten-free flour blend or certified gluten-free oat flour instead of whole wheat flour. Use certified gluten-free rolled oats.

Nut-free: Use a seed butter such as tahini or sunflower butter instead of almond butter. Skip the pecans.

Sheet-Pan Breakfast Pizza

Vegetarian option • Dairy-free option • Nut-free option

Serves 4 to 8

Prep time: 15 minutes (not including making the Magic Dough)

Cook time: 15 minutes

½ batch Magic Dough (page 67)

Extra-virgin olive oil, for the pan and brushing the dough

All-purpose flour, for dusting

1 cup (250 mL) lightly packed baby spinach

1 cup (250 mL) grated cheese or vegan cheese (see combinations at right)

1 tomato, thinly sliced

4 to 6 eggs

Salt and pepper

Fresh basil leaves

1 avocado, pitted, peeled, and sliced, for serving

Toppings

See our favourite combinations (at right)

Vegetarian: Use Veggie Ground (page 309) and other vegetarian toppings.

Dairy-free: Use vegan cheese.

Nut-free: Omit the Veggie Ground or use a store-bought nut-free veggie ground sausage.

We love pizza and breakfast, so combining the two is a win-win. We list our favourite toppings below to help inspire you (add with the spinach), but the sky is the limit! We use a combination of mozzarella and Parmesan cheese, but there are no rules here.

You can make the pizza dough the same day, but we hands-down recommend making it the night before, covering, and refrigerating. Be sure to bring it to room temperature for at least an hour before rolling out so you can get your breakfast pizza on the table at a reasonable time.

1. Preheat the oven to 500°F (260°C). Generously brush a 15 × 10-inch (38 × 25 cm) baking sheet with olive oil.

2. Gently deflate the Magic Dough by pushing it down with your hands. On a lightly floured work surface, use a rolling pin to roll out the Magic Dough to fit the baking sheet. Transfer the dough to the pan, pressing it into the corners of the pan.

3. Brush the top of the dough with olive oil. Scatter the spinach and toppings of choice on the pizza, being careful not to overload it and leaving a ½-inch (1 cm) border of dough around the outer edge. Sprinkle evenly with the cheese and top with the tomato. Bake for 5 minutes.

4. Remove the pan from the oven. Crack the eggs, 1 at a time and evenly spaced, on the pizza. Season the pizza with salt and pepper and continue baking until the eggs are set and cooked to your liking, 5 to 8 minutes.

5. Cut the pizza into squares, with 1 egg per slice, and garnish with the basil. Serve sliced avocado on the side.

FAVOURITE TOPPING COMBINATIONS

• Chopped roasted sweet peppers, cooked turkey sausage or veggie sausage, sliced red onion, mozzarella cheese

• Sliced mushrooms, mozzarella cheese

• Sliced cooked potatoes tossed in olive oil, sliced red onion, thyme, Gouda cheese (no tomato sauce)

• Pesto, cooked turkey sausage or Veggie Ground (page 309), sliced zucchini, feta cheese

Jilly's Breakfast Sandwiches

Vegan • Gluten-free option • Nut-free • Freezer-friendly

Makes 4 sandwiches

Prep time: 15 minutes, plus 1 hour or more for marinating

Cook time: 10 minutes

1 package (12 ounces/350 g) extra-firm tofu, drained

1 cup (250 mL) chicken-flavoured vegetarian stock or vegetable stock

1 teaspoon (5 mL) Himalayan black salt, plus more for seasoning

1 teaspoon (5 mL) garlic powder

1 teaspoon (5 mL) onion powder

¼ teaspoon (1 mL) ground turmeric

1 tablespoon (15 mL) extra-virgin olive oil

4 English muffins, cut in half

1 large tomato, sliced

¼ small red onion, thinly sliced

1 avocado, pitted, peeled, and sliced

2 cups (500 mL) loosely packed baby arugula, lettuce, or spinach

¼ cup (60 mL) fresh basil leaves

Spicy Mayo, Sriracha or chipotle variation (page 328) or vegan mayonnaise, to serve (optional)

Gluten-free: Use gluten-free vegetable stock and gluten-free English muffins.

When we picture the ideal breakfast, we think of a delicious, juicy, crispy sandwich. When Jillian's household first started eating more plant-based meals, they struggled to find satisfying savoury breakfast options. That is, until Jill whipped up a good old-fashioned breakfast sandwich, *vegan*-style. That's right, these breakfast sandwiches are vegan and completely satisfying! Jill makes these for her family every weekend when at the farmhouse.

You can make these sandwiches ahead of time and store them in the freezer (minus the toppings) for up to 2 weeks. They are a great option if you have a busy household and want a quick and nutritious breakfast that can be reheated and devoured on the go. The Himalayan black salt (kala namak), which adds an eggy taste to the tofu, can be bought at health food stores or online. Feel free to use an air-fryer to cook the tofu to crispy perfection. You can easily swap out the tofu for a fried egg.

1. Cut the tofu into four ¾-inch (2 cm) thick equal squares. Pat dry with a paper towel.

2. In a shallow dish that will fit the tofu in one layer, whisk together the vegetarian stock, black salt, garlic powder, onion powder, and turmeric. Place the tofu slices in the mixture to cover and marinate in the fridge for 1 hour or overnight (the longer, the better).

3. Drain the tofu slices (discard the marinade) and season with black salt. Heat the olive oil in a large frying pan, over medium-high heat. Lay the tofu slices in the pan and fry until crispy and golden brown, about 4 minutes per side.

4. Meanwhile, toast the English muffins.

5. To assemble the sandwiches, place the crispy tofu on the bottom halves of the English muffins. Arrange the tomato slices, red onion, avocado, arugula, and basil on top of the tofu. Spread the Spicy Mayo if desired on the top half of the English muffins and close the sandwiches.

6. If you want to freeze the sandwiches for on-the-go breakfasts, top the toasted muffin halves with the tofu (without the toppings) and close the sandwiches. Wrap the sandwiches individually in foil and store in the freezer for up to 2 weeks. To reheat, remove the foil and warm in the microwave. Add the desired toppings.

Everything Bagel Sheet-Pan Hash Browns

Vegan • Gluten-free • Nut-free

Serves **4**

Prep time: **10 minutes**

Cook time: **30 minutes**

2 pounds (900 g) russet potatoes, cut into ½-inch (1 cm) cubes

2 tablespoons (30 mL) olive oil

2 tablespoons (30 mL) Everything Bagel Seasoning (page 330)

¼ teaspoon (1 mL) pepper

Why settle for plain hash browns when you can make this everything bagel version? All the flavour of a perfect seedy, onion-flavoured bagel, in the form of crispy golden hash browns. The only problem will be keeping your hands off them before they hit the table!

To save time, prep the potatoes the night before. Cube the potatoes, place them in an airtight container, cover with water, and refrigerate. (You can peel the potatoes if desired.) In the morning, drain and pat dry the potatoes before using. Easy peasy! Serve these hash browns as a side to Breakfast Burritos (page 25) or Eggs in a French Blanket (page 48). We found these salty enough with the seasoning, but you can add salt at the end if desired.

1. Preheat the oven to 400°F (200°C) and line a baking sheet with parchment paper.

2. In a large bowl, toss the potatoes with the olive oil, Everything Bagel Seasoning, and pepper.

3. Spread the potatoes on the prepared baking sheet and roast until golden brown, about 30 minutes, tossing halfway through. Serve hot.

French Toast Sticks

Vegetarian • Dairy-free option • Gluten-free option • Nut-free option

Serves 4

Prep time: 10 minutes

Cook time: 15 minutes

8 thick slices day-old French or
   Texas toast bread

4 eggs

½ cup (125 mL) 2% milk or
   unsweetened non-dairy milk

1 teaspoon (5 mL) pure vanilla
   extract

Pinch of salt

¼ cup (60 mL) sugar

1 teaspoon (5 mL) cinnamon

4 tablespoons (60 mL) butter
   or vegan butter, divided

To serve

Fresh berries (optional)

Pure maple syrup

Vanilla yogurt or non-dairy vanilla
   yogurt

Dairy-free: Use non-dairy milk
and non-dairy yogurt.

Gluten-free: Use gluten-free
bread.

Nut-free: If using non-dairy
milk, use a nut-free option.

Tori's parents used to own a fast-food restaurant called Arby's, where they offered magical French Toast Sticks on their breakfast menu. (The irony of Tori becoming a dietitian when her parents owned a fast-food restaurant is not lost on us.) We wanted to recreate them in all the same glory that we remembered, and based on our kids' reactions when trying them, we would say mission accomplished. These are brilliant to serve to kids big or small—after all, aren't we all kids at heart?

The trick is to use stale bread or the bread will get too squishy when cut and a little soggy when dipped in the milk mixture. Slicing your bread the night before is an easy way to dry it out if needed. Leftovers of our No-Knead Bread (page 79) work fabulously in this recipe. (Save the crusts to make Garlic Croutons, page 306, or bread crumbs by pulsing in a food processor once dry.)

1. Preheat the oven to 300°F (150°C) and place a large baking sheet lined with parchment paper in the oven.

2. Using a bread knife, slice off the crusts from the bread, then cut the bread into sticks about 1 inch (2.5 cm) thick.

3. In a shallow medium bowl, whisk the eggs. Add the milk, vanilla, and salt and beat until fully combined.

4. In a separate shallow medium bowl, stir together the sugar and cinnamon.

5. Melt 2 tablespoons (30 mL) of the butter in a large frying pan over medium heat. Working in batches of 4 sticks at a time, gently and quickly dip each stick of bread into the milk mixture, turning to coat fully. Be careful not to oversoak the bread. Fry the bread sticks on all sides until golden, about 5 minutes, adding the remaining 2 tablespoons (30 mL) butter as needed. Immediately transfer the fried sticks to the cinnamon sugar mixture and lightly toss to coat. Place the coated sticks on the lined baking sheet in the oven to stay warm while you coat and cook the remaining sticks.

6. Enjoy the French Toast Sticks warm from the oven. Serve with fresh berries along with maple syrup and a side of yogurt, each in small bowls for dipping if desired.

Pierogi Waffles

Vegan option • Vegetarian • Gluten-free option • Nut-free option • Freezer-friendly

Makes 10 waffles

Prep time: 15 minutes (not including making the Pierogi Mashed Potatoes)

Cook time: 10 minutes

1½ cups (375 mL) all-purpose flour

1½ cups (375 mL) grated cheddar cheese or vegan cheddar cheese

1½ tablespoons (22 mL) baking powder

½ teaspoon (2 mL) salt

¼ teaspoon (1 mL) pepper

3 eggs

½ batch (3 cups/750 mL) Pierogi Mashed Potatoes (page 234), warm

1 cup (250 mL) buttermilk or Homemade Buttermilk, non-dairy version (page 324)

⅓ cup (75 mL) butter or vegan butter, melted

For serving

Sour cream or vegan sour cream

Chopped fresh chives and/or dill

For those who reach for the savoury over the sweet, this one's for you. This recipe makes use of leftover Pierogi Mashed Potatoes (page 234), should there be any leftovers. Of course, they truly are good enough to justify making a fresh half batch should you be so inclined—and trust us, you should be. While these are perfect on their own, feel free to add a poached or fried egg on top for a fancy and hearty breakfast.

These waffles freeze well in an airtight container for up to 1 month. See page 324 for how to make your own buttermilk (dairy and dairy-free). Any leftover mashed potato will work for these waffles.

1. Preheat the oven to 200°F (100°C). Heat a waffle iron according to the manufacturer's directions.

2. In a large bowl, stir together the flour, grated cheese, baking powder, salt, and pepper.

3. In a separate large bowl, whisk the eggs. Add the warm mashed potatoes, buttermilk, and melted butter and whisk to combine.

4. Add the wet ingredients to the dry ingredients and stir with a rubber spatula until just combined. Do not overmix. The batter will be slightly lumpy.

5. Coat the hot waffle iron generously with cooking spray. Using a ladle or measuring cup, scoop about ½ cup (125 mL) of batter into the waffle iron, spreading it to cover the entire surface. Close the iron and cook until the waffle is light golden brown, about 3 minutes. Keep the waffles warm in the oven while you cook the remaining waffles.

6. Serve with a dollop of sour cream and garnish with a sprinkle of chopped chives if desired.

Vegan: Use vegan cheese, vegan butter, and vegan sour cream. Use Flax Eggs (page 330) instead of eggs. Follow the vegan option to make the Homemade Buttermilk. Follow the vegan option to make the Pierogi Mashed Potatoes.

Gluten-free: Use a 1:1 gluten-free flour blend instead of all-purpose flour.

Nut-free: Follow the nut-free option to make the Pierogi Mashed Potatoes.

Piña Colada Sheet-Pan Pancakes

Vegetarian • Vegan option • Gluten-free option • Nut-free

Serves 6

Prep time: 15 minutes

Cook time: 25 to 30 minutes

2 cups (500 mL) all-purpose flour

1½ cups (375 mL) sweetened shredded coconut, divided

¼ cup (60 mL) sugar

2½ teaspoons (12 mL) baking powder

½ teaspoon (2 mL) baking soda

¼ teaspoon (1 mL) salt

2 large eggs

1 can (14 ounces/400 mL) full-fat coconut milk

¼ cup (60 mL) coconut oil, melted

1 teaspoon (5 mL) pure vanilla extract

1 teaspoon (5 mL) coconut extract (optional)

8 fresh pineapple rings, ½ inch (1 cm) thick

For serving

Coconut whip

Pure maple syrup

Many years ago, we made a big family trip to Hawaii, grandparents and all. Our memory banks are still filled with giggles as we rolled with Granny in the waves, sang Ukrainian songs, strolled along the streets of Honolulu, snorkelled in Hanauma Bay, and enjoyed endless meals together, laughing so hard we would all cry the whole time. It was, and remains, our happy place. One bite of these piña colada pancakes takes us back to those blissful stress-free days together where the only thing that mattered was which one of us was going to wear Grandma's epic sparkly shirt that day. You can make these as individual pancakes if you don't mind the extra work, but this easier sheet-pan version makes our busy hearts happy.

1. Preheat the oven to 350°F (180°C) and grease or line with parchment paper a 13 × 9-inch (3.5 L) baking dish (the pancakes will be thicker and more cake-like) or a 17 × 11.5-inch (43 × 29 cm) baking sheet.

2. In a large bowl, whisk together the flour, 1 cup (250 mL) of the shredded coconut, sugar, baking powder, baking soda, and salt.

3. In a medium bowl, whisk together the eggs. Add the coconut milk, melted coconut oil, vanilla, and coconut extract (if using) and whisk to combine.

4. Add the wet ingredients to the dry ingredients and stir with a rubber spatula until just mixed. The batter will be lumpy.

5. Pour the batter into the prepared baking dish or baking sheet, spreading evenly with a rubber spatula. Sprinkle with the remaining ½ cup (125 mL) shredded coconut and arrange the pineapple slices on top. Bake until light golden brown and a toothpick inserted into the centre comes out clean, about 30 minutes. Serve with coconut whip and maple syrup if desired.

Vegan: Use Flax Eggs (page 330) instead of eggs.

Gluten-free: Use a 1:1 gluten-free flour blend instead of all-purpose flour.

Eggs in a French Blanket

Vegetarian • Dairy-free option • Nut-free option • Freezer-friendly

Makes 12 to 14 crêpes

Prep time: 10 minutes, plus
1 to 2 hours resting

Cook time: 20 minutes

Crêpe Batter

4 eggs

2¼ cups (550 mL) all-purpose flour

2 cups (500 mL) 2% milk or
    unsweetened non-dairy milk

1 cup (250 mL) club soda

2 teaspoons (10 mL) sugar

1 teaspoon (5 mL) salt

Avocado oil or vegetable oil
    for cooking

Filling

3 cups (750 mL) grated Gouda
    cheese or your favourite
    meltable vegan cheese

12 eggs

½ cup (125 mL) finely chopped fresh
    herbs (we use chives and dill),
    plus more for garnish

Salt and pepper

Dairy-free: Use non-dairy milk
and vegan cheese.

Nut-free: Use a nut-free
non-dairy milk.

The recipe for these crêpes came from Tori's husband Charles's family vault, and it doesn't disappoint. The club soda—yes, you read that right—results in very tender crêpes. And don't skip the resting time—it's 100 percent necessary to relax the protein in the flour. For a sweet variation, fill the crêpes instead with fresh fruit and lightly sweetened whipped cream or coconut whip with a generous spread of our Chia Jam (page 310) before folding them over and devouring. Either way, you'll feel like you've been teleported to the streets of Europe. To save some time, cook the crêpes in advance, cover, and refrigerate for up to 3 days before assembling.

1. MAKE THE CRÊPE BATTER: In a high-speed blender, combine the eggs, flour, milk, club soda, sugar, and salt and blend on medium speed until smooth. Cover and set aside to rest at room temperature for at least 1 hour, or cover and refrigerate overnight.

2. COOK THE CRÊPES: Position the oven racks in the upper and lower thirds of the oven and preheat to 375°F (190°C). Line 2 large baking sheets with parchment paper.

3. Lightly brush the avocado oil in an 8-inch (20 cm) nonstick crêpe pan or a small nonstick frying pan over medium heat. Once the oil is hot, pour a thin layer of batter, about ¼ cup (60 mL), into the pan, swirling the pan to distribute the batter across the bottom and a little up the sides. Cook the crêpe until golden brown on the bottom, 2 to 3 minutes. Gently flip the crêpe and cook for about 2 minutes, until it starts to turn golden brown on the bottom. Slide the crêpe out of the pan and onto a plate. Cover to keep the crêpes from drying out and repeat with the remaining batter, adding more oil to the pan as needed. (See Tip for freezing the crêpes.)

4. ASSEMBLE AND BAKE: Lay a crêpe on a work surface. Sprinkle ¼ cup (60 mL) of the grated cheese in the centre of the crêpe and make a well in the middle of the cheese. Fold in the edges of the crêpe, leaving the centre exposed. Using a large spatula, carefully transfer the crêpe to one of the prepared baking sheets. Crack an egg into the well and sprinkle with 1 to 2 teaspoons (5 to 10 mL) of fresh herbs, salt, and pepper. Repeat to assemble the remaining crêpes, spacing evenly on the baking sheets. Bake the crêpes for about 10 minutes or until the eggs are cooked to your liking. Garnish with more fresh herbs.

Tip: Crêpes, without the filling, can be made ahead. Store cooled crêpes with a piece of parchment paper between each crêpe in a resealable container in the fridge for up to 3 days or in the freezer for up to 1 month. Thaw frozen crêpes on the counter for about 2 hours before using.

Smoked Salmon, Dill, and Cream Cheese Quiche

Vegetarian option • Gluten-free option • Nut-free

Serves 8

Prep time: 20 minutes, plus 1 hour chilling

Cook time: 55 minutes

Pastry Dough

2½ cups (625 mL) all-purpose flour

2 teaspoons (10 mL) sugar

1 teaspoon (5 mL) salt

½ cup (125 mL) vegetable shortening, cut into chunks

½ cup (125 mL) cold butter or vegan butter, cut into ½-inch (1 cm) cubes

2 teaspoons (10 mL) fresh lemon juice or white vinegar

¼ cup (60 mL) + 1 to 2 tablespoons (15 to 30 mL) ice water, divided

Filling

8 eggs

1½ cups (375 mL) table (18%) cream

¼ cup (60 mL) roughly chopped fresh dill

½ teaspoon (2 mL) salt

½ teaspoon (2 mL) pepper

5 ounces (140 g) sliced cold-smoked wild salmon, cut into ½-inch (1 cm) pieces

½ cup (125 mL) cream cheese or vegan cream cheese, room temperature

⅓ cup (75 mL) thinly sliced red onion

¼ cup (60 mL) drained capers

Tori worked at the most adorable artsy diner, the Tomato Fresh Food Café, nestled in the heart of Vancouver, while attending university. The experience helped shape her food philosophy and love of simple yet sophisticated wholesome dishes that are skilfully made. Some variation of smoked salmon with dill, capers, red onions, and a squeeze of lemon could always be found on the café's menu. This quiche is a nod to the talented chefs who, when business was slow, would graciously let Tori loiter in the kitchen to learn their tricks and chat about cooking and life over steaming mugs of freshly brewed chai.

1. MAKE THE PASTRY DOUGH: In a food processor, combine the flour, sugar, and salt. Pulse to mix. Add the shortening and pulse until just incorporated. Add the butter and pulse until the butter is the size of peas.

2. Drizzle the lemon juice and ¼ cup (60 mL) of the water over the flour mixture. Pulse until the dough just starts to stick together in rough clumps, adding the remaining 1 to 2 tablespoons (15 to 30 mL) water if needed.

3. Shape the dough into a disc, wrap tightly in plastic wrap, and refrigerate for at least 1 hour before rolling it out.

4. Preheat the oven to 425°F (220°C).

5. On a lightly floured work surface, use a floured rolling pin to roll out the chilled dough into a 12-inch (30 cm) circle about ⅛ inch (3 mm) thick. Carefully roll the dough around the rolling pin and unroll it over a 9-inch (23 cm) round plain or fluted quiche pan or deep pie plate. Using your hands, gently press the dough into the bottom and up the sides of the dish to fit. Trim the excess dough around the edges and gently crimp or flute the edges using your thumb and index finger.

6. BLIND-BAKE THE CRUST: Line the quiche shell with parchment paper, then fill with dried beans or pie weights up to the brim of the dough. (You can skip this step, but the crust will be a better texture if you blind-bake it first.) Bake until very light golden, about 12 minutes. Use the parchment paper to carefully lift out the beans or pie weights. Let the crust cool. Reduce the oven temperature to 350°F (180°C).

Recipe continues

Smoked Salmon, Dill, and Cream Cheese Quiche continued

7. **MEANWHILE, START THE FILLING:** In a large bowl, whisk the eggs. Add the cream, dill, salt, and pepper and whisk to combine.

8. **ASSEMBLE AND BAKE:** Evenly layer the smoked salmon, cream cheese, red onion, and capers in the pie shell. Pour the egg mixture over top.

9. Bake until the crust is golden brown and the quiche is set in the centre, about 40 minutes. To test doneness, give the dish a gentle nudge—the quiche shouldn't wobble. Cool slightly before serving. Cover and store in the fridge for up to 3 days.

Vegetarian: Skip the smoked salmon.

Gluten-free: Use a gluten-free pie crust or omit the crust for a crustless quiche.

Top Secret Granola

Vegetarian • Vegan option • Gluten-free option • Nut-free option

Makes 7 cups (1.65 L)

Prep time: 10 minutes

Cook time: 15 minutes

5 cups (1.25 L) old-fashioned rolled oats

2 cups (500 mL) unsweetened flaked or shredded coconut

1 cup (250 mL) whole or sliced raw almonds

1 cup (250 mL) whole or chopped raw pecans

1 cup (250 mL) raw pumpkin seeds

1 tablespoon (15 mL) cinnamon

¼ teaspoon (1 mL) salt

1¼ cups (300 mL) avocado oil or vegetable oil

¼ cup (60 mL) pure liquid honey or pure maple syrup

¼ cup (60 mL) lightly packed brown sugar or coconut sugar

1 teaspoon (5 mL) pure vanilla extract

½ cup (125 mL) hemp hearts

1 cup (250 mL) dried fruit (raisins, dried cranberries, or dried apricots; optional)

This one secret was too good not to share. Tori has been making this granola for over fifteen years, to the delight of our families. We keep our granola in a jar within close reach to scoop over yogurt parfaits or just to snack on. Switch up the nuts and seeds for variety, and skip the brown sugar and dried fruit for a less sweet granola. You can replace up to 1 cup (250 mL) of the avocado oil or vegetable oil with apple juice for a lower-fat option, but note that it will alter the flavour. Similarly, melted coconut oil can be substituted for the avocado oil or vegetable oil but will impart more of a coconut flavour.

1. Preheat the oven to 325°F (160°C) and line a baking sheet with parchment paper.

2. In a large bowl, stir together the oats, coconut, almonds, pecans, pumpkin seeds, cinnamon, and salt.

3. In a medium bowl, whisk together the avocado oil, honey, brown sugar, and vanilla.

4. Pour the wet ingredients into the dry ingredients and stir well to combine.

5. Spread the granola evenly on the prepared baking sheet. Bake until light golden brown, about 15 minutes, stirring halfway through.

6. Remove from the oven. Stir in the hemp hearts and dried fruit, if using. Allow the granola to cool completely on the baking sheet before storing in a resealable container at room temperature for up to 1 month.

Vegan: Use maple syrup instead of honey.

Gluten-free: Use certified gluten-free rolled oats.

Nut-free: Omit the nuts and replace with an equal amount of pumpkin seeds or sunflower seeds, rolled oats (certified gluten-free if needed), or coconut.

Fruit Crumble Muffins

Vegan option • Vegetarian • Gluten-free option •
Nut-free option • Freezer-friendly

Streusel Topping

½ cup (125 mL) old-fashioned rolled
   oats

¼ cup (60 mL) whole wheat flour

¼ cup (60 mL) finely chopped raw
   pecans

2 tablespoons (30 mL) lightly
   packed brown sugar

1 teaspoon (5 mL) cinnamon

Pinch of salt

¼ cup (60 mL) butter or vegan
   butter, melted

Muffins

3 eggs

1 cup (250 mL) unsweetened
   applesauce

1 cup (250 mL) avocado oil or
   vegetable oil

¾ cup (175 mL) pure maple syrup

2 teaspoons (10 mL) pure vanilla
   extract

2 cups (500 mL) all-purpose flour

1 cup (250 mL) whole wheat flour

1 cup (250 mL) old-fashioned rolled
   oats

½ cup (125 mL) lightly packed brown
   sugar

2 teaspoons (10 mL) baking powder

1 teaspoon (5 mL) baking soda

½ teaspoon (2 mL) salt

1 tablespoon (15 mL) cinnamon

3 cups (750 mL) fresh or frozen fruit
   (berries, diced pitted plums, or
   diced peeled pitted peaches or
   apples), plus more for garnish

We live for flexible recipes that can pivot based on what we
have in the fridge, and this is one of them. This basic moist,
lightly sweetened muffin recipe can be adjusted depending
on the fruit you have on hand. You can use almost any fruit in these
muffins, making them the perfect base for your own creations! Frozen
(unthawed) and fresh fruit work equally well. We recommend freezing
any extra muffins for quick snacks or on-the-go breakfasts.

1. Preheat the oven to 350°F (180°C) and line 2 muffin tins with paper liners.

2. MAKE THE STREUSEL TOPPING: In a medium bowl, stir together the
oats, whole wheat flour, pecans, brown sugar, cinnamon, and salt. Stir in
the melted butter until combined. Set aside.

3. MAKE THE MUFFINS: In a medium bowl, whisk the eggs well. Add the
applesauce, avocado oil, maple syrup, and vanilla and whisk to combine.

4. In a large bowl, whisk together the all-purpose flour, whole wheat flour,
oats, brown sugar, baking powder, baking soda, salt, and cinnamon.

5. Fold the wet ingredients into the dry ingredients and mix until just
incorporated. Fold in the fruit.

6. Divide the batter among the muffin cups. Top each muffin with a
sprinkle of streusel and more fruit for garnish if desired. Bake until
golden brown and a toothpick inserted into the centre comes out clean,
about 25 minutes. Transfer the muffins to a rack and cool completely.
Store in a resealable container at room temperature for up to 3 days,
in the fridge for up to 1 week, or in the freezer for up to 1 month.

Vegan: Use Flax Eggs (page 330) instead of eggs. Use vegan butter.

Gluten-free: Use a 1:1 gluten-free flour blend instead of all-purpose flour
and whole wheat flour. Use certified gluten-free rolled oats.

Nut-free: Replace the pecans in the streusel with rolled oats (certified
gluten-free if needed).

Baking
and
Bread

Birdie Bars

Vegan • Gluten-free option • Nut-free option • Freezer-friendly

Makes about 20 bars

Prep time: 10 minutes

Cook time: 30 minutes

½ cup (125 mL) unsweetened non-dairy milk

¼ cup (60 mL) ground flaxseed

3 cups (750 mL) old-fashioned rolled oats, divided

2 cups (500 mL) unsweetened shredded coconut

½ cup (125 mL) hemp hearts

¼ cup (60 mL) chia seeds

¼ cup (60 mL) sesame seeds

2 teaspoons (10 mL) cinnamon

¼ teaspoon (1 mL) salt

¾ cup (175 mL) coconut oil

½ cup (125 mL) brown rice syrup

½ cup (125 mL) lightly packed brown sugar

2 teaspoons (10 mL) pure vanilla extract

Gluten-free: Use certified gluten-free rolled oats.

Nut-free: Use a nut-free non-dairy milk.

There is a certain oat bar at one of our favourite coffee shops that we have fallen completely in love with. They are so delicious! Jillian created this wholesome version after getting hooked. This is an utterly perfect seedy oat bar that we both feel pretty darn good about adding to our snack lineup. They are chewy, just sweet enough, and totally school lunch approved (yay, no nuts!). One bite and we are sure you will agree.

You can find brown rice syrup in most health food stores; it is stickier than maple syrup and helps to bind the bars together.

1. Preheat the oven to 325°F (160°C) and line a 13 × 9-inch (3.5 L) baking pan with parchment paper, leaving extra to overhang on the sides to make it easier to remove the bars.

2. In a small bowl, stir together the milk and flaxseed. Set aside for 5 minutes.

3. In a food processor, pulse 2 cups (500 mL) of the oats until finely ground. Add the remaining 1 cup (250 mL) oats, coconut, hemp hearts, chia seeds, sesame seeds, cinnamon, and salt and pulse once or twice just to mix. Transfer the mixture to a large bowl.

4. In a small saucepan, combine the coconut oil, brown rice syrup, and brown sugar. Bring to a simmer over medium heat and cook, stirring, until the sugar has dissolved, about 3 minutes. Remove from the heat and stir in the vanilla.

5. Pour the coconut oil mixture and the flax mixture over the oat mixture. Mix well. Scrape the mixture into the prepared baking pan and evenly and firmly press onto the bottom of the pan with damp hands or the flat bottom of a glass.

6. Bake until light golden brown around the edges, about 30 minutes. Remove from the oven and let cool in the pan for 15 minutes. Use the overhanging parchment paper to gently lift the bars out onto a rack and cool completely.

7. Once cooled, cut into bars using a large, sharp knife. Store in a resealable container at room temperature for up to 1 week or in the freezer for up to 3 months.

Double Chocolate Zucchini Bread

Vegan option • Vegetarian • Gluten-free option • Nut-free option • Freezer-friendly

Makes 2 small loaves

Prep time: 10 minutes

Cook time: 60 minutes

1½ cups (375 mL) all-purpose flour

1 cup (250 mL) whole wheat flour

1 cup (250 mL) sugar or coconut sugar

½ cup (125 mL) chopped raw walnuts (optional)

½ cup (125 mL) Dutch-processed cocoa powder, sifted

⅓ cup (75 mL) hemp hearts

1 teaspoon (5 mL) baking soda

½ teaspoon (2 mL) baking powder

¼ teaspoon (1 mL) salt

3 eggs

3 cups (750 mL) packed grated unpeeled zucchini

¾ cup (175 mL) extra-virgin olive oil

2 teaspoons (10 mL) pure vanilla extract

⅔ cup (150 mL) dark or semi-sweet chocolate chips

Prepare to be dazzled by this moist, chocolate-packed healthier zucchini bread. This quick bread earns extra points for the plant-based omega-3s thanks to the walnuts, hemp hearts, and olive oil. Though it may seem odd to use olive oil in baking, we chose it over other oils for its healthier profile, and we promise that you won't be able to tell! While you can use natural cocoa in this recipe, we suggest using Dutch-processed cocoa powder for the richest chocolate flavour and deep colour. These loaves freeze beautifully, and the batter can also be made into muffins: bake for about 25 minutes or until a toothpick comes out clean.

1. Preheat the oven to 350°F (180°C). Grease two 8 × 4-inch (1.5 L) loaf pans, then dust with flour or line with parchment paper, leaving extra to overhang on the sides to make it easier to remove the loaves.

2. In a large bowl, stir together the all-purpose flour, whole wheat flour, sugar, walnuts (if using), cocoa powder, hemp hearts, baking soda, baking powder, and salt.

3. In a medium bowl, beat the eggs. Stir in the zucchini, olive oil, and vanilla.

4. Add the zucchini mixture to the flour mixture and mix with a rubber spatula until just incorporated. Fold in the chocolate chips.

5. Divide the batter evenly between the prepared loaf pans and bake until a toothpick inserted into the centre comes out clean, 50 to 60 minutes. Cool for 5 minutes in the pan, then turn the loaves out onto a rack and cool completely. Store in a resealable container in the fridge for up to 1 week or in the freezer for up to 1 month.

Vegan: Use Flax Eggs (page 330) instead of eggs and dairy-free chocolate.

Gluten-free: Use 1:1 gluten-free flour blend instead of all-purpose flour and whole wheat flour.

Nut-free: Skip the nuts.

Beer Bread

Vegan option • Vegetarian • Gluten-free option • Nut-free • Freezer-friendly

Makes 1 loaf

Prep time: 10 minutes

Cook time: 50 minutes

3 cups (750 mL) all-purpose flour

½ cup (125 mL) grated cheddar cheese or vegan cheddar cheese

2 tablespoons (30 mL) chopped fresh dill

2 tablespoons (30 mL) sugar

1 tablespoon (15 mL) + 1 teaspoon (5 mL) baking powder

1 teaspoon (5 mL) salt

1 teaspoon (5 mL) dried oregano

1 teaspoon (5 mL) dried thyme

½ teaspoon (2 mL) garlic powder

1 can (12 ounces/355 mL) lager beer

½ cup (125 mL) butter or vegan butter, melted, divided

What's better than combining our two favourite things, beer and bread, into one recipe? We have loved beer bread for as long as we can remember. In fact, Jillian's mom Peggy owned a home decor store in Peace River, Alberta, called Beyond the Picket Fence and she always carried beer bread mix in the store. Jillian would whip up a loaf in the little kitchen in the back. This recipe has long since replaced the old bread mix, but the nostalgia and joy we feel each time we bake it remains.

On one of her many trips to Vancouver, Jillian had the pleasure of indulging in the irresistible beer bread at the Fairmont Vancouver Airport. The hotel's recipe, along with Jillian's childhood memories, helped inspire this final masterpiece. We'd be shocked if you leave a single crumb behind.

1. Preheat the oven to 375°F (190°C). Grease a 9 × 5-inch (2 L) loaf pan and line it with parchment paper, leaving extra to overhang on the sides to make it easier to remove the loaf.

2. In a medium bowl, stir together the flour, cheese, dill, sugar, baking powder, salt, oregano, thyme, and garlic powder. Add the beer and ¼ cup (60 mL) of the melted butter and stir with a rubber spatula just to combine. The dough will be lumpy.

3. Transfer the dough into the prepared loaf pan and bake until golden brown and a toothpick inserted into the centre comes out clean, 50 to 60 minutes. Pour the remaining ¼ cup (60 mL) melted butter evenly over the warm loaf. Remove the loaf from the pan, transfer to a rack, and cool slightly before slicing. Store in a resealable container in the fridge for up to 3 days or in the freezer for up to 1 month.

Vegan: Use vegan butter and vegan shredded cheese or omit the cheese.

Gluten-free: Use a 1:1 gluten-free flour blend instead of all-purpose flour and use gluten-free beer.

Magic Dough

Vegan • Nut-free

Prep time: 20 minutes, plus 3 hours rising

2 cups (500 mL) lukewarm water

2 tablespoons (30 mL) sugar

1 tablespoon (15 mL) active dry yeast

¼ cup (60 mL) extra-virgin olive oil, avocado oil, or vegetable oil

2 teaspoons (10 mL) salt

4 to 4¾ cups (1 to 1.12 L) all-purpose flour, plus more for dusting

Homemade bread is a magical thing, especially when it's this easy! This recipe can be used to create a wide range of breads, from pita, pizza, and naan-style flatbreads to classic dinner rolls, Granny's Cinnamon Buns (page 81), and our Dilly Buns (page 75). Although the Magic Dough flatbreads aren't exact replicas of the authentic versions, this dough does offer a simplified, versatile recipe that is so easy you will have it memorized in no time—with delicious results. The dough is easy to work with and is ready to bake in just a few hours.

1. In a large bowl, whisk together the water and sugar to dissolve. Sprinkle in the yeast and let it sit for about 10 minutes, until it activates and foams up.

2. Stir the olive oil and salt into the yeast mixture and add 4 cups (1 L) of the flour. Stir with a wooden spoon until stirring gets too difficult.

3. Transfer the dough to a well-floured work surface. Using the palms of your hands, knead the dough until it is smooth and elastic, slowly adding more flour as needed to prevent the dough from sticking to your hands. Form the dough into a smooth round ball. Place in a greased medium bowl, cover with a kitchen towel, and let it sit in a warm, draft-free place until doubled in size, about 3 hours.

4. Proceed with making your chosen bun or flatbread recipe.

Dinner Buns

Vegan • Nut-free • Freezer-friendly

Makes 15 buns

Prep time: 15 minutes (not including making the Magic Dough), plus 45 minutes rising

Cook time: 25 minutes

1 batch Magic Dough (page 67)

All-purpose flour, for dusting

Served warm from the oven, dinner buns are one of the most comforting foods to enjoy alongside a bowl of hot soup like our Autumn Rice Soup (page 148) or Lentil Soup (page 151). You will feel like a baking pro when you pull these beautiful fluffy buns out of the oven.

1. Grease a 13 × 9-inch (3.5 L) baking dish or pan.

2. Gently deflate the Magic Dough by pushing it down with your hands. Tip the dough out onto a lightly floured work surface and divide it into 15 equal portions. With floured hands, shape the dough pieces into balls, tucking the edges under and pinching at the bottom to make the tops smooth. Evenly space the buns in the prepared baking dish, dust the tops with flour if desired, cover with a kitchen towel, and let rise until doubled in size, about 45 minutes.

3. Meanwhile, preheat the oven to 375°F (190°C).

4. Bake the buns until golden brown on the bottoms and tops, about 25 minutes. Transfer the buns to a rack and cool slightly before serving. Store in a resealable container at room temperature for up to 3 days or in the freezer for up to 1 month.

Pita-Style Flatbreads

Vegan • Nut-free

Makes 12 to 14 pitas

Prep time: 15 minutes (not including making the Magic Dough), plus 35 minutes rising

Cook time: 15 minutes

---

1 batch Magic Dough (page 67)

All-purpose flour, for dusting

This pita-style flatbread is such a great companion to Classic Chickpea Hummus (page 110) and Loaded Hummus (page 113). These are so fluffy and mouthwatering served fresh out of the oven that once you try them, you won't ever go back to store-bought!

1. Position a rack in the middle of the oven. Place a pizza stone on the rack and preheat the oven to 500°F (260°C). (If you do not have a pizza stone, you can use a rimless or upside-down baking sheet.)

2. Gently deflate the Magic Dough by pushing it down with your hands. Divide the Magic Dough into 12 or 14 equal portions (depending on how large you want your pitas). Shape each portion of dough into a smooth ball.

3. On a lightly floured work surface, use a rolling pin to flatten the dough slightly until ¼ to ½ inch (5 mm to 1 cm) thick. Place the pita on a square of parchment paper large enough to fit the pita and transfer to a baking sheet. Repeat with the remaining dough. Cover the pitas with a kitchen towel and let rise until almost doubled in size, 30 to 35 minutes.

4. Working in batches, transfer the pitas with the parchment paper to the pizza stone. Bake until puffed and very lightly browned, 3 to 4 minutes. Serve immediately.

Naan-Style Flatbreads

Vegetarian • Vegan option • Nut-free

Makes 14 naan

Prep time: 15 minutes (not including making the Magic Dough)

Cook time: 20 minutes

1 batch Magic Dough (page 67)

All-purpose flour, for dusting

Garlic Butter

¼ cup (60 mL) butter or vegan butter

1 clove garlic, minced

This Indian flatbread traditionally contains yogurt and is baked in a clay tandoor oven. We've created a vegan version that cooks in a cast-iron pan on the stovetop that we make on a regular basis to serve with curries such as our Coconut Curry (page 185).

1. Gently deflate the Magic Dough by pushing it down with your hands. Dust a work surface with flour. Divide the Magic Dough into 14 equal portions. Use a rolling pin lightly dusted with flour to roll out the balls until very thin, about ⅛ inch (3 mm).

2. Heat a large cast-iron or heavy-bottomed frying pan over medium-high heat. Once the pan is hot, working in batches so as not to overcrowd the pan, cook the naan until the surface is full of air bubbles and the bottom is golden brown and blistered in spots, about 1 minute. Flip and cook for about 1 minute more, until the bottom is golden brown. Transfer the naan to a plate and cover with a kitchen towel to keep warm. Repeat with the remaining naans.

3. In a small saucepan over low heat, melt the butter. Add the garlic and cook until the garlic is fragrant, 1 to 2 minutes. Brush the naan with the warm garlic butter just before serving.

Vegan: Use vegan butter.

Dilly Buns

Vegan option • Vegetarian • Nut-free

Makes about 12 buns

Prep time: 15 minutes (not including making the Magic Dough), plus 1 hour rising

Cook time: 30 minutes

1 batch Magic Dough (page 67)

All-purpose flour, for dusting

Filling

½ cup (125 mL) butter or vegan butter, softened

¼ cup (60 mL) finely chopped fresh dill

½ teaspoon (2 mL) salt

2 cloves garlic, minced

These little buns are fluffy pieces of heaven that were inspired by our sweet friend Cara. They remind us of a Ukrainian bun that our grandma used to make many years ago. We tried these with a filling of 1 cup (250 mL) of cream cheese and double the dill (no butter) and they were pretty awesome—in case the thought crosses your mind. Serve them with a hot bowl of soup or as a side at your next dinner or lunch for a jaw-dropping reaction from your guests.

1. Lightly grease a 13 × 9-inch (3.5 L) baking pan.

2. In a small bowl, mix together the butter, dill, salt, and garlic. Set aside.

3. Gently deflate the Magic Dough by pushing it down with your hands. Lightly sprinkle a work surface with flour and scrape the dough onto it. Use a rolling pin dusted with flour to roll out the dough into a 12 × 24-inch (30 × 60 cm) rectangle (it doesn't have to be exact) with the longer side facing you.

4. Evenly spread the filling with a rubber spatula lengthwise across the lower half of the dough, leaving a 1-inch (2.5 cm) border at the edge closest to you.

5. Starting at the long edge closest to you, tightly roll the dough up into a log. Using a sharp knife, cut the log into 2-inch (5 cm) pieces. (You should have about 12 pieces.)

6. Place the buns cut side down in the prepared baking pan. Cover with a kitchen towel and let sit in a warm, draft-free place until doubled in size, about 1 hour.

7. Meanwhile, preheat the oven to 350°F (180°C).

8. Bake the buns until golden brown, about 30 minutes. Invert the buns onto a rack or parchment paper. Serve warm. Leftover buns can be stored in a resealable container at room temperature for up to 3 days and reheated if desired.

Vegan: Use vegan butter.

No-Knead Bread

Vegan • Nut-free • Freezer-friendly

Makes 1 large loaf or 2 small loaves

Prep time: 5 minutes, plus 8 hours rising

Cook time: 45 minutes

---

2 cups (500 mL/350 g) whole wheat bread flour

2 cups (500 mL/350 g) all-purpose flour or white bread flour, plus extra for dusting

2 teaspoons (10 mL) active dry yeast

2 teaspoons (10 mL) salt

2 teaspoons (10 mL) sugar

2 cups (500 mL) lukewarm water

There is nothing quite like the smell of baking bread. For anyone who has felt too intimidated to make bread from scratch or simply doesn't have the time, this dough is for you. We experimented with different ratios of whole wheat and all-purpose flour, and a 50/50 mix was our preference, giving it a wholesome touch without making it too dry and dense. Make the dough the night before to enjoy freshly baked bread for breakfast or whip it up in the morning to serve alongside a hearty bowl of soup for a cozy dinner.

While a bread cloche or Dutch oven yields the best results, we also provide directions for using a baking sheet.

1. In a large bowl, stir together the whole wheat flour, all-purpose flour, yeast, salt, and sugar. Add the water and stir with a wooden spoon until well combined, using your hands if needed to work in all the flour.

2. Sprinkle the dough with all-purpose flour and cover the bowl tightly with plastic wrap. Let sit in a warm, draft-free place until doubled in size, 6 to 7 hours.

3. Gently deflate the dough by pushing it down with your hands. Dust a work surface with all-purpose flour and turn the dough out onto it.

4. IF USING A BREAD CLOCHE OR DUTCH OVEN: Use your hands to shape the dough into a round loaf and place it on a large piece of parchment paper. Trim the paper around the loaf, leaving a 2-inch (5 cm) border of parchment. Cover the loaf with a kitchen towel and let sit in a warm, draft-free place until doubled in size, about 1 hour.

5. Thirty minutes before you are ready to bake, place the bread cloche or Dutch oven in the middle of the oven and a small ovenproof dish with hot water on the lower rack and preheat the oven to 450°F (230°C).

6. Once the dough has doubled in size, score the top of the loaf with a sharp knife or lame if desired. Carefully transfer the loaf with the parchment paper to the preheated cloche or Dutch oven, cover with the lid, and bake for 30 minutes. Remove the lid and bake for another 10 to 15 minutes, until golden brown. Transfer the bread to a rack to cool. (Skip steps 7 to 9.)

Recipe continues

7. IF USING A BAKING SHEET: Line a baking sheet with parchment paper. Divide the dough into 2 equal portions. Working with 1 piece of dough at a time, use your hands to shape the dough into a round loaf and place on the prepared baking sheet, leaving ample space between the loaves. Cover the loaves with a kitchen towel and let sit in a warm, draft-free place until doubled in size, about 1 hour.

8. About 30 minutes before you are ready to bake, position a rack in the middle of the oven and place a small ovenproof dish with hot water on the lower rack. Preheat the oven to 450°F (230°C).

9. Once the dough has doubled in size, score the top of the loaf with a sharp knife or lame if desired. Bake for about 30 minutes, until golden brown. Transfer the bread to a rack to cool.

10. Store the bread, covered, at room temperature for up to 3 days or in a resealable bag in the freezer for up to 1 month.

Granny's Cinnamon Buns

Vegan option • Vegetarian • Nut-free

Makes about 12 cinnamon buns

Prep time: 15 minutes (not including making the Magic Dough), plus 1 hour rising

Cook time: 25 minutes

Cinnamon Buns

1 batch Magic Dough (page 67)

All-purpose flour, for dusting

1 cup (250 mL) butter or vegan butter, softened

1½ cups (375 mL) lightly packed brown sugar

1 tablespoon (15 mL) cinnamon

Cream Cheese Icing (optional)

¼ cup (60 mL) butter or vegan butter, softened

½ package (8 ounces/250 g) cream cheese or vegan cream cheese, room temperature

2 cups (500 mL) icing sugar, sifted

1 teaspoon (5 mL) pure vanilla extract

Vegan: Use vegan butter and vegan cream cheese.

Tori's grandma Martha was famous for her cinnamon buns. Soft and fluffy, sticky, and perfectly sweet, it's no accident that friends and family would drop in knowing there was a chance these cinnamon buns would be served. This recipe was inspired by her old-fashioned and very indulgent cinnamon bun recipe and landed somewhere between a cinnamon bun and sticky bun. They certainly are sweet enough on their own, but should you be inclined, we include a cream cheese icing recipe.

1. MAKE THE CINNAMON BUNS: Grease a 13 × 9-inch (3.5 L) baking dish.

2. Gently deflate the Magic Dough by pushing it down with your hands. Tip the dough out onto a lightly floured work surface. Use a rolling pin dusted with flour to roll out the dough into a 12 × 24-inch (30 × 60 cm) rectangle (it doesn't have to be exact) with the longer side facing you.

3. Evenly spread the butter on the dough with a rubber spatula, leaving a ½-inch (1 cm) border at the edge closest to you. Evenly sprinkle the brown sugar over the butter, then sprinkle the cinnamon evenly over the brown sugar.

4. Starting at the long edge closest to you, carefully and tightly roll the dough up into a log. With the log seam side down, use a sharp knife to cut it into 2-inch (5 cm) pieces. (You should have about 12 pieces.)

5. Place the buns cut side down in the prepared baking dish. Cover with a kitchen towel and let sit in a warm, draft-free place until doubled in size, about 1 hour.

6. Meanwhile, preheat the oven to 350°F (180°C). Place a large piece (bigger than your baking dish) of foil or parchment paper on a work surface.

7. MAKE THE CREAM CHEESE ICING (IF USING): In a medium bowl, using an electric mixer, beat the butter until smooth and fluffy. Add the cream cheese and continue beating until smooth. Add the icing sugar and vanilla and beat again until smooth. Cover and refrigerate until ready to use.

8. Bake the buns until the brown sugar mixture bubbles and the tops of the buns are golden brown, about 25 minutes. Immediately invert the baking dish onto the foil or parchment paper and let the buns cool slightly before serving.

9. Spread the Cream Cheese Icing (if using) evenly over the cinnamon buns. Store cooled cinnamon buns in a resealable container in the fridge for up to 3 days.

Veggie Cornmeal Muffins

Vegan option • Vegetarian • Gluten-free option • Nut-free option • Freezer-friendly

Makes about 20 muffins

Prep time: 20 minutes

Cook time: 30 minutes

1¼ cups (300 mL) all-purpose flour

1 cup (250 mL) fine yellow cornmeal (we use Purity brand)

¼ cup (60 mL) sugar

1 tablespoon (15 mL) baking powder

1 teaspoon (5 mL) salt

1 teaspoon (5 mL) garlic powder

1 teaspoon (5 mL) onion powder

½ teaspoon (2 mL) baking soda

2 cups (500 mL) grated Tex-Mex or Monterey Jack cheese or vegan cheese

2 eggs

1 cup (250 mL) milk or unsweetened non-dairy milk

½ cup (125 mL) extra-virgin olive oil

1½ cups (375 mL) grated unpeeled zucchini

1 cup (250 mL) frozen corn kernels, unthawed

¼ cup (60 mL) sliced green onions (white and light green parts only)

½ cup (125 mL) finely diced yellow, orange, or red sweet pepper (optional)

¼ cup (60 mL) finely chopped fresh cilantro (optional)

2 to 3 tablespoons (30 to 45 mL) finely diced seeded jalapeño pepper (optional)

Jillian has never loved sweet things, but a savoury muffin always has a place on her table. Loaded with veggies, these cornmeal muffins make for a tasty snack, breakfast on the go, or a nice touch served with a steaming bowl of soup like our Broccoli Cheeze Soup (page 152). Basically, you can serve them with anything and you'll have a happy crowd. They freeze well and are perfect for sneaking into school lunches.

The jalapeño, cilantro, or sweet peppers can be omitted if desired without compromising the texture of the muffin.

1. Preheat the oven to 375°F (190°C) and line a muffin tin with paper liners. (You may need 2 tins, depending on their size.)

2. Into a large bowl, sift the flour, cornmeal, sugar, baking powder, salt, garlic powder, onion powder, and baking soda. Stir in the grated cheese.

3. In a medium bowl, whisk the eggs. Add the milk and olive oil and whisk to combine. Stir in the grated zucchini, corn, green onions, and sweet peppers, cilantro, and jalapeños, if using.

4. Add the wet ingredients to the dry ingredients and fold with a rubber spatula until combined.

5. Divide the batter among the muffin cups. Bake until the tops are golden brown and a toothpick inserted into the centre comes out clean, about 30 minutes. Transfer the muffins to a rack to cool. Store in a resealable container in the fridge for up to 5 days or in the freezer for up to 1 month.

Vegan: Use Flax Eggs (page 330) instead of eggs, use vegan cheese, and use non-dairy milk.

Gluten-free: Use a 1:1 gluten-free flour blend instead of all-purpose flour.

Nut-free: If using non-dairy milk, use a nut-free option.

Pull-Apart Garlic Bread Biscuits

Vegetarian • Vegan option • Gluten-free option • Nut-free

Makes 8 biscuits

Prep time: 10 minutes

Cook time: 20 minutes

Biscuits

2 cups (500 mL) all-purpose flour

4 teaspoons (20 mL) baking powder

1 teaspoon (5 mL) salt

1 teaspoon (5 mL) garlic powder

1 teaspoon (5 mL) dried parsley

½ cup (125 mL) cold butter or vegan butter, diced

½ cup (125 mL) grated Parmesan cheese or vegan parm

1 tablespoon (15 mL) finely chopped fresh chives or parsley

1 egg

¾ to 1 cup (175 to 250 mL) buttermilk or Homemade Buttermilk, non-dairy version (page 324)

Garlic Butter

¼ cup (60 mL) butter or vegan butter

1 clove garlic, smashed or minced (see headnote)

Vegan: Use a Flax Egg (page 330) instead of egg and vegan cheese or omit. Follow the vegan option to make the Homemade Buttermilk.

Gluten-free: Use a 1:1 gluten-free flour blend instead of all-purpose flour.

These moist pull-apart biscuits taste just like traditional garlic bread. Served warm from the oven, they are beyond perfect for dunking in a steaming bowl of soup. The trick is in the method: the batter is scooped into mounds that are nestled next to each other on the pan, allowing the soft biscuits to bake together in one picture-perfect mound.

For the garlic butter, mince the garlic for a more pronounced flavour, or for a milder touch of garlic, simply smash the clove to infuse the butter before brushing it on the warm biscuits. Omit the cheese if you wish. We loved them both ways!

1. MAKE THE BISCUITS: Preheat the oven to 425°F (220°C) and line a baking sheet with parchment paper.

2. In a large bowl, whisk together the flour, baking powder, salt, garlic powder, and parsley. Add the butter and, using your fingers or a pastry blender, break up the butter until the pieces are the size of peas. Stir in the Parmesan and chives.

3. In a measuring cup, whisk the egg. Add the buttermilk to the 1-cup (250 mL) mark and whisk to combine.

4. Add the buttermilk mixture to the flour mixture and mix together with a rubber spatula until just combined (do not overmix). If the mixture is too dry add a couple of tablespoons of buttermilk and give it a stir. It should be thick enough to scoop.

5. Using a 4-ounce (115 g/size 8) cookie scoop, scoop 8 portions of dough and arrange on the prepared baking sheet, 1 in the middle and 7 in a circle, just touching each other. Bake until they are golden brown on the bottom, about 20 minutes.

6. MEANWHILE, MAKE THE GARLIC BUTTER: Melt the butter with the garlic in a small saucepan over low heat (or in a microwave-safe container in the microwave).

7. Brush the warm biscuits with the Garlic Butter and serve. Store any extras in a resealable container in the fridge for up to 2 days.

Appetizers

Creamy Buffalo Chick'n Dip

Vegetarian • Vegan option • Gluten-free option • Nut-free

Serves 6

Prep time: 15 minutes

Cook time: 55 minutes

1 can (20 ounces/565 g) green
jackfruit in brine, drained

1 tablespoon (15 mL) avocado oil
or vegetable oil

1 cup (250 mL) diced yellow onion

¼ cup (60 mL) + 1 tablespoon (15 mL)
hot sauce, divided (we use
Frank's Red Hot Original)

1 tablespoon (15 mL) butter or vegan
butter, melted

1 package (8 ounces/250 g) cream
cheese or vegan cream cheese,
room temperature

¾ cup (175 mL) grated cheddar
cheese or vegan cheddar
cheese, divided

½ cup (125 mL) sour cream or vegan
sour cream

1 teaspoon (5 mL) garlic powder

Salt and pepper

For garnish

¼ cup (60 mL) sliced green onions
(white and light green parts
only)

Chopped fresh cilantro

Sliced jalapeño peppers

For serving

Tortilla chips

Sliced baguette

Our cousin Sam makes the best buffalo chicken dip appetizer for all our family celebrations. It is always the first thing to disappear, and we all look forward to it every time we have a get-together. This dip is completely indulgent, creamy, spicy, and, needless to say, so addictive. We took Sam's original with chicken and gave it a plant-based makeover—it was too good not to!

The secret to this dip is canned jackfruit, a terrific replacement for chicken. Dare we even say it's better than chicken in this dip? See if your friends and family (or you!) can even tell it's not chicken! Be sure to purchase jackfruit in brine, not in syrup, for this dish. You can prepare this dip ahead of time and simply bake just before serving.

1. Preheat the oven to 400°F (200°C) and line a baking sheet with parchment paper.

2. In a medium bowl, use 2 forks to roughly shred the jackfruit. Toss the jackfruit with the avocado oil.

3. Spread the jackfruit on the prepared baking sheet and bake for 15 minutes. Remove from the oven and add the onions, 1 tablespoon (15 mL) of the hot sauce, and the melted butter. Toss to coat the jackfruit. Return to the oven and bake until golden and slightly crisp, 10 to 15 minutes. Transfer the jackfruit and onion mixture to a medium bowl. Reduce the oven to 350°F (180°C).

4. Add the remaining ¼ cup (60 mL) hot sauce, cream cheese, ½ cup (125 mL) of the cheddar, sour cream, and garlic powder to the jackfruit and onion mixture. Using a spoon or electric mixer, mix together until well combined. Season with salt and pepper to taste.

5. Transfer the mixture to a 9.5 × 6.5-inch (24 × 15 cm) oval baking dish (or similar size dish). Sprinkle the remaining ¼ cup (60 mL) cheddar over top. Bake until the cheddar has melted and the dip is bubbling around the edges, 20 to 25 minutes. Garnish with the green onions, cilantro, and sliced jalapeños if desired. Serve hot with tortilla chips and sliced baguette.

Vegan: Use vegan butter, vegan cream cheese, vegan cheddar, and vegan sour cream.

Gluten-free: Use gluten-free tortilla chips and a gluten-free baguette.

Asparagus Bundles

Vegetarian • Vegan option • Gluten-free option • Nut-free

Serves 8

Prep time: 20 minutes

Cook time: 15 minutes

1 pound (450 g) asparagus, trimmed

1 tablespoon (15 mL) extra-virgin olive oil

1 clove garlic, minced

Salt and pepper

1 sheet or block (8 ounces/225 g) puff pastry, thawed

1 cup (250 mL) grated Gouda cheese or meltable vegan cheese

1 egg

1 teaspoon (5 mL) water

Vegan: Use vegan puff pastry and vegan cheese. Skip the egg wash.

Gluten-free: Use gluten-free puff pastry.

Shortly after Jill and Justin purchased their eleven-acre farm, they were out for a walk one day and met their neighbour Glen, who had lived in the area for quite some time. He mentioned to them that their farm had many hidden gems, including wild blackberries, saskatoon bushes, wild crabapple trees, huckleberry bushes, and wild asparagus. They'd never heard of wild asparagus and thought he must be mistaken. A few months later, Justin stumbled on a patch on the side of the road, and once they knew what to look for, they realized Glen was right: wild asparagus was everywhere! Jill estimates they picked over 15 pounds of it in their first year! They found themselves eating asparagus for breakfast, lunch, and dinner, gifting it to visitors, and freezing extras. These asparagus bundles were one of their favourite recipes.

Of course, you can use store-bought asparagus, assuming you don't have it growing wild in your yard! Once picked, asparagus starts to form a woody stem called lignan at the cut end. Trim the asparagus ends just before cooking to prevent the woody lignan from reforming.

1. Preheat the oven to 425°F (220°C) and line a baking sheet with parchment paper.

2. In a large bowl, toss together the asparagus, olive oil, and garlic. Season with salt and pepper.

3. On a lightly floured work surface and with a lightly floured rolling pin, roll out the puff pastry into a 12-inch (30 cm) square. Using a sharp knife, cut the pastry into sixteen 3-inch (8 cm) squares.

4. To make the bundles, place 2 or 3 asparagus spears in the centre of a pastry square, corner to corner, with the asparagus tips slightly hanging off one end. Sprinkle the pastry lightly with about 1 tablespoon (15 mL) of cheese. Fold over the opposite corners of the pastry to enclose the asparagus, pressing to seal.

5. Transfer the asparagus bundle seam side up to the prepared baking sheet. Repeat with the remaining asparagus and pastry to make the remaining bundles.

6. Whisk together the egg and water in a small bowl. Brush the pastry with the egg wash. Bake until golden brown, about 15 minutes. Serve hot.

Baked Tofu Jalapeño Popper Bites

Vegan • Gluten-free option • Nut-free option

Serves 6 to 8

Prep time: 20 minutes (not including making the Jalapeño Pepper Jelly)

Cook time: 20 minutes

2 packages (12 ounces/350 g each) extra-firm tofu, drained

1 cup (250 mL) cornstarch

1 cup (250 mL) unsweetened non-dairy milk

2 cups (500 mL) panko crumbs

1 teaspoon (5 mL) garlic powder

1 teaspoon (5 mL) salt

½ teaspoon (2 mL) sweet paprika

¼ cup (60 mL) avocado oil

½ cup (125 mL) Jalapeño Pepper Jelly (page 96) or store-bought hot pepper jelly

Sliced jalapeño peppers, for garnish

Spicy Mayo, Sriracha variation (page 328), for drizzling or dipping

Crispy, sweet, and spicy—we can't think of any better way to eat tofu. Baking instead of frying tofu is a simple, fuss-free way to prepare this dish, but you can shallow-fry these poppers on the stovetop if you prefer. While our homemade Jalapeño Pepper Jelly (page 96) is our first choice, store-bought hot pepper jelly will work just fine. You can find hot pepper jelly in most grocery stores in the deli section or look for it at your local farmers' market. Serve these poppers hot out of the oven to keep them crunchy.

1. Preheat the oven to 400°F (200°C) and line a baking sheet with parchment paper.

2. Press the tofu between 2 sheets of paper towel or a kitchen towel to remove excess liquid. Cut the pressed tofu into ½-inch (1 cm) cubes.

3. Set out 3 medium shallow bowls. Put the cornstarch in one bowl. Put the milk in the second bowl. In the third bowl, stir together the panko crumbs, garlic powder, salt, and paprika until combined. Add the avocado oil and stir to combine.

4. To prepare the tofu, working in batches, place the tofu cubes in the cornstarch and toss to coat. Remove from the cornstarch, shaking off the excess, and place them in the milk, turning to coat. Place them in the panko coating, lightly pressing the crumb mixture on all sides to coat. Arrange on the prepared baking sheet.

5. Bake the tofu until golden brown, about 20 minutes, turning halfway through.

6. Heat the Jalapeño Pepper Jelly in a microwave-safe bowl in the microwave or in a small saucepan on the stovetop.

7. Transfer the baked tofu to a large bowl. Add the Jalapeño Pepper Jelly and toss until coated. Transfer to a serving platter and garnish with sliced jalapeños if desired. Serve hot with Spicy Mayo drizzled over top or served on the side.

Gluten-free: Use gluten-free panko crumbs.

Nut-free: Use a nut-free non-dairy milk.

Jalapeño Pepper Jelly

Vegan • Gluten-free • Nut-free

Makes about 4 cups (1 L)

Prep time: 20 minutes

Cook time: 20 minutes, plus 24 hours resting

1 cup (250 mL) finely diced seeded green sweet peppers

1 cup (250 mL) finely diced seeded jalapeño peppers

1 cup (250 mL) white vinegar

½ teaspoon (2 mL) salt

4 cups (1 L) sugar

2 packages (3 ounces/85 mL each) liquid fruit pectin

We grew up having this jalapeño pepper jelly on crackers with cream cheese every single holiday and special occasion. Our grandma and Tori's mom Patsy would make up batches every fall to have on hand year-round. We created a new appetizer, Baked Tofu Jalapeño Popper Bites (page 95), using this pepper jelly and it was devoured in minutes!

The jelly can be made with either red or green hot peppers: we suggest either red chili peppers or jalapeño peppers. If you want to kick up the spice level, simply replace the sweet peppers with the same volume of hot peppers. A food processor makes easy work of the prep but isn't quite as pretty as hand-dicing the peppers. Consider wearing food prep gloves to protect your hands while preparing hot peppers.

1. In a medium pot, combine the sweet peppers, jalapeños, vinegar, and salt. Bring to a boil over medium-high heat. Once the mixture is boiling, reduce the heat to low, cover, and simmer for 10 minutes.

2. MEANWHILE, STERILIZE MASON JARS AND LIDS: Place 4 clean 2-cup (500 mL) mason jars on a rack in a boiling water canning pot. Add 4 sealing discs (but not screw bands). Cover the jars with water, bring to a simmer, and simmer for 10 minutes. Turn off the heat and keep the jars and sealing discs in the water until ready to use.

3. Stir the sugar into the pepper mixture. Increase the heat to medium-high and return the mixture to a boil, stirring constantly, until the sugar dissolves. Remove from the heat and stir in the pectin, stirring continuously for 10 minutes. The jelly will look slightly thickened at this point.

4. Pour the hot jelly into the sterilized jars, leaving ½-inch (1 cm) headspace. Remove any air bubbles in the jelly by passing a clean thin wooden or plastic utensil between the jelly and the sides of the jars.

5. Wipe the jar rims with a clean cloth. Centre a hot sealing disc on a rim and twist on a screw band just until fingertip tight. Unprocessed jars can be stored in the refrigerator for up to 1 month.

6. TO PROCESS THE JALAPEÑO PEPPER JELLY: Return the sealed jars to the rack in the canning pot and add enough water to cover them by 1 to 2 inches (2.5 to 5 cm). Return the water to a boil, cover, and boil for 15 minutes. Remove the jars from the bath (canning tongs will help for this) and place them on a kitchen towel on the counter. Cool, undisturbed, at room temperature for 24 hours.

7. Once the jars have cooled, check the seals. If sealed properly, the centre of the lid will be concave and not pop up when pressed. Store any jars that have not sealed properly in the fridge for up to 1 month. Label and date the well-sealed jars and store in a cool, dark, dry place for up to 2 years.

Mushroom Arancini

Vegan option • Vegetarian • Gluten-free option • Nut-free

Serves 8 to 10

Prep time: 10 minutes (not including making the Mushroom Risotto)

Cook time: 15 minutes

½ batch cold Mushroom Risotto (page 189; about 4 cups/1 L)

1 cup (250 mL) panko crumbs

Avocado oil or vegetable oil, for frying

¼ cup (60 mL) thinly sliced fresh basil, for garnish

Pizza sauce or tomato sauce, for dipping

Arancini are Sicilian rice balls stuffed, coated with bread crumbs, and deep-fried. They're a fabulous way to use up leftover risotto. What a great excuse to make extra risotto! These flavourful mushroom rice balls can be enjoyed on their own, but we love them served with a warm pizza sauce for dipping. Our Sheet-Pan Tomato Sauce (page 314) is perfect as a dip if you want to make your own. Traditional arancini is stuffed with mozzarella cheese. We enjoyed them just as much unstuffed, but you can stuff each arancini with a ¼-inch (5 mm) cube of mozzarella cheese before breading and frying.

To bake these instead of frying, simply mix 2 tablespoons (30 mL) of extra-virgin olive oil into the panko crumbs before coating the arancini, then bake in the oven at 400°F (200°C) until golden brown, about 25 minutes.

1. Roll 2-tablespoon (30 mL) portions of chilled risotto into balls. You should get about 40 golf-ball-sized balls.

2. Put the panko crumbs in a shallow medium bowl. Working with 1 risotto ball at a time, roll the balls in the panko to completely coat in crumbs.

3. Pour avocado oil into a deep medium frying pan to a depth of 1 inch (2.5 cm) and heat over medium heat to 350°F (180°C) on a deep-frying thermometer.

4. Working in batches so as not to overcrowd the pan, fry the arancini until golden brown all over, about 4 minutes total. Using a slotted spoon, transfer the arancini to a plate lined with paper towel or a rack set over a baking sheet to drain excess oil.

5. Place the rice balls on a serving platter and sprinkle with the basil. Serve with pizza sauce or tomato sauce (warmed if desired) on the side for dipping.

Vegan: Follow the vegan option to make the Mushroom Risotto.

Gluten-free: Use gluten-free panko crumbs.

Cheese Toast

Vegan option • Vegetarian • Gluten-free option • Nut-free

Makes 6 toasts

Prep time: 10 minutes

Cook time: 10 minutes

3 cups (750 mL) mixed grated cheese or mixed meltable vegan cheese

¼ cup (60 mL) mayonnaise or vegan mayonnaise

½ teaspoon (2 mL) dried basil

½ teaspoon (2 mL) dried oregano

½ loaf country bread, cut into six 1-inch (2.5 cm) thick slices (or 6 slices of Texas toast bread)

1 cup (250 mL) sliced cherry tomatoes

Salt and pepper

When we lived in the small town of Peace River, Alberta, we only had a few restaurant options to choose from, and Boston Pizza was one of them. They had the best cheese toast, loaded with fresh tomatoes and herbs, and we devoured our fair share on a regular basis. We were beside ourselves when they took it off the menu. Cheese toast is our definition of comfort food and happens to be Jill's go-to snack for the kids when they're hungry and she's pinched for time. This recipe is by no means high on the health barometer, but trust us when we say you will love it! Any firm cheese works in this recipe. We default to Gouda, mozzarella, and cheddar cheese, but there are no rules.

1. Position an oven rack about 6 inches (15 cm) under the broiler and preheat the broiler. Line a baking sheet with parchment paper.

2. In a medium bowl, stir together the cheese, mayonnaise, basil, and oregano.

3. Place the slices of bread on the prepared baking sheet. Broil the bread on one side until lightly toasted, 2 to 3 minutes. Remove from the oven and turn over the slices of bread.

4. Spread an even thick layer of the cheese mixture on each toast (untoasted side). Top with the sliced tomatoes and return to the oven.

5. Broil until golden brown and the cheese is melted, about 4 minutes. Sprinkle the toasts with salt and pepper to taste. Serve hot.

Vegan: Use vegan cheese and vegan mayonnaise.

Gluten-free: Use gluten-free bread.

Devilled Spuds

Vegan • Gluten-free • Nut-free

Makes 24 devilled spuds

Prep time: 15 minutes

Cook time: 15 minutes

14 large baby potatoes (about 12 ounces/340 g)

¼ cup (60 mL) vegan mayonnaise

1 tablespoon (15 mL) dill pickle brine

2 teaspoons (10 mL) yellow mustard

½ teaspoon (2 mL) Himalayan black salt, plus more for garnish

Pinch of sweet paprika, plus more for garnish

1 tablespoon (15 mL) finely chopped fresh chives, for garnish

For those who grew up in the '80s, chances are you remember the popularity of devilled eggs! We remember a platter of devilled eggs served at almost every party on ornate plates specially designed to hold them. We still love this nostalgic appetizer, but now that Jilly's partner Justin has moved away from eating eggs, we decided to try a different twist—devilled spuds! There is something so satisfying about these delicious morsels of perfection that transport us directly back to our childhood. Slip on those gel shoes and start back-combing your bangs as you prepare to be thrown back a few decades with this one.

The Himalayan black salt adds an egg flavour; if you don't have it, simply use regular salt. For best results look for baby potatoes that are on the large side and symmetrical (think egg!). The two extra potatoes in the filling guarantee you'll have enough to fill the potatoes.

1. Add the potatoes to a large pot of water, cover with the lid slightly ajar, and boil over high heat until fork-tender, 12 to 15 minutes. Drain the potatoes.

2. Once cool enough to handle, cut 12 of the potatoes in half lengthwise. Using a melon baller or teaspoon, scoop out most of the potato, transferring the scooped-out potato to a medium bowl. Remove and discard the skin from the remaining 2 potatoes, cut in half, and add to the bowl.

3. Add the mayonnaise, pickle brine, mustard, black salt, and paprika to the bowl. Using an electric mixer, blend the mixture until smooth.

4. Transfer the potato mixture to a pastry bag fitted with a large star tip or to a resealable plastic bag with one corner cut out. Pipe the potato mixture into the potato shells.

5. Garnish with a sprinkle of paprika, more black salt, and chives.

Deep-Fried Pickles with Avocado Ranch Dip

Vegan • Gluten-free option • Nut-free

Serves 8 to 10

Prep time: 20 minutes (includes making batter)

Cook time: 15 minutes

Avocado Ranch Dip

½ ripe avocado, pitted and peeled

½ cup (125 mL) vegan mayonnaise

1 tablespoon (15 mL) fresh lemon juice

1½ teaspoons (7 mL) apple cider vinegar

Dash of Worcestershire sauce

Dash of hot sauce (optional; we use Tabasco)

¼ teaspoon (1 mL) dried dill

¼ teaspoon (1 mL) onion powder

¼ teaspoon (1 mL) garlic powder

Pinch of sweet paprika

1 teaspoon (5 mL) finely chopped fresh flat-leaf parsley

1 teaspoon (5 mL) finely chopped fresh chives

1 teaspoon (5 mL) finely chopped fresh tarragon (or ½ teaspoon/ 2 mL dried tarragon)

Salt and pepper

Deep-Fried Pickles

12 to 14 large whole dill pickles

¼ cup (60 mL) cornstarch, more as needed

1 batch Batter from Patsy's Fried Fish (page 190)

Avocado oil or canola oil, for deep-frying

Years ago, when Jillian was living in Calgary, Alberta, every Thursday night she would go to a pub with one of her best friends, Angela, and order hot wings and fried pickles. It was a weekly tradition they both looked forward to. However, as the years passed, somewhere along the way they forgot just how awesome fried pickles were. On a Team Jilly trip to Vancouver and a pit stop at Joe Fortes restaurant, Jill spotted fried pickles on the menu. She wasn't sure if her taste buds would do the same happy dance they did before . . . until she took her first bite. They were so outstanding, they needed to be in the cookbook! The amazing team at Joe Fortes helped us create this recipe inspired by their version, including a delicious avocado ranch dip.

Be sure to thoroughly dry the pickles before frying to help the batter stick. A deep-fryer is ideal for cooking these.

1. MAKE THE AVOCADO RANCH DIP: In a medium bowl, mash the avocado with a fork until smooth. Add the mayonnaise, lemon juice, apple cider vinegar, Worcestershire sauce, hot sauce (if using), dill, onion powder, garlic powder, paprika, parsley, chives, and tarragon. Whisk until combined. Season with salt and pepper to taste. Store in a resealable container in the fridge until ready to use or up to 1 day.

2. DEEP-FRY THE PICKLES: Pour avocado oil into a deep-fryer or large, heavy-bottomed pot to a depth of 3 inches (8 cm) and heat over medium-high heat to 350°F (180°C) on a deep-frying thermometer. It is important to monitor the temperature of your oil; the pickles will burn if the oil is too hot, and not be crisp if too cool. We suggest using a deep-frying thermometer.

3. Slice the pickles lengthwise into quarters. If the pickles are small, cut them in half. Pat the pickles dry with paper towel.

4. In a medium bowl, working in batches, toss the pickles in the cornstarch to coat, adding more cornstarch if needed so that each pickle spear is well coated.

5. Using tongs, dip the pickles in the batter and deep-fry the pickles in small batches (about 6 pickles) until golden brown. Be careful not to overcrowd the pot. If the pickles sink to the bottom of the pot, let them cook for 30 seconds before nudging them to avoid disturbing the batter. Using tongs, transfer the fried pickles to a large plate or baking sheet lined with paper towel to absorb excess oil. Serve hot with the Avocado Ranch Dip on the side.

Gluten-free: Use gluten-free Worcestershire sauce. Follow the gluten-free option to make the batter.

Fried Green Tomatoes

Vegan • Gluten-free option • Nut-free option

Serves 8 to 10

Prep time: 20 minutes

Cook time: 15 minutes

Dipping Sauce

¾ cup (175 mL) vegan mayonnaise

3 cloves garlic, minced

1 tablespoon (15 mL) chopped fresh
    dill (or 1 teaspoon/5 mL dried dill)

1 tablespoon (15 mL) fresh lime juice

1 to 2 teaspoons (5 to 10 mL) hot
    sauce, to taste

Salt

Fried Green Tomatoes

8 to 10 medium green tomatoes

1 cup (250 mL) + 2 tablespoons
    (30 mL) cornstarch, divided

½ cup (125 mL) vegan mayonnaise

½ cup (125 mL) unsweetened non-
    dairy milk

2 teaspoons (10 mL) salt, divided

2 teaspoons (10 mL) garlic powder,
    divided

1 cup (250 mL) panko crumbs

½ cup (125 mL) yellow cornmeal

1 teaspoon (5 mL) sweet paprika

1 teaspoon (5 mL) pepper

Avocado oil, for frying

We remember watching that scene in *Fried Green Tomatoes* where they actually ate fried green tomatoes, finding ourselves salivating at the thought of devouring a plate of our own, even though we had never had them before. A few years ago, Jillian ended up with a basket of beautiful green tomatoes from her garden and decided to give them a shot. They lived up to her expectations after all those years! The crunchy coating contrasting with the firm bright green tomato, dipped in this highly addictive sauce, had us weak in the knees. This recipe is a great way to use up those green tomatoes in your garden in the warmer late summer months.

Even though it may be tempting, we recommend not using red tomatoes, as they won't hold up during cooking.

1. MAKE THE DIPPING SAUCE: In a small bowl, whisk together the mayonnaise, garlic, dill, lime juice, and hot sauce. Season with salt and refrigerate until ready to use.

2. MAKE THE FRIED GREEN TOMATOES: Slice the tomatoes horizontally into ¼-inch (5 mm) thick slices. Set aside.

3. Set out 3 shallow medium bowls. Put 1 cup (250 mL) of the cornstarch in one bowl. In the second bowl, whisk together the mayonnaise, milk, 1 teaspoon (5 mL) of the salt, and 1 teaspoon (5 mL) of the garlic powder. In the third bowl, stir together the panko crumbs, cornmeal, the remaining 2 tablespoons (30 mL) cornstarch, paprika, the remaining 1 teaspoon (5 mL) garlic powder, the remaining 1 teaspoon (5 mL) salt, and pepper.

4. Pour avocado oil into a medium frying pan to a depth of ½ inch (1 cm) and heat over medium heat to 350°F (180°C) on a deep-frying thermometer.

5. To prepare the tomatoes, working with 1 slice at a time, dredge the tomato in the cornstarch, turning to lightly coat. Place the tomato in the mayonnaise mixture, turning to coat. Finish with the seasoned panko, coating both sides.

6. Working in small batches, fry the tomatoes until golden brown, about 2 minutes per side. Using tongs, transfer the fried tomatoes to a baking sheet or plate lined with paper towel to absorb excess oil. Place on a serving platter and serve immediately with the Dipping Sauce on the side.

Gluten-free: Use gluten-free panko crumbs.

Nut-free: Use a nut-free non-dairy milk.

Heirloom Tomato Pie

Vegetarian • Vegan option • Gluten-free option • Nut-free option

Serves 6

Prep time: 10 minutes

Cook time: 20 minutes

1 sheet or block (8 ounces/225 g) puff pastry, thawed

¾ cup (175 mL) soft goat cheese or vegan cream cheese, room temperature

2 to 3 tablespoons (30 to 45 mL) 2% milk, half-and-half (10%) cream, or unsweetened non-dairy milk

2 tablespoons (30 mL) pesto or Carrot-Top Pesto (page 305)

3 or 4 large heirloom tomatoes, sliced ¼ inch (5 mm) thick

Salt and pepper

¼ cup (60 mL) chopped fresh basil

⅓ cup (75 mL) grated Asiago cheese or vegan parm

Tori has learned a couple of things about Jillian over the years. First, she doesn't like sweet things. Second, she *loves* tomatoes. It's a serious obsession, and always has been. Tori created this tomato pie for Jillian using beautiful heirloom tomatoes fresh from the farmers' market at the height of summer. This recipe uses puff pastry for a simple fuss-free base. If you don't have access to heirloom tomatoes, use the best quality fresh tomatoes you can find. Serve this as a light lunch with a green salad or as an elegant appetizer with a glass of crisp white wine.

1. Preheat the oven to 400°F (200°C). Have a baking sheet on hand.

2. Place a large piece of parchment paper (about 12 × 20 inches/30 × 50 cm) on a work surface. Place the puff pastry on the parchment paper and use a lightly floured rolling pin to roll it out into a 10 × 15-inch (25 × 38 cm) rectangle. It doesn't have to be exact. Carefully slide the parchment and pastry onto the baking sheet.

3. In a medium bowl, stir together the goat cheese, milk (just enough to make it spreadable), and pesto until smooth. Spread the mixture evenly over the pastry, leaving a ½-inch (1 cm) border of pastry around the outer edge.

4. Arrange the tomato slices in rows (or however you want; this is a rustic tart), slightly overlapping, to cover the cheese mixture. Season with salt and pepper. Sprinkle with the basil leaves and top with the Asiago cheese. Bake until the pastry is golden brown and the cheese starts to bubble, about 20 minutes. Serve immediately.

Vegan: Use vegan puff pastry, vegan cheese, and non-dairy milk.

Gluten-free: Use gluten-free puff pastry.

Nut-free: Use nut-free pesto and nut-free non-dairy milk.

Classic Chickpea Hummus

Vegan • Gluten-free option • Nut-free

Serves 4 to 6

Prep time: 5 minutes

1 can (19 ounces/540 mL) chickpeas, drained and chickpea liquid reserved

¼ cup (60 mL) extra-virgin olive oil, plus more for garnish

3 to 4 tablespoons (45 to 60 mL) fresh lemon juice, to taste

2 tablespoons (30 mL) tahini

2 to 3 cloves garlic

½ teaspoon (2 mL) salt

Chopped fresh flat-leaf parsley, for garnish (optional)

Pita Crisps (page 117) or warmed pita bread, for serving

Hummus is a protein-packed Middle Eastern chickpea dip (hummus actually means "chickpea" in Arabic) that is traditionally served with pita bread and often topped with a drizzle of olive oil, olives, paprika, and parsley. We'll be the first to admit that we are extremely picky when it comes to hummus. We like it smooth and creamy, not too thick, and walking that fine line between just the right amounts of lemon, garlic, and salt. This is the recipe we turn to every time.

You can easily make this ahead and use it in a variety of ways, including as a dip on a veggie platter, a spread for your favourite sandwich, with Pita Crisps (page 117), or simply with fresh pita like our Pita-Style Flatbreads (page 71) for dipping. It's a perfect snack staple for a busy week!

Add just enough of the liquid from the canned chickpeas to get a creamy consistency and adjust the amount of garlic to your taste; we are fans so we always add that extra clove! To dress up your hummus, check out our Loaded Hummus recipes (page 113).

1. In a high-speed blender or small food processor, combine the chickpeas, olive oil, lemon juice, tahini, garlic, and salt. Mix on low speed and slowly increase the speed, gradually adding the reserved chickpea liquid (⅓ to ½ cup/75 to 125 mL) while blending, until you reach a smooth, creamy consistency. Add more salt to taste if desired.

2. Transfer the hummus to a serving dish. Garnish with a drizzle of olive oil and a sprinkle of parsley, if using. Serve with Pita Crisps or warmed pita bread. Store the hummus in a resealable container in the fridge for up to 3 days.

Gluten-free: Serve with gluten-free pita bread.

Loaded Hummus

Vegetarian • Vegan option • Gluten-free • Nut-free

Serves 4 to 6

Prep time (for each variation): 15 minutes (not including making the Classic Chickpea Hummus)

Turn that dip into a meal by dressing up a batch of Classic Chickpea Hummus (page 110) with a heap of fresh toppings served with a stack of freshly baked Pita-Style Flatbreads (page 71). We were inspired by the way hummus is often served in the Middle East—topped with vibrant, flavourful garnishes. It's simple, beautiful, and healthy. Need we say more? Be creative with your toppings! These two variations are our favourites.

¼ cup (60 mL) diced English cucumber

¼ cup (60 mL) sliced pitted Kalamata olives

¼ cup (60 mL) diced tomatoes or cherry tomatoes cut in half

¼ cup (60 mL) Quick Pickled Red Onions (page 320)

2 tablespoons (30 mL) crumbled feta cheese or vegan feta cheese

1 batch Classic Chickpea Hummus (page 110)

Garnishes

¼ teaspoon (1 mL) dried oregano

¼ teaspoon (1 mL) red chili flakes (optional)

Extra-virgin olive oil, for drizzling

2 tablespoons (30 mL) finely chopped fresh flat-leaf parsley

Mediterranean Loaded Hummus

1. In a medium bowl, stir together the cucumber, olives, tomatoes, Pickled Red Onions, and feta until combined.

2. Spread the Classic Chickpea Hummus in a shallow serving bowl or plate. Spoon the mixture over the hummus. Garnish with the oregano, chili flakes (if using), a drizzle of olive oil, and parsley.

Vegan: Use vegan feta cheese.

Tex-Mex Loaded Hummus

¼ cup (60 mL) diced tomatoes or cherry tomatoes cut in half

¼ cup (60 mL) diced white or red onion

½ avocado, pitted, peeled, and diced

¼ cup (60 mL) canned or frozen corn kernels, cooked and cooled

1 tablespoon (15 mL) diced seeded jalapeño pepper (optional)

1 tablespoon (15 mL) chopped fresh cilantro, plus more for garnish

Pinch of ground cumin

Pinch of chili powder

1 teaspoon (5 mL) lime zest

Juice of ½ lime

1 teaspoon (5 mL) extra-virgin olive oil

Salt

1 batch Classic Chickpea Hummus (page 110)

¼ cup (60 mL) crumbled feta cheese or vegan feta cheese

Lime wedges, for garnish

1. In a medium bowl, combine the tomatoes, onion, avocado, corn, jalapeño (if using), cilantro, cumin, chili powder, lime zest, lime juice, and olive oil. Stir together to combine. Season with salt.

2. Spread the Classic Chickpea Hummus in a shallow serving bowl or plate. Spoon the mixture over the hummus. Sprinkle with the feta and garnish with more cilantro and lime wedges.

Vegan: Use vegan feta cheese.

Pita Crisps

Vegetarian • Vegan option • Gluten-free option • Nut-free

Serves 6

Prep time: 5 minutes

Cook time: 10 minutes

6 pitas, each cut into 6 wedges

2 tablespoons (30 mL) extra-virgin olive oil

2 tablespoons (30 mL) butter or vegan butter, melted

Seasoning Variations

Garlic Lover's

½ teaspoon (2 mL) garlic powder

½ teaspoon (2 mL) onion powder

½ teaspoon (2 mL) salt, or to taste

Italian Herb and Cheese

1 teaspoon (5 mL) Italian seasoning

¼ cup (60 mL) grated Parmesan cheese or vegan parm

½ teaspoon (2 mL) salt, or to taste

Cinnamon Sugar

1 teaspoon (5 mL) cinnamon

2 tablespoons (30 mL) sugar

Your favourite dips have just met their soulmate. These pita crisps are very addictive! We love how versatile they are and how ridiculously simple they are to make. The sky's the limit when it comes to how creative you can get with the seasonings. Serve the Garlic Lover's Pita Crisps with our Loaded Hummus (page 113), Creamy Buffalo Chick'n Dip (page 91), or any of the flavour variations on their own as a satisfying snack. You can also cut the pitas into 1-inch (2.5 cm) squares to use them as croutons.

1. Position the oven racks in the upper and lower thirds of the oven and preheat to 350°F (180°C). Line 2 baking sheets with parchment paper.

2. In a large bowl, mix together the olive oil and melted butter. Add the pita wedges and toss until evenly coated. Sprinkle in the desired seasoning, depending on the variation you wish to make, and toss to combine. Transfer the pitas to the prepared baking sheets in a single layer.

3. Bake until just golden, 8 to 10 minutes, flipping the pitas and rotating the pans halfway through. Cool on the baking sheet. The pita crisps will continue to get crispy as they cool. Store in a resealable container at room temperature for up to 3 weeks.

Vegan: Use vegan butter and vegan parm.

Gluten-free: Use gluten-free pita bread.

Pizza Seed Crackers

Vegan • Gluten-free option • Nut-free

Makes about 20 crackers

Prep time: 10 minutes

Cook time: 35 minutes

1 cup (250 mL) sunflower seeds

½ cup (125 mL) pumpkin seeds

½ cup (125 mL) hemp hearts

3 tablespoons (45 mL) all-purpose flour

2 tablespoons (30 mL) ground flaxseed

2 tablespoons (30 mL) chia seeds

1 tablespoon (15 mL) nutritional yeast

1 teaspoon (5 mL) dried oregano

1 teaspoon (5 mL) dried basil

1 teaspoon (5 mL) garlic powder

1 teaspoon (5 mL) onion powder

1 teaspoon (5 mL) flaky sea salt, plus more for garnish

½ teaspoon (2 mL) ground fennel seeds

½ teaspoon (2 mL) black pepper

Red chili flakes (optional)

1 cup (250 mL) boiling water

2 tablespoons (30 mL) tomato paste

1 tablespoon (15 mL) olive oil

Jillian started making these crackers when her family went plant-based so they'd have a wholesome, fibre-rich, and protein-packed snack and a source of healthy fats. They're filled to the brim with nutritious seeds and have a subtle pizza flavour. Once you start eating them, we dare you to stop! Plus, they are so simple to make. Our favourite way to enjoy these crackers is topped with a spread of cream cheese or vegan cream cheese and sliced cherry tomatoes with a sprinkle of flaky sea salt.

1. Preheat the oven to 350°F (180°C) and line a baking sheet with parchment paper.

2. In a large bowl, stir together the sunflower seeds, pumpkin seeds, hemp hearts, flour, flaxseed, chia seeds, nutritional yeast, oregano, basil, garlic powder, onion powder, flaky sea salt, fennel seeds, black pepper, and chili flakes to taste, if using.

3. In a medium bowl, whisk together the boiling water, tomato paste, and olive oil until well combined.

4. Pour the tomato mixture into the seed mixture and mix with a wooden spoon until well combined.

5. Transfer the mixture to the prepared baking sheet and spread evenly in a thin layer using the back of a large spoon. Sprinkle with more flaky sea salt if desired.

6. Bake until golden brown around the edges, 30 to 35 minutes. Let the cracker cool completely on the baking sheet before breaking it into large pieces. Store in a resealable container at room temperature for up to 1 week.

Gluten-free: Use a 1:1 gluten-free flour blend instead of all-purpose flour.

Fraiche Fruit Salsa

Vegan • Gluten-free • Nut-free

Serves 4 to 6

Prep time: 10 minutes

2 cups (500 mL) diced fresh fruit

¾ cup (175 mL) loosely packed chopped fresh cilantro

¼ cup (60 mL) finely diced red onion

1 clove garlic, minced

1 tablespoon (15 mL) extra-virgin olive oil

½ teaspoon (2 mL) salt

Juice of 1 lime

½ jalapeño pepper, seeded and finely diced (optional)

This vibrant sweet and spicy salsa is extremely versatile. Make it with peaches, pineapple, mango, or even kiwi, depending on what's in season or on hand. It's ideal at the peak of peach season to elevate simple grilled fish or chicken or try it as part of the Tropical Tofu Bowls (page 186) or with Coconut-Crusted Halibut (page 176). Of course, you can also enjoy the salsa solo with stacks of tortilla chips or Pita Crisps (page 117). Any way you serve it, you'll feel like you're taking a vacay with each scoop!

1. In a medium bowl, mix together all the ingredients. Cover and refrigerate until ready to serve. This salsa is best enjoyed when freshly made but can be stored, covered, in the fridge for up to 2 days.

Prawn Potstickers

Dairy-free • Nut-free • Freezer-friendly

Makes about 70 potstickers

Prep time: 45 minutes

Cook time: 20 minutes

Sesame Soy Dipping Sauce

¼ cup (60 mL) soy sauce

2 teaspoons (10 mL) pure maple syrup

1 tablespoon (15 mL) unseasoned rice vinegar

1 teaspoon (5 mL) sesame oil

½ teaspoon (2 mL) sesame seeds

Pinch of red chili flakes (optional)

Potstickers

2 cups (500 mL) roughly chopped napa cabbage

1 can (8 ounces/227 g) sliced water chestnuts, drained

1 cup (250 mL) chopped peeled carrots

½ pound (225 g) cremini or mixed mushrooms

1 pound (450 g) fresh prawns, peeled and deveined

2 tablespoons (30 mL) avocado oil or vegetable oil

2 tablespoons (30 mL) grated peeled fresh ginger

4 cloves garlic, minced

⅓ cup (75 mL) sliced green onions (white and light green parts only), plus more for garnish

One of Jillian's favourite places to eat when she visits Maui is Monkeypod Kitchen. Not only do they have the world's best mai tais (try our version on page 287), but they also have amazing potstickers. Potstickers are Chinese dumplings steamed on one side, then fried to crispy perfection on the other. According to legend, they were invented when a chef in China's imperial court accidentally burned a batch of dumplings after leaving them on the stove too long. The best kind of accident, if you ask us!

These crispy yet tender dumplings, filled with a vegetable prawn filling and dunked in a mouthwatering Sesame Soy Dipping Sauce, take a bit of time to make but are worth the effort. A food processor saves you buckets of time here. Note that you can freeze filled but uncooked potstickers on a baking sheet, then store in a resealable container in the freezer for up to 1 month. Fry and steam just slightly longer than the times given below.

1. MAKE THE SESAME SOY DIPPING SAUCE: In a small bowl, whisk together the soy sauce, maple syrup, rice vinegar, sesame oil, sesame seeds, and chili flakes, if using. Set aside.

2. MAKE THE POTSTICKERS: In a food processor, combine the cabbage, water chestnuts, and carrots and pulse until finely chopped. Transfer the mixture to a large bowl. Add the mushrooms to the food processor and pulse just until finely chopped (be careful not to turn them into a paste). Add the mushrooms to the cabbage mixture.

3. Add the prawns to the food processor and pulse until just minced.

4. Heat the avocado oil in a large frying pan over medium-high heat. Add the ginger and cook, stirring constantly, until fragrant, 1 to 2 minutes. Add the cabbage and mushroom mixture and cook, stirring occasionally, until softened, 4 to 5 minutes. Add the garlic, green onions, soy sauce, sesame oil, rice vinegar, and sugar. Stir to combine and cook for 1 minute. Remove from the heat and stir in the minced prawns.

Recipe and ingredients continue

3 tablespoons (45 mL) soy sauce

2 tablespoons (30 mL) sesame oil

1½ teaspoons (7 mL) unseasoned
rice vinegar

1 teaspoon (5 mL) sugar

2 packages (8 ounces/225 g each)
round dumpling wrappers
(about 70 wrappers)

Avocado oil or vegetable oil,
for frying

Sesame seeds, for garnish (optional)

5. Fill a small bowl with water and line a baking sheet with parchment paper or waxed paper. To fill the potstickers, working with 1 dumpling wrapper at a time, scoop 2 to 3 teaspoons (10 to 15 mL) of the filling into the middle of the wrapper. Dip your finger in the water and wet the outer edge of the wrapper.

6. Fold the wrapper over the filling to create a half-moon shape, then pinch the edges together to seal. If the edges are not sticking together, wet your fingers with a little water and pinch again. Place the potsticker seam side up on the prepared baking sheet. Repeat with the remaining potstickers.

7. COOK THE POTSTICKERS: Heat about 1 tablespoon (15 mL) of the avocado oil in a large frying pan with a lid over medium heat. Working in batches so as not to overcrowd the pan, add the potstickers in a single layer, seam side up, and cook until golden brown and crisp on the bottom, 2 to 3 minutes.

8. Pour ¼ cup (60 mL) water into the pan, cover with the lid, and steam until the potstickers are slightly translucent, about 3 minutes. Transfer the cooked potstickers to a serving platter. Repeat with the remaining potstickers, adding more oil to the pan as needed.

9. Sprinkle the potstickers with sesame seeds (if using) and sliced green onions. Serve warm with the Sesame Soy Dipping Sauce for dipping.

Sweet and Spicy Vegan Lettuce Wraps

Vegan • Gluten-free option • Nut-free option

Serves 4 to 6

Prep time: 25 minutes (not including soaking the soy curls)

Cook time: 45 minutes

Lettuce Wraps

1 package (8 ounces/225 g) dried soy curls

½ cup (125 mL) cornstarch

¼ cup (60 mL) avocado oil or vegetable oil

1 cup (2 ounces/50 g) dried chow mein noodles

½ cup (125 mL) sliced green onions (white and light green parts only), divided

1 teaspoon (5 mL) sesame seeds

1 to 2 heads iceberg lettuce or butter lettuce, leaves separated

Spicy Mayo, Sriracha variation (page 328)

¼ cup (60 mL) roughly chopped unsalted peanuts

⅓ cup (75 mL) roughly chopped fresh cilantro, for garnish

Lime wedges, for serving

Sweet Chili Sauce

½ cup (125 mL) water, divided

¼ cup (60 mL) unseasoned rice vinegar

¼ cup (60 mL) sugar

2 teaspoons (10 mL) soy sauce

¼ to ½ teaspoon (1 to 2 mL) red chili flakes

3 cloves garlic, minced

1 teaspoon (5 mL) cornstarch

Before her TV debut, Jillian worked at Cactus Club Café in Vancouver, making her way from server to head designer at warp speed. One of the perks of her promotion was a Cow Card, earning her (and her tag-along Tori) a much-appreciated discount. We ate our way through the menu and developed a couple of food crushes along the way, including their lettuce wraps. On any given girls' night, you could often find us at Cactus Club, eating our weight in lettuce wraps.

After years of ordering them, we were finally inspired to create our own version, replacing the chicken with baked crispy soy curls. These are so good! We double-dare you to tell us this doesn't taste like chicken! Transform this addictive appetizer into a heartier main dish simply by adding steamed rice or rice noodles to the filling, or chop the lettuce and serve on rice to create a bowl.

1. Preheat the oven to 450°F (230°C) and line a baking sheet with parchment paper.

2. START THE LETTUCE WRAPS—SOAK THE SOY CURLS: Place the soy curls in a large bowl and cover with boiling water. Let soak to rehydrate, 10 to 15 minutes.

3. MEANWHILE, MAKE THE SWEET CHILI SAUCE: In a small saucepan, combine ¼ cup (60 mL) of the water, rice vinegar, sugar, soy sauce, chili flakes, and garlic. Bring to a simmer over medium heat and cook for 2 to 3 minutes, until the sugar dissolves.

4. Add the cornstarch to a measuring cup. Pour in the remaining ¼ cup (60 mL) water while stirring to create a slurry. Add the slurry to the pot, bring back to a simmer, and cook, stirring, for 2 minutes to thicken the sauce. Remove from the heat and set aside until ready to serve.

5. COAT AND BAKE THE SOY CURLS: Drain the soy curls and squeeze them to remove excess water. Pat dry with a kitchen towel or paper towel. Wipe the bowl dry. Return the soy curls to the bowl and toss with the cornstarch until coated. Drizzle with the avocado oil and toss again to combine.

Recipe and ingredients continue

Ginger Hoisin Sauce

1 tablespoon (15 mL) avocado oil or vegetable oil

1 tablespoon (15 mL) grated peeled fresh ginger

1 tablespoon (15 mL) minced garlic (about 5 cloves)

½ cup (125 mL) hoisin sauce

6. Evenly spread the coated soy curls on the prepared baking sheet and bake for 10 minutes, turning halfway through, until crispy and lightly browned.

7. MEANWHILE, MAKE THE GINGER HOISIN SAUCE: Heat the avocado oil in a small frying pan over medium heat. Add the ginger and garlic and cook, stirring occasionally, until fragrant, about 2 minutes. Add the hoisin sauce and cook, stirring occasionally, until just heated. Remove from the heat.

8. ASSEMBLE THE LETTUCE WRAPS: In a large bowl, combine the baked soy curls with the chow mein noodles. Add the warm Ginger Hoisin Sauce and toss to coat. Transfer to a serving dish. Garnish with half of the green onions and the sesame seeds.

9. Serve with the lettuce leaves, Sweet Chili Sauce, Spicy Mayo, peanuts, the remaining green onions, cilantro, and lime wedges.

Gluten-free: Use gluten-free soy sauce or tamari and gluten-free hoisin sauce. Skip the chow mein noodles.

Nut-free: Skip the peanuts.

Salads and Soups

Okanagan Coleslaw

Vegetarian • Vegan option • Gluten-free • Nut-free

Serves 4 to 6

Prep time: 10 minutes

2 cups (500 mL) finely shredded purple cabbage

2 cups (500 mL) finely shredded green cabbage

1 cup (250 mL) shredded peeled carrot

1 Ambrosia apple, unpeeled and diced

2 tablespoons (30 mL) sunflower seeds

¼ cup (60 mL) dried cranberries or cherries (optional)

Creamy French Dressing (page 327)

Everyone needs a trusty coleslaw recipe, and this is ours, Okanagan-style! The apples and dried fruit add just the right amount of sweetness with extra crunch and flavour thanks to the sunflower seeds. Serve this coleslaw (omit the sunflower seeds and dried fruit and add cilantro) with Patsy's Fried Fish (page 190) and Salt and Vinegar Potatoes (page 237). Ambrosia apples are the best variety for resisting browning once cut, making them perfect for this salad, but in a pinch any sweet, crisp apple will do—just add it shortly before tossing with the dressing. Should you be short for time, feel free to use a coleslaw mix as a base instead of the cabbage and carrot.

1. In a large bowl, combine the purple cabbage, green cabbage, carrots, apple, sunflower seeds, and cranberries, if using. At this stage, the coleslaw can be stored in a resealable container in the fridge for up to 3 days.

2. When ready to serve, toss with enough Creamy French Dressing to coat. The coleslaw tossed with the dressing can be stored in a resealable container in the fridge for up to 1 day.

Vegan: Follow the vegan option to make the Creamy French Dressing.

Dill Pickle Potato Salad

Vegetarian • Vegan option • Gluten-free • Nut-free

Serves 8

Prep time: 30 minutes

Cook time: 15 minutes

3 pounds (1.4 kg) baby white or red potatoes

½ cup (125 mL) mayonnaise or vegan mayonnaise

½ cup (125 mL) sour cream, vegan sour cream, or plain full-fat Greek yogurt

½ cup (125 mL) finely chopped red onion

½ cup (125 mL) chopped fresh dill, plus more for garnish

3 tablespoons (45 mL) grainy Dijon mustard

1 teaspoon (5 mL) dill pickle brine

3 stalks celery, thinly sliced

1 cup (250 mL) thinly sliced dill pickles

½ cup (125 mL) thinly sliced radishes, divided

Salt and pepper

This salad is what all potatoes want to be when they grow up (ironically, it's made with baby potatoes). Every summer gathering of our childhood included some version of potato salad. This one wins the gold medal thanks to the added crunch of dill pickles, a splash of pickle brine, and an extra handful of fresh herbs for good measure. It's basically perfect, if we do say so ourselves. If you prefer a milder onion flavour, use green onions instead of red ones.

1. Bring a large pot of salted water to a boil. Add the potatoes and cook until fork-tender, 12 to 15 minutes. Drain the potatoes and rinse under cold running water. Drain again and set aside to cool to room temperature.

2. Meanwhile, in a large bowl, whisk together the mayonnaise, sour cream, red onion, dill, mustard, and pickle brine.

3. Once the potatoes are cool, cut into halves or quarters (depending on their size) and add them to the dressing. Add the celery, dill pickles, and ¼ cup (60 mL) of the radishes and mix until well combined. Season with salt and pepper. Transfer the potato salad to a serving dish.

4. Garnish with the remaining ¼ cup (60 mL) radishes and fresh dill. Refrigerate the potato salad, covered, until serving or for up to 3 days.

Vegan: Use vegan mayonnaise and vegan sour cream.

Goat Cheese Croquettes

Vegan option • Vegetarian • Gluten-free option • Nut-free

Makes about 12 croquettes

Prep time: 10 minutes, plus
30 minutes to 1 hour chilling

Cook time: 12 minutes

---

1 log (11 ounces/300 g) goat cheese
    or vegan cream cheese

¾ cup (175 mL) panko crumbs

¼ teaspoon (1 mL) salt

¼ teaspoon (1 mL) pepper

¼ cup (60 mL) all-purpose flour

2 eggs

Avocado oil or canola oil, for frying

Crunchy on the outside and irresistibly creamy on the inside, discs of goat cheese fried to crispy perfection create the most incredible crouton imaginable. We use these goat cheese croquettes in our Autumn Beet Salad with Honey Mustard Dressing (page 139) and our Grilled Romaine Salad with Roasted Tomatoes (page 136). They are just as great on top of any salad, such as our Spring Garden Salad (page 140), or any grain bowl.

1. Unwrap the goat cheese log and freeze it on a small baking sheet lined with parchment paper for 30 minutes to 1 hour. This will keep the cheese firm during frying.

2. When the cheese is cold, use a sharp knife to cut the log crosswise into ½-inch (1 cm) thick slices. If needed, reshape the cheese slices into smooth patties with your hands. If using vegan cream cheese, scoop 1-tablespoon (15 mL) balls onto a baking sheet and freeze for 30 minutes to 1 hour before pressing into patties.

3. Set out 1 shallow medium bowl and 2 shallow small bowls. In the medium bowl, stir together the panko crumbs, salt, and pepper. In the first small bowl, place the flour. In the second small bowl, beat the eggs.

4. To prepare the croquettes, dredge 3 or 4 goat cheese rounds in the flour, coating all sides. Place the cheese in the egg, turning to coat and letting excess drip off. Finish with the panko, coating both sides. Transfer to a large plate. Repeat to coat the remaining goat cheese rounds.

5. Pour ¼ inch (5 mm) of avocado oil into a small, heavy-bottomed frying pan over medium heat. Working in batches, fry the croquettes until golden brown, about 2 minutes per side, adding more oil to the pan as needed. Transfer the croquettes to a plate lined with paper towel to absorb excess oil or to a rack. Serve hot or at room temperature. Store the croquettes in a resealable container in the fridge for up to 2 days and reheat in the oven if desired.

Vegan: Use vegan cream cheese instead of goat cheese. Use ½ cup (125 mL) unsweetened non-dairy milk instead of eggs.

Gluten-free: Use gluten-free panko crumbs. Use a 1:1 gluten-free flour blend instead of all-purpose flour.

Grilled Romaine Salad with Roasted Tomatoes

Vegan option • Vegetarian • Gluten-free option • Nut-free

Serves 4

Prep time: 20 minutes (not including making the Goat Cheese Croquettes)

Cook time: 10 minutes

Dressing

¼ cup (60 mL) extra-virgin olive oil

1 tablespoon (15 mL) white wine vinegar

2 teaspoons (10 mL) Dijon mustard

½ teaspoon (2 mL) Worcestershire sauce

2 cloves garlic, minced

1 teaspoon (5 mL) minced drained capers

3 tablespoons (45 mL) grated Parmesan cheese, vegan parm, or nutritional yeast

3 tablespoons (45 mL) mayonnaise or vegan mayonnaise

Juice of 1 lemon

Salt and pepper

Salad

2 hearts of romaine lettuce

3 tablespoons (45 mL) extra-virgin olive oil, divided

Salt and pepper

10 ounces (280 g) small tomatoes

1 batch Goat Cheese Croquettes (page 135), room temperature or warmed

---

Much like for Tori, many of Jill's jobs leading up to today were in the service industry. One of the restaurants she worked at was the iconic 4th Street Rose in Calgary, known for its high-end rustic vibe. They served a grilled romaine Caesar salad, and one bite of this updated version takes Jill right back!

We suggest making the dressing and the croquettes ahead of time, reheating in the oven if desired, and blistering the tomatoes and grilling the lettuce just before it's time to eat.

1. MAKE THE DRESSING: In a mason jar with a lid, combine the olive oil, vinegar, mustard, Worcestershire sauce, garlic, capers, Parmesan, mayonnaise, lemon juice, and salt and pepper to taste. Seal the jar and shake until smooth. (Alternatively, you can blend with an immersion blender until smooth.) Adjust seasoning if needed. Store in the fridge until ready to use. The dressing can be stored, covered, in the fridge for up to 3 days.

2. Preheat a grill for direct cooking over medium heat.

3. MAKE THE SALAD: Cut the hearts of romaine lengthwise down the middle. Brush the lettuce all over with 2 tablespoons (30 mL) of the olive oil. Season with salt and pepper.

4. In a small bowl, toss the tomatoes with the remaining 1 tablespoon (15 mL) olive oil. Season with salt and pepper.

5. Using tongs, place the tomatoes and romaine, cut side down, directly on the hot grill. (Keep the bowl nearby.) Grill, turning the tomatoes occasionally, until charred and blistered and the romaine is lightly charred on the cut side, about 3 minutes. Transfer the grilled tomatoes to the bowl. Turn the lettuce and continue grilling for another 2 minutes. Transfer the grilled romaine to a plate.

6. For serving, arrange the grilled romaine on a platter. Top with the grilled tomatoes and Goat Cheese Croquettes. Drizzle with the dressing and serve.

Vegan: Use vegan mayonnaise and vegan parm or nutritional yeast in the dressing. Follow the vegan option to make the Goat Cheese Croquettes.

Gluten-free: Use gluten-free Worcestershire sauce. Follow the gluten-free option to make the Goat Cheese Croquettes.

Autumn Beet Salad
with Honey Mustard Dressing

Vegan option • Vegetarian • Gluten-free option • Nut-free option

Serves 4 to 6

Prep time: 15 minutes (not including making the Goat Cheese Croquettes)

Cook time: 40 minutes

Autumn Beet Salad

2 large red beets, peeled and cut into ½-inch (1 cm) thick wedges

1 tablespoon (15 mL) extra-virgin olive oil

Salt and pepper

8 cups (2 L) lightly packed torn curly kale (stems removed)

2 Bartlett pears, cored and thinly sliced

1 batch Goat Cheese Croquettes (page 135)

½ cup (125 mL) raw walnuts

¼ cup (60 mL) pumpkin seeds

Honey Mustard Dressing

¼ cup (60 mL) mayonnaise or vegan mayonnaise

2 tablespoons (30 mL) fresh lemon juice

2 tablespoons (30 mL) pure liquid honey or pure maple syrup

2 teaspoons (10 mL) Dijon mustard

1 teaspoon (5 mL) yellow mustard

Pinch of salt

We both grow beets in our gardens and admit that we're really after what most people throw out—the beet leaves. Our Ukrainian heritage taught us how to be resourceful with food, and as such, there is no part of a beet (or pretty much any food) that goes unused. Come fall, we are both looking for ways to use the buckets of beets that are spilling out of our gardens. This hearty salad always comes to the rescue. It features all the flavours we know and love about fall. The Honey Mustard Dressing is perfectly sweet and creamy. But the Goat Cheese Croquettes (page 135) are the true star.

You can easily make all the components ahead of time and assemble just before serving (slice the pear just before serving so it doesn't turn brown). We typically use red beets, though other varieties such as yellow beets will work just as nicely.

1. ROAST THE BEETS: Preheat the oven to 400°F (200°C) and line a baking sheet with parchment paper.

2. In a large bowl, toss the beet wedges in the olive oil. Season with salt and pepper. Spread the beets in a single layer on the prepared baking sheet and roast until fork-tender, 35 to 40 minutes. Let the beets cool slightly on the baking sheet. The beets can be served warm or stored in a resealable container in the fridge for up to 2 days. (You can reheat the beets before serving if desired but you don't have to.)

3. MEANWHILE, MAKE THE HONEY MUSTARD DRESSING: In a small bowl, combine the mayonnaise, lemon juice, honey, Dijon mustard, yellow mustard, and salt. Whisk together until smooth.

4. ASSEMBLE THE SALAD: In a large serving bowl or on a platter, layer the kale, sliced pears, roasted beets, and Goat Cheese Croquettes. Sprinkle with the walnuts and pumpkin seeds. Drizzle with the Honey Mustard Dressing and serve.

Vegan: Follow the vegan option to make the Goat Cheese Croquettes. Use vegan mayonnaise and maple syrup instead of honey to make the dressing.

Gluten-free: Follow the gluten-free option to make the Goat Cheese Croquettes.

Nut-free: Use more pumpkin seeds instead of walnuts.

Spring Garden Salad

Vegan option • Vegetarian • Gluten-free • Nut-free

Serves 6

Prep time: 15 minutes

---

8 cups (2 L) mixed greens

1 cup (250 mL) thinly sliced
English cucumber

6 to 8 edible pansies (optional)

4 radishes, thinly sliced

1 cup (250 mL) spring peas in
their pods

1 cup (250 mL) halved cherry
tomatoes

Creamy French Dressing
(page 327)

2 tablespoons (30 mL) roughly
chopped fresh dill, plus
more for garnish

This is not your grandma's boring green salad. (Actually, neither of us can recall our grandma making a salad, ever.) Jill loves to whip up this stunning dish with vibrant veggies straight from her garden. Perfect for a brunch or a picnic, it's prepared with fresh mixed greens and garnished with spring peas in their pods and beautiful edible pansies. The peas in their pods make eating this salad so much more fun, but don't eat the pods. This is so incredibly easy to put together, but it looks like something straight from a magazine. It is truly a feast for the stomach and the eyes.

Be sure to use edible pansies (with no pesticides).

1. In a large shallow serving bowl, layer the mixed greens, cucumber, pansies (if using), radishes, spring peas, and cherry tomatoes.

2. Stir the chopped dill into the Creamy French Dressing.

3. Garnish the salad with more dill and serve with the Creamy French Dressing on the side to keep the salad fresh and pretty.

Vegan: Follow the vegan option to make the Creamy French Dressing.

Prawn Chopped Salad

Gluten-free • Nut-free

Serves 4

Prep time: 15 minutes

Cook time: 20 minutes

Tarragon Dressing

⅓ cup (75 mL) extra-virgin olive oil

2 tablespoons (30 mL) white wine vinegar

2 tablespoons (30 mL) finely diced shallots

2 tablespoons (30 mL) chopped fresh tarragon (or 2 teaspoons/ 10 mL dried tarragon)

1 tablespoon (15 mL) fresh lemon juice

1½ teaspoons (7 mL) pure liquid honey

Salt and pepper

Poached Prawns

2 tablespoons (30 mL) sea salt or kosher salt

2 teaspoons (10 mL) cracked black peppercorns

1 teaspoon (5 mL) lime zest

2 teaspoons (10 mL) fresh lime juice

1 sprig fresh tarragon (or 1 teaspoon/ 5 mL dried tarragon), plus more for garnish

1 pound (450 g) fresh prawns, peeled and deveined

Salad

1½ cups (375 mL) thinly sliced celery

1 cup (250 mL) fresh or frozen corn kernels, cooked and cooled

¼ cup (60 mL) diced red onion

1 head butter lettuce

At a previous job years ago, Jillian had a weekly lunch with her boss, and they always ordered the same thing: a chopped prawn salad. She *still* thinks about that salad. Although she hasn't tasted it since or been able to get her hands on the recipe, she recreated it just how she imagines it tasted twenty-some years ago. This salad is the definition of fresh, with crisp sliced celery, and it's packed full of flavour thanks to an aromatic tarragon dressing. It is light and vibrant, perfect for a spring or summer picnic or lunch.

1. MAKE THE TARRAGON DRESSING: In a small bowl, whisk together the olive oil, vinegar, shallots, tarragon, lemon juice, and honey. Season with salt and pepper. Cover and refrigerate until ready to serve. You can make the dressing up to 2 days in advance and store in a resealable container in the fridge.

2. POACH THE PRAWNS: Prepare an ice bath by filling a large bowl half-full with ice. Fill the bowl with cold water to cover the ice.

3. Fill a large pot with water. Add the salt, peppercorns, lime zest, lime juice, and tarragon. Bring to a boil over medium-high heat, then reduce the heat to low and simmer for about 15 minutes. Add the prawns and cook until they just turn pink and are cooked through, 3 to 5 minutes depending on their size.

4. Drain the prawns and immediately transfer to the ice bath to chill. Once chilled, drain the prawns, pat dry with paper towel, and transfer to a medium bowl.

5. ASSEMBLE THE PRAWN CHOPPED SALAD: Add the celery, corn, and red onion to the prawns and mix together. Drizzle in the Tarragon Dressing. (You may not need all the dressing.)

6. Separate the lettuce leaves and arrange them to line a medium serving platter. Spoon the prawn mixture into the centre. Garnish with more tarragon if desired and serve.

Soba Noodle Salad

Vegan • Gluten-free option • Nut-free

Soba Noodle Salad

1 package (12.8 ounces/363 g) soba noodles

1 cup (250 mL) shredded purple cabbage

1 cup (250 mL) shredded romaine lettuce or savoy cabbage

1 cup (250 mL) cooked shelled edamame

1 cup (250 mL) diced English cucumber

1 cup (250 mL) thinly sliced red, orange, or yellow sweet pepper

½ cup (125 mL) shredded peeled carrots

½ cup (125 mL) roughly chopped fresh cilantro

½ cup (125 mL) thinly sliced green onions (white and light green parts only)

¼ cup (60 mL) sesame seeds

Lime wedges, for serving

Wafu-Inspired Dressing

3 tablespoons (45 mL) vegan mayonnaise

2 tablespoons (30 mL) soy sauce

2 tablespoons (30 mL) unseasoned rice vinegar

1 tablespoon (15 mL) sesame oil

1 tablespoon (15 mL) fresh lime juice

1 tablespoon (15 mL) sugar

1 tablespoon (15 mL) grated yellow onion or white onion

1 tablespoon (15 mL) grated peeled fresh ginger

When introduced to wafu dressing, Jill instantly fell in love with its flavour profile. Wafu is a Japanese-style dressing typically made with soy sauce, rice vinegar, and vegetable oil. We were inspired by it to create this soba noodle salad that is so fresh and flavourful. Our dressing is creamy thanks to the addition of mayonnaise, with the flavour of ginger peeking through.

This salad can be made with either romaine lettuce or savoy cabbage—either is great but we love the crispness of the savoy. If you want to take this recipe to the next level, try toasting your sesame seeds to bring out their flavour. You can add tofu or cooked shrimp to turn this into a complete meal.

1. START THE SOBA NOODLE SALAD: Cook the soba noodles according to the package directions. Drain the noodles and rinse under cold running water. Let cool.

2. MEANWHILE, MAKE THE WAFU-INSPIRED DRESSING: In a small bowl, whisk together the mayonnaise, soy sauce, rice vinegar, sesame oil, lime juice, sugar, onion, and ginger.

3. ASSEMBLE THE SALAD: In a large bowl, combine the cooled soba noodles, cabbage, lettuce, edamame, cucumber, sweet peppers, and carrots. Toss together. Drizzle with the Wafu-Inspired Dressing. Garnish with the cilantro, green onion, and sesame seeds. Serve with the lime wedges on the side.

Gluten-free: Use 100% buckwheat soba noodles and gluten-free soy sauce or tamari.

Grilled Halloumi Watermelon Salad

Vegetarian • Vegan option • Nut-free

Serves 4 to 6

Prep time: 20 minutes

Cook time: 6 minutes

1 tablespoon (15 mL) avocado oil

1 package (8.8 ounces/250 g) halloumi cheese, cut into ½-inch (1 cm) thick slices

3 cups (750 mL) lightly packed arugula

1 cup (250 mL) snow peas

½ small watermelon (1.3 pounds/ 600 g), cubed or cut into small triangles (4 cups/1 L)

1 avocado, pitted, peeled, and sliced

½ cup (125 mL) sprouts (see headnote)

¼ cup (60 mL) raw pumpkin seeds

¼ cup (60 mL) thinly sliced red onion

¼ cup (60 mL) thinly sliced radishes

Creamy French Dressing (page 327)

If summertime were a salad, this would be it. It's salty, crunchy, sweet, and super refreshing. It's the kind of salad you would serve to your best friend, since it's basically the food equivalent of going to the spa. We fell in love with a similar watermelon salad on a trip to Honolulu for Jillian's birthday and haven't stopped thinking about it since.

If you haven't had cooked halloumi cheese before, you are in for such a treat! Halloumi has a high melting point, making it easy to grill or sear. Instead of grilling it on the stovetop, feel free to fire up the barbecue to medium heat, brush the halloumi with the olive oil, and sear for 2 to 3 minutes per side. There are so many interesting types of sprouts available; we used pea sprouts but you can use whatever you have available.

1. Heat the avocado oil in a large nonstick grill pan or frying pan over medium-high heat. Sear the halloumi slices until crispy and browned, 2 to 3 minutes per side.

2. To assemble the salad, arrange the arugula, snow peas, watermelon, avocado, sprouts, pumpkin seeds, red onion, and radishes on a large platter or in a shallow serving dish. Top with the grilled halloumi and drizzle with the Creamy French Dressing to taste.

Vegan: Skip the cheese. Follow the vegan option to make the Creamy French Dressing.

Autumn Rice Soup

Vegan option • Gluten-free option • Nut-free option

Serves 6 to 8

Prep time: 20 minutes

Cook time: 45 minutes

2 tablespoons (30 mL) extra-virgin olive oil, butter, or vegan butter

1 cup (250 mL) finely chopped yellow onion

4 cloves garlic, minced

8 ounces (225 g) sliced cremini mushrooms (about 3 cups/750 mL)

1 butternut squash (1½ pounds/675 g), peeled and cut into ½-inch (1 cm) cubes (4 cups/1 L)

2 stalks celery, sliced

2 bay leaves

1 can (19 ounces/540 mL) white beans, drained and rinsed

2 tablespoons (30 mL) chopped fresh flat-leaf parsley (or 2 teaspoons/ 10 mL dried parsley)

1 tablespoon (15 mL) chopped fresh sage

½ teaspoon (2 mL) chopped fresh thyme

10 cups (2.4 L) vegetable stock

1 cup (250 mL) rice (we use jasmine)

1 cup (250 mL) Cashew Cream (page 324)

1 cup (250 mL) roughly chopped curly kale leaves (stems removed)

½ cup (125 mL) grated Parmesan cheese or vegan parm

Salt and pepper

This rustic soup tastes like fall in a bowl, according to one of our recipe testers, and we couldn't agree more. Filled with hearty vegetables and earthy herbs, this creamy vegan soup is filling enough to be called dinner. Serve with thick slices of our No-Knead Bread (page 79) or a batch of Pull-Apart Garlic Bread Biscuits (page 87) for a match made in heaven.

1. Heat the olive oil in a large, heavy-bottomed pot over medium heat. Add the onions and cook, stirring occasionally, until soft and translucent, 3 to 4 minutes.

2. Add the garlic and mushrooms and cook, stirring occasionally, until fragrant and the mushrooms have softened, 3 to 5 minutes.

3. Add the squash, celery, bay leaves, beans, parsley, sage, thyme, and vegetable stock. Stir to combine. Bring to a boil, then reduce the heat to a simmer, cover, and cook for 15 minutes. Stir in the rice, cover, and continue to simmer, stirring occasionally, until the rice is cooked, about 20 minutes.

4. Add the Cashew Cream, kale, and Parmesan and stir until combined. Remove from the heat and season with salt and pepper. Remove and discard the bay leaves.

Vegan: Use vegan butter and vegan parm.

Gluten-free: Use gluten-free vegetable stock.

Nut-free: Use table (18%) cream or unsweetened soy creamer instead of Cashew Cream. (If using table cream, the recipe will not be vegan.)

Lentil Soup

Vegan • Gluten-free option • Nut-free • Freezer-friendly

Serves 4 to 6

Prep time: 15 minutes, plus soaking

Cook time: 1 hour

1½ cups (375 mL) dried green lentils

1 tablespoon (15 mL) extra-virgin olive oil

1 cup (250 mL) finely diced yellow onion

2 cloves garlic, minced

¾ cup (175 mL) diced peeled carrot

¾ cup (175 mL) diced celery

3 medium tomatoes, roughly chopped

1 teaspoon (5 mL) ground coriander

1 teaspoon (5 mL) ground cumin

1 bay leaf (optional)

8 cups (2 L) chicken-flavoured vegetarian stock or vegetable stock

Salt and pepper

There is something so satisfying about a pot of soup full of vegetables simmering on the stove. Lentils are packed with fibre and protein, making this a perfect vegetarian dish to add to your repertoire of quick, healthy meals. Jill was not a lentil fan until one day she came by the Jillian Harris Design headquarters and Shay was eating this soup—one of Tori's recipes she made all the time! Jill took one taste and the soup was instantly a staple in her house. So of course it had to make its way into the cookbook. For anyone trying to lean into more plant-based eating, this soup is a great place to start.

You can use canned lentils to shave time off the cooking. Simply stir in 1 can (19 ounces/540 mL) drained lentils with the stock, simmer for 10 minutes, and you're done!

1. Rinse the lentils and soak in water for at least 3 hours or preferably overnight. (You can skip the soaking step, but they will take about twice as long to cook.)

2. Heat the olive oil in a large, heavy-bottomed pot over medium heat. Add the onions and cook, stirring occasionally, until soft and translucent, 3 to 4 minutes. Stir in the garlic, carrots, and celery and cook, stirring occasionally, until the vegetables soften, about 4 minutes. Stir in the tomatoes, coriander, cumin, and bay leaf (if using) and cook, stirring occasionally, until the tomatoes start to break down, about 5 minutes.

3. Drain the lentils and add to the pot. Stir in the vegetarian stock, cover with the lid slightly ajar, and simmer until the lentils are soft, about 45 minutes. Do not overcook or the lentils will be mushy. Season with salt and pepper. Store in a resealable container in the fridge for up to 3 days or in the freezer for up to 1 month.

Gluten-free: Use gluten-free vegetable stock.

Broccoli Cheeze Soup

Vegan • Gluten-free option • Nut-free option

Serves 6 to 8

Prep time: 20 minutes (not including making the Garlic Croutons)

Cook time: 30 minutes

---

1 tablespoon (15 mL) extra-virgin olive oil

1 tablespoon (15 mL) vegan butter

1 cup (250 mL) finely chopped yellow onion

2 cloves garlic, minced

1 cup (250 mL) finely chopped celery (2 stalks)

¼ cup (60 mL) dry white wine or vegetable stock

8 cups (2 L) roughly chopped broccoli (keep florets and tender stems separate)

6 cups (1.5 L) vegetable stock, plus more to thin if needed

1 cup (250 mL) thickly sliced peeled carrots

1 pound (450 g) russet potatoes (about 2 medium potatoes), peeled and cut into ½-inch (1 cm) cubes

½ cup (125 mL) raw cashews

½ cup (125 mL) nutritional yeast

1 tablespoon (15 mL) apple cider vinegar

Salt and pepper

1 batch Garlic Croutons (page 306)

Broccoli cheese soup was an absolute staple in our households growing up. We are always looking for ways to reinvent our favourite dishes into plant-forward versions and just had to try our hand with this soup. This soup is loaded with veggies (broccoli stalks included, so no waste!) and gets its creamy texture from raw cashews and potatoes that are cooked right in the soup and blended for zero hassle (unlike traditional cashew cream). We like to serve this soup sprinkled with Garlic Croutons (page 306) or with our Dinner Buns (page 68).

1. Melt the olive oil and vegan butter in a large, heavy-bottomed pot over medium heat. Add the onions and cook, stirring occasionally, until soft and translucent, 3 to 4 minutes. Add the garlic and celery and cook, stirring occasionally until fragrant, 2 to 3 minutes. (Be careful not to burn the garlic.)

2. Deglaze the pot with the white wine and cook, stirring occasionally, until reduced by half, 2 to 3 minutes. Stir in the broccoli stems, vegetable stock, carrots, potatoes, and cashews. Bring to a boil over medium-high heat, then reduce the heat to low, cover, and simmer, stirring occasionally, until the veggies are soft, about 20 minutes.

3. Meanwhile, in a steamer basket set over a pot of boiling water, steam the broccoli florets until tender, about 4 minutes. Drain and rinse under cold running water. Set aside.

4. Remove the soup from the heat and stir in the nutritional yeast and apple cider vinegar. Season with salt and pepper. Using an immersion blender, blend the soup until smooth. Add half the broccoli florets and pulse the soup with the immersion blender just until small broccoli bits are visible. (Alternatively, you can blend the soup, working in batches, in a high-speed blender with a vented lid to let the steam escape. Be careful; the soup is hot.)

5. Stir the remaining broccoli florets into the soup. Thin with more stock if needed for desired consistency. Serve hot with Garlic Croutons for sprinkling on top.

Gluten-free: Use gluten-free vegetable stock. Follow the gluten-free option to make the Garlic Croutons or skip them.

Nut-free: Use ½ cup (125 mL) table (18%) cream or unsweetened soy creamer instead of cashews. (If using table cream, the recipe will not be vegan.)

Thai Coconut Soup

Vegan option · Gluten-free option · Nut-free

1 tablespoon (15 mL) coconut oil

1 cup (250 mL) diced yellow onion

3 cloves garlic, minced

1 (1-inch/2.5 cm) piece fresh galangal or fresh ginger, thinly sliced

2 tablespoons (30 mL) red curry paste

2 stalks lemongrass, trimmed and sliced crosswise into 3-inch (8 cm) pieces

3 cups (750 mL) chicken-flavoured vegetarian stock or vegetable stock

1 can (14 ounces/400 mL) full-fat coconut milk

1 can (14 ounces/400 mL) coconut cream

1 tablespoon (15 mL) palm sugar or light brown sugar

1 tablespoon (15 mL) fish sauce

2 makrut lime leaves (optional)

1 can (15 ounces/425 mL) whole peeled straw mushrooms, sliced (or 2 cups/500 mL sliced shiitake or cremini mushrooms)

1 package (12 ounces/350 g) firm tofu, diced

14 ounces (400 g) fresh prawns, peeled and deveined

½ cup (125 mL) chopped fresh cilantro, divided

½ package (8 ounces/225 g) dried flat rice noodles (optional)

Salt

2 limes, 1 juiced and 1 cut into wedges

Tori started making this soup many years ago after she attended a cooking course in Chiang Mai, northern Thailand (what an experience!). We created this Thai coconut soup that was inspired by this same soup that Tori learned how to make during her travels, filled with aromatic Thai flavours. Add rice noodles for a heartier meal and a couple of sliced fresh red bird's eye Thai chilies to dial up the heat if you prefer.

To source the harder-to-find ingredients, pop by an Asian grocery store or well-stocked grocery store, or purchase the ingredients online. We've included substitutes should you need them.

1. Heat the coconut oil in a large, heavy-bottomed pot over medium heat. Add the onions and cook, stirring occasionally, until soft and translucent, 3 to 4 minutes. Add the garlic, galangal, curry paste, and lemongrass and cook, stirring occasionally, until fragrant, 3 to 4 minutes.

2. Stir in the vegetarian stock, coconut milk, coconut cream, palm sugar, fish sauce, and lime leaves, if using. Reduce the heat to low, stir, cover, and simmer for 15 minutes. Add the mushrooms, stir to combine, cover, and continue simmering until the mushrooms have softened, about 5 minutes. Add the tofu, prawns, and ¼ cup (60 mL) of the cilantro and stir to combine. Simmer until the prawns are cooked through, about 5 minutes, depending on their size. Remove from the heat.

3. Meanwhile, if adding rice noodles, cook the noodles according to the package directions, drain, and divide the noodles among the bowls.

4. Season the soup with salt and add the juice of 1 lime. Remove and discard the galangal or ginger, lemongrass, and the lime leaves, if used.

5. Ladle the soup into the bowls and garnish with the remaining ¼ cup (60 mL) cilantro. Serve with lime wedges.

Vegan: Skip the fish sauce and prawns.

Gluten-free: Use gluten-free vegetable stock.

Coconut Seafood Chowder

Vegan option · Gluten-free option · Nut-free

Serves 6

Prep time: 15 minutes

Cook time: 20 minutes

---

3 tablespoons (45 mL) extra-virgin olive oil

1½ cups (375 mL) finely chopped yellow onion

1 cup (250 mL) diced celery

4 cloves garlic, minced

4 cups (1 L) vegetable stock, plus more to thin if needed

1 pound (450 g) baby potatoes, quartered

1 bay leaf

1 teaspoon (5 mL) fresh thyme leaves

1 pound (450 g) skinless, boneless wild salmon fillet

Salt and pepper

1 can (14 ounces/400 mL) full-fat coconut milk

1 cup (250 mL) frozen corn kernels

½ pound (225 g) large fresh prawns, peeled and deveined

2 tablespoons (30 mL) roughly chopped fresh dill, plus more for garnish

Lemon wedges, for garnish

You will never believe that this creamy Maritime-inspired seafood chowder is dairy-free! This recipe is unbelievably simple but beyond impressive, coming together in a few short steps. Delicately cooked salmon and prawns simmer in a coconut broth filled with tender baby potatoes, sweet corn kernels, and fresh dill.

Pair this soup with glasses of crisp rosé wine and a basket of Pull-Apart Garlic Bread Biscuits (page 87) to soak up all of the flavourful broth. We are both passionate about using wild-caught spot prawns and line-caught wild salmon—local, if you can!

1. Heat the olive oil in a large, heavy-bottomed pot over medium heat. Add the onions, celery, and garlic and cook, stirring occasionally, until fragrant, 3 to 4 minutes.

2. Stir in the vegetable stock, potatoes, bay leaf, and thyme. Bring to a boil, then reduce the heat to low, cover, and simmer until the potatoes are fork-tender, 8 to 10 minutes.

3. Meanwhile, cut the salmon fillet into 1 to 1½-inch (2.5 to 4 cm) wide pieces. Season with salt and pepper.

4. Once the potatoes are fork-tender, stir in the coconut milk, frozen corn, prawns, salmon, and dill. Continue to simmer over low heat until the seafood is just cooked through, about 5 minutes. Remove and discard the bay leaf. Season with salt and pepper. Add more stock to thin to the desired consistency if needed.

5. Ladle the chowder into bowls. Garnish with a sprinkle of dill and a lemon wedge.

Vegan: Substitute 1 can (19 ounces/540 mL) chickpeas, drained and rinsed, for the salmon and prawns.

Gluten-free: Use gluten-free vegetable stock.

Ramen Bar

Vegan option • Vegetarian • Gluten-free option • Nut-free

Serves 4

Prep time: 30 minutes

Cook time: 20 minutes

Broth

2 tablespoons (30 mL) sesame oil

8 ounces (225 g) cremini or shiitake mushrooms, sliced

4 cloves garlic, minced

2 tablespoons (30 mL) grated peeled fresh ginger

8 cups (2 L) chicken-flavoured vegetarian stock or vegetable stock

¼ cup (60 mL) soy sauce

2 tablespoons (30 mL) white (shiro) miso paste

2 packages (3 ounces/85 g each) instant ramen noodles

Ramen Bar Add-Ins

Nori

Sliced red or yellow sweet peppers

Sprouts

Enoki mushrooms

Peas or snap peas

Broccoli florets

Purple cabbage

Corn kernels

Firm tofu, cubed

Shelled edamame

Baby bok choy, chopped

Matchstick carrots or zucchini

Fresh cilantro, chopped

Soft-boiled eggs, peeled and halved

Sambal oelek or Sriracha sauce

Sliced green onions (white and light green parts only)

Sesame seeds

Lime wedges

Ramen is a Japanese soup that originated in China. It is a combination of a flavourful broth (meat- or sometimes fish-based), wheat-based noodles, and a selection of meats or vegetables, and often soft-boiled eggs. Along with different kinds of broths, toppings, and noodle styles, regional variations are plentiful in Japan.

We love this ramen recipe for so many reasons. This broth isn't exactly a mirror of a traditional version, but we can't get enough of the flavours and endless ingredients that can be added to create a wholesome one-bowl meal that everyone loves.

Set out the add-ins in separate bowls to create a "bar" so everyone can customize their own ramen. If adding eggs, we recommend boiling them for 7 minutes to yield a perfect runny yolk for this soup; you can adjust the time depending on your preference. We enjoyed pairing this meal with a lovely chardonnay.

1. MAKE THE BROTH: Heat the sesame oil in a large pot over medium heat. Add the mushrooms and cook, stirring occasionally, 3 to 4 minutes. Add the garlic and ginger and cook, stirring constantly, until fragrant, 2 to 3 minutes.

2. Stir in the vegetarian stock, soy sauce, and miso paste and stir until the miso is dissolved and the broth comes to a boil. Reduce the heat to low, cover, and simmer for 15 minutes. Add the ramen noodles and cook until done, 2 to 3 minutes. Remove from the heat.

3. ASSEMBLE: While the broth is simmering, add the desired add-ins to 4 bowls. Ladle the hot broth into the bowls, allowing the vegetables to get slightly tender. Cool slightly before enjoying.

Vegan: Omit the eggs.

Gluten-free: Use gluten-free vegetable stock, gluten-free ramen noodles, and gluten-free soy sauce or tamari.

Main Dishes

Fish Tacos

Gluten-free option • Nut-free

Serves 4 to 6

Prep time: 15 minutes (not including making Patsy's Fried Fish and Cilantro Lime Rice)

Cilantro Vinaigrette

½ cup (125 mL) loosely packed cilantro, plus more for garnish

¼ cup (60 mL) fresh lime juice

1 tablespoon (15 mL) grated peeled fresh ginger

1 tablespoon (15 mL) pure liquid honey

½ teaspoon (2 mL) sesame oil

¼ teaspoon (1 mL) salt

½ cup (125 mL) extra-virgin olive oil

Fish Tacos

1 batch Cilantro Lime Rice (page 225)

2 cups (500 mL) finely shredded red or green cabbage

1 batch Patsy's Fried Fish (page 190), using 1 cod fillet (2 pounds/900 g) cut into ½-inch (1 cm) strips or pieces

8 to 12 (6-inch/15 cm) flour tortillas, warmed

Sliced fresh or pickled jalapeño peppers or Cowboy Candy (page 316; optional)

Quick Pickled Red Onions (page 320)

We could write a book about all of the life events that have gone down at Two Eagles Golf Course in Kelowna. It was where Tori and Charles met, and between the open-bar weddings (never a good idea!), baby showers, and Jill and our cousin Sam driving a golf cart into a pond, it's a mini miracle that they even let us in the doors. Thank goodness they do, because we cannot get enough of their fish tacos. For years, we have been begging Neil, owner of the golf course restaurant 19 Okanagan Grill + Bar, for the recipe. We are thrilled to share a very slightly modified version of Chef Geoff's recipe—we could not resist using Patsy's Fried Fish (page 190) for our tacos! The cilantro vinaigrette is so good that you'll want to make a double batch—you won't regret it. We love you, Neil. Thanks for putting up with all our shenanigans!

1. MAKE THE CILANTRO VINAIGRETTE: In a high-speed blender, combine the cilantro, lime juice, ginger, honey, sesame oil, and salt and blend until smooth. With the motor running, slowly pour in the olive oil and blend until emulsified and creamy. Transfer to a resealable container and refrigerate until ready to use.

2. ASSEMBLE THE FISH TACOS: Layer the Cilantro Lime Rice, cabbage, and Patsy's Fried Fish in the centre of each tortilla. Top with the jalapeños (if using), Pickled Red Onions, and a generous drizzle of the Cilantro Vinaigrette. Garnish with more cilantro.

Gluten-free: Use gluten-free tortillas. Follow the gluten-free option to make Patsy's Fried Fish.

Baked Crispy Cauliflower Sandwiches

Vegan • Gluten-free option • Nut-free option

Serves 4

Prep time: 25 minutes

Cook time: 30 minutes

Baked Crispy Cauliflower

1 large head cauliflower

1 cup (250 mL) vegan mayonnaise

2 tablespoons (30 mL) water or unsweetened non-dairy milk

1 cup (250 mL) all-purpose flour

2 teaspoons (10 mL) sweet paprika, divided

2 teaspoons (10 mL) garlic powder, divided

2 teaspoons (10 mL) salt, divided

½ teaspoon (2 mL) pepper, divided

2 cups (500 mL) panko crumbs

¼ cup (60 mL) extra-virgin olive oil

Sandwiches

4 large hamburger buns or ciabatta rolls

Vegan mayonnaise or Spicy Mayo (page 328)

Lettuce

Sliced dill pickles

Thinly sliced red onion

Sliced tomatoes

Hot sauce (optional)

These sandwiches are so crispy and satisfying and make for such a fun dinner! Toasting the panko crumbs is the secret to golden, crispy cauliflower steaks that are perfectly crunchy. If you love hot sauce as much as we do, make these sandwiches buffalo-style by coating the baked cauliflower steaks with your favourite hot sauce just before serving. Load them up with all of your favourite toppings, grab a napkin, and dig in.

Reserve for another recipe any cauliflower florets that fall away while cutting the steaks (freeze to use in your next smoothie; see page 27). Serve these sandwiches with our Dill Pickle Potato Salad (page 132), Salt and Vinegar Potatoes (page 237), or Okanagan Coleslaw (page 131).

1. Preheat the oven to 400°F (200°C) and line a large baking sheet with parchment paper.

2. PREPARE THE CAULIFLOWER STEAKS: Remove and discard the leaves from the cauliflower. Using a large, sharp knife, trim the stem end so the cauliflower sits flat on the cutting board. Cut the cauliflower from top to bottom, making the first cut through the centre and keeping the stem intact, into four ¾-inch (2 cm) thick steaks. Save the remainder for another use.

3. Set out 3 shallow medium bowls. In one bowl, whisk together the mayonnaise and water. In the second bowl, stir together the flour, 1 teaspoon (5 mL) of the paprika, 1 teaspoon (5 mL) of the garlic powder, 1 teaspoon (5 mL) of the salt, and ¼ teaspoon (1 mL) of the pepper. In the third bowl, stir together the panko crumbs and the remaining 1 teaspoon (5 mL) paprika, 1 teaspoon (5 mL) garlic powder, 1 teaspoon (5 mL) salt, and ¼ teaspoon (1 mL) pepper.

4. TOAST THE PANKO MIXTURE: Heat the olive oil in a large frying pan over medium heat. Scatter in the panko mixture and cook, stirring constantly, until the panko is lightly toasted and fragrant, about 3 minutes. Return the toasted panko to the bowl.

Recipe continues

5. COAT AND BAKE THE CAULIFLOWER STEAKS: Using your hands, coat each cauliflower steak on both sides in the flour mixture, shaking off the excess. (If the flour mixture doesn't stick, lightly rinse the cauliflower under running water, then coat again.) Place the cauliflower in the mayo mixture, turning to coat. Finish with the panko coating, lightly pressing it into both sides. Place the cauliflower steaks 1 inch (2.5 cm) apart on the prepared baking sheet. Bake until the cauliflower steaks are golden brown, about 30 minutes, turning halfway through.

6. ASSEMBLE THE SANDWICHES: Toast the buns if desired. Spread some mayonnaise on the bun halves. Place a cauliflower steak on the bottom half of each bun, then top each with lettuce, pickles, red onions, tomatoes and any other desired toppings. Finish the sandwiches with the tops.

Gluten-free: Use 1:1 gluten-free flour blend instead of all-purpose flour, gluten-free panko crumbs, and gluten-free buns.

Nut-free: If using non-dairy milk, use a nut-free option.

Butternut Squash Gyros

Vegetarian • Vegan option • Gluten-free option • Nut-free

Serves 4

Prep time: 20 minutes

Cook time: 40 minutes

Butternut Squash Filling

1 medium butternut squash
(2½ pounds/1.125 kg), peeled
and cut into ½-inch (1 cm)
cubes (6½ cups/1.625 mL)

3 tablespoons (45 mL) avocado oil
or vegetable oil

1 teaspoon (5 mL) ground coriander

1 teaspoon (5 mL) ground cumin

1 teaspoon (5 mL) garlic powder

1 teaspoon (5 mL) sweet paprika

½ teaspoon (2 mL) salt

¼ teaspoon (1 mL) pepper

Salad

1 English cucumber, diced

2 tomatoes, diced

2 tablespoons (30 mL) finely diced
red onion

1 clove garlic, minced

2 tablespoons (30 mL) extra-virgin
olive oil

2 tablespoons (30 mL) chopped
fresh dill, plus more for garnish

1 tablespoon (15 mL) pickled red
onion brine or white vinegar

Salt

Finding wholesome, hearty plant-based meals that are approved by everyone is not always easy. One day Jillian tried a vegan spin on gyros, a Greek dish traditionally made with roasted meat served in a folded pita. Rather than filling them with the traditional meat, Jillian decided to fill hers with roasted butternut squash, and they were an instant hit with her family! Both the kids and Justin loved these squash gyros, and they have since earned a permanent slot in their dinner rotation.

These gyros taste great with a side of Classic Chickpea Hummus (page 110), and should you feel ambitious, try making Pita-Style Flatbreads (page 71). Use hot paprika instead of sweet paprika to add heat to the gyros. Pepperoncini peppers will also do the trick!

1. MAKE THE BUTTERNUT SQUASH FILLING: Preheat the oven to 425°F (220°C) and line a baking sheet with parchment paper.

2. In a large bowl, combine the squash, avocado oil, coriander, cumin, garlic powder, paprika, salt, and pepper. Toss to mix well. Spread the squash mixture evenly on the prepared baking sheet. Roast until the squash is golden brown and tender, about 30 minutes, tossing halfway through.

3. MEANWHILE, MAKE THE SALAD: In a medium bowl, mix together the cucumber, tomatoes, red onion, garlic, olive oil, dill, and pickled red onion brine. Season with salt.

Recipe and ingredients continue

Garlic Dill Sauce

1 cup (250 mL) plain full-fat Greek
    yogurt or non-dairy plain yogurt

2 tablespoons (30 mL) mayonnaise
    or vegan mayonnaise

2 tablespoons (30 mL) fresh lemon
    juice

4 cloves garlic, minced

1 tablespoon (15 mL) chopped
    fresh dill

Pinch of salt

For serving

4 large Greek pitas

Olive oil, for toasting the pita

Quick Pickled Red Onions
    (page 320)

Feta cheese or vegan feta
    cheese, crumbled (optional)

Fresh dill

4. MAKE THE GARLIC DILL SAUCE: In a small bowl, stir together the yogurt, mayonnaise, lemon juice, garlic, dill, and salt.

5. ASSEMBLE THE GYROS: Heat a dry medium nonstick frying pan over medium-high heat. Working with 1 pita at a time, drizzle a little olive oil on each side and heat in the pan until lightly toasted, about 1 minute per side.

6. In the centre of each pita, layer the roasted butternut squash, salad, Garlic Dill Sauce, Pickled Red Onions, and a sprinkle of feta , if using. Garnish with the dill and fold the sides together.

Vegan: Use non-dairy yogurt, vegan mayonnaise, and vegan feta cheese.

Gluten-free: Use gluten-free Greek pitas.

Chicken Paprikash with Nokedli

Nut-free

Serves 4

Prep time: 20 minutes

Cook time: 1 hour

Chicken Paprikash

2 pounds (900 g) skin-on, bone-in chicken thighs

Salt

3 tablespoons (45 mL) extra-virgin olive oil, divided

1 large sweet onion, chopped

1 clove garlic, minced

1 teaspoon (5 mL) Hungarian sweet paprika

2 tomatoes, chopped

1 green sweet pepper, chopped

1 tablespoon (15 mL) all-purpose flour

¼ cup (60 mL) sour cream

Black pepper

Chopped fresh flat-leaf parsley, for garnish

Nokedli (dumplings)

3 cups (750 mL) all-purpose flour

1½ teaspoons (7 mL) salt

3 eggs

1½ cups (375 mL) water

This traditional Hungarian chicken paprikash (paprikás csirke) is straight from Tori's husband Charles's family recipe files in Debrecen, Hungary. Tori was introduced to this dish when she met his family for the very first time on their European honeymoon, and what an adventure that was. Stepping into Debrecen was the most authentic version of farm-to-table that either Tori or Charles had ever witnessed. From raising their own chickens that were cooked on an open fire to growing grapes to make their own wine, everything happened in the family's little backyard. Nothing was wasted and everything was precious, the way it should be. Tori and Charles sat around that fire learning how to make this dish, sipping homemade pálinka (a Hungarian fruit spirit), and soaking up Charles's family history from his aunts and uncles. Fast-forward many years later, this nostalgic and utterly mouthwatering dish with tender pieces of chicken and a creamy sauce remains a staple in the Wesszer home, and Charles often makes it for family and friends.

The homemade dumplings, tender with the perfect texture to soak up the sauce, are truly worth the effort. Though you can make the dumplings by hand, a Hungarian (or German) dumpling maker or spaetzle maker will make it much easier. The large holes of a colander can also be used.

1. START THE CHICKEN PAPRIKASH: Pat the chicken dry with paper towel and season with salt.

2. Heat 1 tablespoon (15 mL) of the olive oil in a large frying pan with high sides or a medium, heavy-bottomed pot with a lid over medium-high heat. Place the chicken skin side down in the pan and cook until golden brown on all sides, 3 to 4 minutes per side. Transfer to a plate.

3. Reduce the heat to medium-low (no need to wipe the pan) and add 1 tablespoon (15 mL) of the olive oil and the onions. Cook, stirring occasionally, until the onions are soft and golden brown, 6 to 8 minutes, to bring out their sweetness. Add the garlic and paprika and cook, stirring, until fragrant, 1 to 2 minutes. Add the tomatoes and green peppers, return the chicken to the pan, and season with salt. Reduce the heat to low, cover, and cook until the vegetables are softened, 8 to 10 minutes.

Recipe continues

4. Add cold water to just cover the chicken. Stir, cover, and simmer for 30 minutes.

5. MEANWHILE, MAKE THE NOKEDLI: Bring a large pot of salted water to a boil over high heat.

6. In a medium bowl, whisk together the flour, salt, eggs, and water to combine. The dough will be thick.

7. Once the water is boiling, place the dumpling maker over the pot. Working with ⅓ cup (75 mL) of the batter at a time, allow the batter to flow through the dumpling maker, sliding the square section as you go. Cook until the dumplings float. Drain the dumplings and toss with a drizzle of oil to prevent them from sticking together. Set aside, keeping warm.

8. FINISH THE CHICKEN PAPRIKASH: While the sauce continues to simmer, transfer the cooked chicken to a plate or bowl. Cover to keep warm.

9. In a small frying pan, heat the remaining 1 tablespoon (15 mL) olive oil over medium heat. Add the flour, whisk vigorously to combine, and cook, stirring occasionally, until golden brown with a nutty aroma, about 3 minutes. Scrape the flour mixture into the simmering sauce and cook, stirring constantly, for 1 to 2 minutes to slightly thicken.

10. Remove the pan from the heat. Add the sour cream and, using an immersion blender, blend until smooth.

11. Carefully (it may still be hot) remove and discard the skin and bones from the chicken. Stir the meat back into the sauce. Season with salt and pepper.

12. Serve the Chicken Paprikash over the Nokedli and garnish with the parsley.

Chip-Crusted Baked Tenders

Vegan option • Gluten-free option • Nut-free • Freezer-friendly

Serves 4

Prep time: 20 minutes

Cook time: 15 minutes (or 30 minutes if baking chicken from frozen)

1 bag (8 ounces/ 225 g) tortilla chips or salted potato chips

1 teaspoon (5 mL) taco seasoning (if using tortilla chips) or 1 teaspoon (5 mL) garlic powder (if using potato chips)

⅔ cup (150 mL) mayonnaise or vegan mayonnaise

2 pounds (900 g) skinless, boneless chicken breasts, cut into ½-inch (1 cm) thick strips or 1 large head cauliflower, cut into florets

Spicy Mayo, Chipotle variation (page 328) or your favourite dipping sauce, for dipping

Finger food is king, no matter your age. We put a little twist on the crowd-pleasing chicken fingers that Tori's husband Charles makes regularly and created a cheeky version using crushed chips that everyone loves! Potato or tortilla chips are the perfect coating for either chicken or cauliflower, and of course you can use any flavour of chip your heart desires.

Uncooked coated chicken fingers can be frozen on a baking sheet, then stored in a resealable container in the freezer for up to 1 month. Bake from frozen until cooked through, about 30 minutes.

1. Position the oven racks in the upper and lower thirds of the oven and preheat the oven to 400°F (200°C). Line 2 baking sheets with parchment paper.

2. Use a rolling pin to crush the chips in their bag. Alternatively, you can pulse the chips in a food processor until they are the texture of coarse crumbs.

3. In a shallow bowl, stir together the crushed chips and taco seasoning (if using tortilla chips) or garlic powder (if using potato chips). Put the mayonnaise in a second shallow bowl.

4. Working with 1 chicken strip or cauliflower floret at a time, dip in the mayonnaise to lightly coat all over, then coat in the crushed chip mixture, pressing the chip coating onto the chicken or cauliflower florets. As they are coated, transfer to the prepared baking sheets.

5. Bake until the chicken or cauliflower is golden brown and the internal temperature of the chicken is 165°F (74°C), about 15 minutes, flipping the chicken and rotating the pans halfway through. Serve with the Spicy Mayo.

Vegan: Use cauliflower florets instead of chicken and vegan mayonnaise.

Gluten-free: Use gluten-free chips.

Coconut-Crusted Halibut

Gluten-free option • Nut-free option

Serves 4

Prep time: 15 minutes

Cook time: 15 minutes

2 tablespoons (30 mL) avocado oil or vegetable oil

1 cup (250 mL) panko crumbs

1 cup (250 mL) unsweetened shredded coconut

½ cup (125 mL) unsalted macadamia nuts, roughly chopped (optional)

1 teaspoon (5 mL) salt

½ cup (125 mL) mayonnaise or vegan mayonnaise

4 skinless halibut fillets (6 ounces/ 170 g each)

For serving

Cilantro Lime Rice (page 225)

Spicy Mayo, Sriracha variation (page 328)

Fraiche Fruit Salsa (page 120)

You can throw coconut on pretty much anything and consider us sold, but this particular dish is a total showstopper. This tropical-inspired Coconut-Crusted Halibut is a light but satisfying dinner any time of the year and is dressed up with a refreshing tropical fruit salsa that you can get creative with—mango, kiwi, and pineapple all work beautifully. The macadamia nuts add a crunch and nutty tropical flavour to the crust that we love!

Serve the fish on a bed of Cilantro Lime Rice (page 225) with a drizzle of Spicy Mayo (page 328) if desired.

1. Preheat the oven to 425°F (220°C) and line a baking sheet with parchment paper.

2. Heat the avocado oil in a small frying pan over medium heat. Add the panko crumbs and cook, stirring occasionally, until golden. Transfer the toasted panko crumbs to a medium shallow dish.

3. In the same pan, lightly toast the coconut over medium heat, stirring constantly to prevent it from burning. Add the toasted coconut to the panko crumbs. Add the macadamia nuts (if using) and salt and stir to mix.

4. Put the mayonnaise in a second medium shallow dish.

5. Working with 1 fillet at a time, dip the fillets in the mayonnaise to thinly coat, then coat in the panko coconut mixture. Transfer the coated fillets to the prepared baking sheet.

6. Bake the fish until golden brown on the bottom and cooked through, 10 to 15 minutes (the bake time will depend on the thickness of the fish).

7. Serve the fish on a bed of Coconut Lime Rice with a drizzle of Spicy Mayo and a scoop of Fraiche Fruit Salsa.

Gluten-free: Use gluten-free panko crumbs.

Nut-free: Use more unsweetened shredded coconut instead of nuts.

Chow Mein

Vegetarian option • Vegan option • Gluten-free option • Nut-free option

Serves 4 to 6

Prep time: 20 minutes, plus 1 to 3 hours marinating

Cook time: 30 minutes

1½ pounds (675 g) skinless, boneless chicken thighs, thinly sliced
or 2 packages (12 ounces/350 g each) extra-firm tofu, cubed
or 1 pound (450 g) fresh prawns, peeled and deveined

Marinade

¾ cup (175 mL) water

½ cup (125 mL) sliced green onions

1 tablespoon (15 mL) soy sauce

1 tablespoon (15 mL) oyster sauce

1 tablespoon (15 mL) sesame oil

1 tablespoon (15 mL) cornstarch

2 teaspoons (10 mL) Knorr Powdered Chicken Broth or vegetarian stock concentrate

1 teaspoon (5 mL) grated peeled fresh ginger

2 cloves garlic, minced

½ teaspoon (2 mL) salt

½ teaspoon (2 mL) white pepper

Chinese food was such a special treat when we were growing up in Peace River, Alberta. Sam and Frank from the Golden Palace restaurant, our favourite place to dine out, would warmly greet us in typical small-town fashion, knowing everyone by name and our order by heart. We sure do miss them. One dish that was always part of our order was their chow mein. Chow mein literally means "stir-fried noodles," and it's a traditional Chinese dish made with stir-fried vegetables and sometimes meat or tofu.

Victoria from Team Fraîche asked her mom Anita if she would let us include her family recipe in our book; we were thrilled and honoured when she said yes! This is her coveted family recipe, a veggie-heavy chow mein that is off-the-charts delicious. Anita makes it with chicken, but we love it just as much with tofu or prawns. The choice is yours! You can find packaged fresh thin, wavy chow mein noodles in the refrigerated section at most grocery stores.

1. MARINATE THE CHICKEN, TOFU, OR PRAWNS: Place the chicken, tofu, or prawns in a large bowl or resealable container.

2. In a small bowl, whisk together the water, green onions, soy sauce, oyster sauce, sesame oil, cornstarch, powdered chicken broth, ginger, garlic, salt, and white pepper. Pour the sauce over the chicken, tofu, or prawns. Marinate chicken or tofu, covered, in the fridge for at least 3 hours or up to overnight. Marinate prawns for 1 hour.

3. FRY THE CHOW MEIN NOODLES: Bring a large pot of water to a boil over high heat. Add the chow mein noodles and cook until tender, 1 to 2 minutes. Drain the noodles and transfer to a large bowl. Add the soy sauce, oyster sauce, and avocado oil and mix until combined.

4. Heat a large nonstick frying pan over medium-high heat. Once the pan is hot, add the chow mein noodles and cook, stirring occasionally, until golden brown, about 5 minutes. Transfer the fried noodles to a large serving dish and set aside, keeping them warm. Set aside the frying pan (no need to wipe it clean).

Recipe and ingredients continue

Fried Chow Mein Noodles

1 package (1 pound/454 g) fresh
  chow mein noodles

¼ cup (60 mL) soy sauce

¼ cup (60 mL) oyster sauce

2 tablespoons (30 mL) avocado oil
  or vegetable oil

Chow Mein

4 eggs

2 tablespoons (30 mL) 2% milk or
  unsweetened non-dairy milk

Salt and pepper

2 tablespoons (30 mL) avocado oil
  or vegetable oil, divided

1 cup (250 mL) water

1 clove garlic, minced

4 cups (1 L) shredded green
  cabbage

1 cup (250 mL) thinly sliced peeled
  carrots

4 cups (1 L) chopped baby bok choy

1 cup (250 mL) thinly sliced red,
  yellow, or orange sweet peppers

2 cups (500 mL) bean sprouts

3 green onions (white and light
  green parts only), sliced,
  for garnish

5. MAKE THE CHOW MEIN: In a small bowl, whisk the eggs with the milk and salt and pepper to taste.

6. Heat 1 tablespoon (15 mL) of the avocado oil in the frying pan over medium heat. Pour in the egg mixture and tilt the pan so the eggs fully cover the bottom. As the eggs start to set, use a rubber spatula to drag the cooked edges into the centre of the pan. Tilt the pan again so the uncooked egg moves to the edge of the pan. Carefully flip the omelette and continue cooking until just set. Transfer the omelette to a cutting board. Cut the omelette into ½-inch (1 cm) strips.

7. Heat the pan (no need to wipe it clean) over medium heat. Add the chicken, prawns, or tofu along with their marinade and cook, stirring occasionally, until the chicken or prawns are just cooked through, or until the tofu is heated through. Reduce the heat to medium-low, add the water, and simmer, stirring occasionally, until the sauce thickens, 2 to 3 minutes.

8. Heat the remaining 1 tablespoon (15 mL) avocado oil in a wok or stir-fry pan over medium-high heat. Once the oil is hot, add the garlic, cabbage, and carrots and cook, stirring occasionally, 3 to 5 minutes. Add the bok choy, sweet peppers, and bean sprouts and cook, stirring occasionally, until tender, about 3 minutes. Add the cooked chicken, prawn, or tofu mixture and stir to combine.

9. Spoon the mixture over the fried chow mein noodles. Top with the egg and garnish with the green onions.

Vegetarian: Use vegetarian stock concentrate and tofu.

Vegan: Use tofu and egg-free noodles. Replace the oyster sauce with equal parts soy sauce and water, use vegetarian stock concentrate, and skip the egg or use a store-bought egg replacer.

Gluten-free: Use gluten-free soy sauce or tamari, gluten-free oyster sauce, gluten-free noodles, and gluten-free broth mix.

Nut-free: If using non-dairy milk, use a nut-free option.

Ginger "Beef"

Vegan • Gluten-free option • Nut-free

Serves 4

Serves 4

Prep time: 25 minutes (not including soaking the soy curls)

Cook time: 20 minutes

Ginger "Beef"

1 package (8 ounces/225 g) soy curls

4 cups (1 L) hot beef-flavoured vegetarian stock

1 cup (250 mL) cornstarch

¼ cup (60 mL) avocado oil

Ginger Sauce

2 tablespoons (30 mL) cornstarch

¼ cup (60 mL) water

1 tablespoon (15 mL) avocado oil

3 cloves garlic, minced

2 tablespoons (30 mL) minced peeled fresh ginger

½ cup (125 mL) fresh orange juice

¼ cup (60 mL) soy sauce

3 tablespoons (45 mL) packed brown sugar

2 tablespoons (30 mL) rice wine vinegar

¼ to ½ teaspoon (1 to 2 mL) red chili flakes (optional)

The Golden Palace restaurant opened in 1977 (the year Tori was born) and quickly became the hub in our hometown Peace River, Alberta. One of northern Alberta's first Chinese fine-dining restaurants, the Golden Palace was opened by Sam Chow, who immigrated to Canada from Hoiping, China, in the 1950s. It was probably our entire family's introduction to Chinese cuisine and we *loved* it! This is where we tried escargot and crab for the first time, indulged in the most incredible pineapple chicken balls, and could not get enough of their ginger beef, a family favourite from day one. Jillian loves ginger beef so much that sometimes she will cheat on her plant-based diet, just to curb the craving!

Inspired by our memories of the Golden Palace's ginger beef, we created a plant-based version. Soy curls are an incredible replacement for the beef! We are so happy that we figured out a way to get that same crispy texture without deep-frying them. This ginger "beef" is delicious on a bed of rice, served with Chow Mein (page 179), or wrapped in lettuce leaves. The sauce and the soy curls can be made up to 2 hours ahead. Reheat the sauce and toss in the soy curls just before serving.

1. MAKE THE GINGER "BEEF"—BAKE THE SOY CURLS: Preheat the oven to 450°F (230°C) and line a baking sheet with parchment paper.

2. In a large bowl, cover the soy curls with the hot vegetarian stock. Soak for 10 to 15 minutes to rehydrate the soy curls.

3. Drain the soy curls in a sieve and squeeze out the excess liquid. Pat the soy curls dry with a kitchen towel or paper towel. Dry the bowl. Return the soy curls to the bowl and toss with the cornstarch until coated. Drizzle with the avocado oil and toss again to combine.

4. Evenly spread the coated soy curls on the prepared baking sheet and bake for 20 to 25 minutes, until crispy and lightly browned, turning half-way through.

5. MEANWHILE, MAKE THE GINGER SAUCE: Put the cornstarch in a small bowl and whisk in the water to make a slurry.

Recipe and ingredients continue

Ginger "Beef" continued

Garnishes

1 tablespoon (15 mL) sesame seeds

2 green onions (white and light
  green parts only), sliced

Steamed jasmine rice and steamed
  broccoli, for serving

6. Heat the avocado oil in a small saucepan over medium heat. Add the garlic and ginger and cook, stirring constantly, until fragrant, about 2 minutes. Add the orange juice, soy sauce, brown sugar, rice wine vinegar, and chili flakes, if using. Simmer, stirring occasionally, until the sugar dissolves, 2 to 3 minutes. Give the cornstarch slurry another stir, add it to the sauce, and cook, stirring constantly, until slightly thickened, about 2 minutes. Remove from the heat.

7. ASSEMBLE THE DISH: In a large bowl, toss the fried soy curls with the Ginger Sauce. Transfer the soy curls to a medium serving dish. Garnish with the sesame seeds and green onions. Serve with steamed rice and steamed broccoli.

Gluten-free: Use gluten-free soy sauce or tamari.

Coconut Curry

Vegan option • Gluten-free option • Nut-free

Serves 4

Prep time: 10 minutes

Cook time: 30 minutes

2 tablespoons (30 mL) avocado oil or vegetable oil

1 cup (250 mL) finely chopped yellow onion

3 cloves garlic, minced

1 tablespoon (15 mL) grated peeled fresh ginger

2 teaspoons (10 mL) cumin seeds (or 1 teaspoon/5 mL ground cumin)

1 teaspoon (5 mL) ground turmeric

1 teaspoon (5 mL) ground coriander

1 teaspoon (5 mL) garam masala

4 ripe tomatoes, finely chopped (or one 28-ounce/796 mL can diced tomatoes)

2 cups (500 mL) quartered white mushrooms

1 teaspoon (5 mL) salt

1 can (14 ounces/400 mL) coconut cream or full-fat coconut milk

2 teaspoons (10 mL) packed brown sugar

1 package (12 ounces/350 g) extra-firm tofu, cut into ½-inch (1 cm) cubes *or* 14 ounces (400 g) fresh prawns, peeled and deveined *or* 1 can (19 ounces/540 mL) chickpeas, rinsed and drained

1 cup (250 mL) frozen peas

Salt and pepper

Chopped fresh cilantro, for garnish

For serving

Plain yogurt or non-dairy yogurt

Steamed jasmine or basmati rice or Cilantro Lime Rice (page 225)

Naan-Style Flatbreads (page 72) or store-bought naan

Jillian first experienced Indian food when Tori took her to Vij's restaurant in Vancouver, where they both lived at the time. The aromas and flavours were like nothing she had ever experienced. Fast-forward a few years to one day when Jillian was craving this delicious curry. Not having the recipe, she tried to recreate it from memory, and the rest is history. This mild curry made with South Indian flavours is a staple on Jillian's table and is very quick to make. We love that our kids enjoy it as much as we do.

Feel free to add more spice to taste, a few handfuls of fresh spinach with the peas for extra greens, or a couple of cups of cauliflower florets with the mushrooms. Serve this curry with steamed basmati rice or Cilantro Lime Rice (page 225).

1. Heat the avocado oil in a large, heavy-bottomed pot over medium heat. Add the onions and cook, stirring occasionally, until golden brown, 5 to 7 minutes. Stir in the garlic, ginger, cumin, turmeric, coriander, and garam masala, and cook, stirring occasionally, until fragrant, about 3 minutes. Add the fresh tomatoes (if using), mushrooms, and salt and stir until the tomatoes have started to break down and the mushrooms have softened, about 10 minutes. (If using canned tomatoes, stir them in now.)

2. Stir in the coconut cream and brown sugar. Bring to a boil over medium-high heat, then reduce the heat to low and simmer, stirring occasionally, 10 to 15 minutes. Add the protein of choice (tofu, prawns, or chickpeas) and continue simmering, stirring occasionally, until the curry has slightly thickened, about 8 minutes. (If using prawns, ensure they are cooked through.)

3. Stir in the peas and cook for 2 minutes. Remove from the heat. Season with salt and pepper. Garnish with the cilantro. Serve with yogurt, rice, and naan.

Vegan: Use tofu and non-dairy yogurt.

Gluten-free: Serve with gluten-free naan.

Tropical Tofu Bowls

Vegan • Gluten-free option • Nut-free option

Serves 4

Prep time: 15 minutes

Cook time: 25 minutes

1 cup (250 mL) rice (we use jasmine)

Crispy Tofu

1 package (12 ounces/350 g) extra-firm tofu, drained and patted dry

1 cup (250 mL) cornstarch

½ cup (125 mL) unsweetened non-dairy milk

1 cup (250 mL) panko crumbs

1 teaspoon (5 mL) sweet paprika

1 teaspoon (5 mL) garlic powder

1 teaspoon (5 mL) salt

Avocado oil or vegetable oil, for frying

½ cup (125 mL) teriyaki sauce

For assembly

8 fresh pineapple rings

2 cups (500 mL) cooked shelled edamame

Fraiche Fruit Salsa (page 120)

1 avocado, pitted, peeled, and sliced

Spicy Mayo, Sriracha variation (page 328)

Quick Pickled Red Onions (page 320)

Sesame seeds

Lime wedges

Tori created these bowls while we were in Maui for Jillian's fortieth birthday, to feed the crew of hungry gals after a day of snorkelling. They were a *hit*! They are packed with wholesome veggies and protein. We love serving them à la carte so that everyone can create their own bowl.

We made ours with tofu, but you can use chicken or prawns should you wish. To bake the crispy tofu instead of frying, simply add 2 tablespoons (30 mL) of avocado oil to the panko mixture and bake them at 400°F (200°C) until golden, 15 to 20 minutes. Double the ingredients for the crispy tofu to make a heartier meal, and feel free to add toasted nori for extra crunch.

1. COOK THE RICE: Cook the rice until tender according to the package directions. (The cooking time will depend on the type of rice you use.)

2. MEANWHILE, MAKE THE CRISPY TOFU: Cut the tofu into 1-inch (2.5 cm) cubes. Press the cubes between sheets of paper towel or a kitchen towel to remove excess liquid.

3. Set out 3 medium shallow bowls. Put the cornstarch in one bowl. Put the milk in the second bowl. In the third bowl, stir together the panko crumbs, paprika, garlic powder, and salt.

4. Place half the tofu cubes in the cornstarch and toss to coat. Remove them from the cornstarch and place them in the milk, turning to coat. Finish with the panko coating, lightly pressing the crumbs into all sides. Transfer to a plate. Repeat to coat the remaining tofu cubes.

5. Heat ½ inch (1 cm) of avocado oil in a medium frying pan over medium heat. Working in batches so as not to overcrowd the pan, cook the tofu until golden brown on all sides, 4 to 5 minutes. Transfer the tofu to a large plate lined with paper towel. Repeat with the remaining tofu, adding more oil if needed. Once all the tofu is cooked, transfer to a medium bowl and toss with the teriyaki sauce to coat. (Alternatively, you can drizzle the teriyaki sauce on top of the tofu once the bowls are assembled.)

6. ASSEMBLE THE BOWLS: Divide the rice among bowls. Top with the Crispy Tofu, pineapple, edamame, Fraiche Fruit Salsa, avocado, a drizzle of Spicy Mayo, Pickled Red Onions, and a sprinkle of sesame seeds. Serve with lime wedges.

Gluten-free: Use gluten-free panko crumbs and gluten-free teriyaki sauce.

Nut-free: If using non-dairy milk, use a nut-free option.

Mushroom Risotto

Vegetarian • Vegan option • Gluten-free option • Nut-free

Serves 6 to 8

Prep time: 15 minutes

Cook time: 45 minutes

9 cups (2.25 L) chicken-flavoured vegetarian stock or vegetable stock

6 tablespoons (90 mL) butter or vegan butter, divided

1½ pounds (675 g) thinly sliced mixed mushrooms (8 cups/2 L)

4 cloves garlic, minced

Salt and pepper

2 tablespoons (30 mL) extra-virgin olive oil

2 cups (500 mL) finely chopped yellow onion

2½ cups (625 mL) arborio rice (or other risotto rice)

½ cup (125 mL) dry white wine

1 teaspoon (5 mL) chopped fresh thyme (optional)

1 cup (250 mL) grated Parmesan cheese or vegan parm, plus more for garnish

Chopped fresh thyme and/or curly parsley, for garnish

Vegan: Use vegan butter and vegan parm.

Gluten-free: Use gluten-free vegetable stock.

Risotto, a northern Italian dish, is a bit of a labour of love, but well worth the time and elbow grease. The creaminess of risotto comes from the slow release of the rice starch through regular stirring and the gradual addition of stock. It's the definition of a food hug, and the perfect thing to serve on a cold winter day with a glass of wine. In fact, we highly recommend pouring yourself a glass to sip and cranking up the Dean Martin while you make this dish. While it takes some time to cook, it will hands-down be the best babysitting job you've ever had.

We recommend using a mix of mushroom varieties, including shiitake, oyster, and cremini, but you can use white or brown mushrooms that are easier to find. Substitute stock for the wine if desired. Do yourself a favour and use any leftover risotto (or make extra) to make Mushroom Arancini (page 99)!

1. In a medium pot, bring the vegetarian stock to a boil, then reduce the heat to low, cover, and keep at a simmer.

2. Melt 4 tablespoons (60 mL) of the butter in a large, heavy-bottomed pot over medium heat. Add the mushrooms and garlic and cook, stirring occasionally, until the mushrooms are soft and slightly browned, 8 to 10 minutes. Season with salt and pepper and transfer the mushrooms to a bowl.

3. In the same pot (no need to wipe it clean), heat the remaining 2 tablespoons (30 mL) butter and the olive oil over medium heat. Add the onions and cook, stirring occasionally, until soft and fragrant, 3 to 4 minutes.

4. Add the rice and cook, stirring occasionally, until it is lightly toasted and it smells nutty, 3 to 4 minutes.

5. Add the white wine and cook, stirring, until the wine is mostly absorbed into the rice.

6. Reduce the heat to medium-low. Add the thyme (if using) and a ladleful (about ¾ cup/175 mL) of hot stock. Stir frequently until the stock is absorbed into the rice, about 3 minutes. Repeat, adding a ladleful of stock at a time and stirring until each addition has been fully absorbed, 20 to 25 minutes. The rice should be velvety but still have a slight bite to it.

7. Stir in the Parmesan and sautéed mushrooms. Season with salt and pepper. Garnish with more Parmesan and thyme and/or parsley.

Patsy's Fried Fish

Dairy-free • Gluten-free option • Nut-free

Serves 4

Prep time: 10 minutes (not including making the Dill Tartar Sauce)

Cook time: 15 minutes

2 pounds (900 g) skinless, boneless fish (pickerel, cod, halibut, or salmon), cut into 3-inch (8 cm) pieces, patted dry

Batter

1 cup (250 mL) all-purpose flour

3 tablespoons (45 mL) cornstarch

2 teaspoons (10 mL) baking powder

2 teaspoons (10 mL) sugar

1 teaspoon (5 mL) salt

1 cup (250 mL) ice-cold water

2 tablespoons (30 mL) soy sauce

2 tablespoons (30 mL) avocado oil or vegetable oil, plus more for frying

For serving

1 batch Dill Tartar Sauce (page 328)

Lemon wedges

This is Tori's mom Patsy's famous recipe for fried fish, used for dozens of dinners up at Sturgeon Lake in northern Alberta where we grew up. The boys would head out on the lake early in the morning in their aluminum boats and spend the day chatting and fishing (more chatting than fishing, we suspect) before bringing in their catch.

We traditionally use pickerel, but any fish, such as cod, halibut, or salmon, will work. Serve with our Salt and Vinegar Potatoes (page 237), Okanagan Coleslaw (page 131), and Dill Tartar Sauce (page 328). You can cut the fish into nugget shapes or strips for making Fish Tacos (page 163). We recommend using two sets of tongs, one for the batter and one for frying. It will save you time and kitchen mess, we promise!

1. Preheat the oven to 250°F (120°C). Line a baking sheet with parchment paper.

2. In a large bowl, whisk together the flour, cornstarch, baking powder, sugar, and salt. Form a well in the centre. Pour the water, soy sauce, and avocado oil into the well and whisk until the batter is smooth.

3. Heat at least 2 inches (5 cm) of avocado oil in a large pot or deep-fryer to 350°F (180°C) on a deep-frying thermometer. (Keep the temperature steady.)

4. Using tongs, dip the fish pieces, 1 at a time, in the batter to coat and allow any excess to drip back into the bowl. Working in batches (being careful not to overcrowd the pot), carefully place the battered fish in the hot oil and fry until golden, 2 to 3 minutes per side. Using tongs or a slotted spoon, transfer the fried fish to a plate lined with paper towel or to a wire rack to drain excess oil. Once drained, transfer the fish to the prepared baking sheet and keep warm in the oven until ready to serve. Repeat with the remaining fish.

5. Serve hot with Dill Tartar Sauce and lemon wedges.

Gluten-free: Use a 1:1 gluten-free flour blend instead of all-purpose flour and use gluten-free soy sauce or tamari.

Mushroom French Dip Sandwiches

Vegetarian • Vegan option • Gluten-free option • Nut-free

Serves 6

Prep time: 15 minutes

Cook time: 20 minutes

Dip

1½ tablespoons (22 mL) beef-flavoured vegetarian stock concentrate

2 tablespoons (30 mL) dry red wine

2 tablespoons (30 mL) butter or vegan butter

1½ cups (375 mL) water

Sandwiches

¼ cup (60 mL) butter or vegan butter, plus more for the buns

1½ pounds (675 g) portobello mushrooms (about 8 large mushrooms), thinly sliced

2 cloves garlic, minced

1 large yellow onion, thinly sliced

2 green sweet peppers, sliced

¼ cup (60 mL) dry red wine

2 tablespoons (30 mL) beef-flavoured vegetarian stock concentrate

6 crusty buns, cut in half

6 slices Gruyère cheese or vegan cheese (optional)

Although these mushroom sandwiches are not made with meat, they are absolutely a cut above the fast-food beef version that inspired this recipe and are just as satisfying. Filled with sautéed mushrooms, onions, and green peppers, they are so comforting after a cold day outside. When we were kids, Tori's parents owned the Arby's in Kelowna, and it did not take us long to fall in love with their menu, especially the French dip sandwiches (with a shout-out to curly fries!). This plant-based version is superior to the original—think French dip meets Philly cheesesteak. Pure *heaven!* This sandwich is messy to eat, but so worth it!

Sliced French loaves or baguettes work as an alternative to the crusty buns should you wish, and any other cheese will work in place of Gruyère. The red wine can be replaced with stock if desired.

1. MAKE THE DIP: In a medium saucepan, combine the vegetarian stock concentrate, red wine, butter, and water. Stir together and bring to a simmer over medium heat, then reduce the heat to low, cover, and keep warm until ready to serve.

2. MAKE THE SANDWICHES: Position an oven rack about 6 inches (15 cm) under the broiler and preheat the broiler. Line 2 large baking sheets with parchment paper.

3. Melt the butter in a large saucepan over medium heat. Add the mushrooms, garlic, onions, and green peppers and cook, stirring occasionally, until softened, about 8 minutes.

4. Add the red wine and vegetarian stock concentrate and cook, stirring occasionally, until reduced by about a quarter, 3 to 4 minutes. Remove from the heat.

5. Butter the bun halves and place the bottom halves cut side up on one of the prepared baking sheets. Place the top halves cut side up on the second baking sheet. Broil until the buns are lightly toasted, 1 to 2 minutes.

6. Divide the mushroom mixture evenly among the bottom halves. Top with a slice of cheese if desired. Broil for 1 to 2 minutes, until the cheese is melted.

7. Close the sandwiches and cut crosswise in half. Serve with the hot Dip in small bowls alongside.

Vegan: Use vegan butter and skip the Gruyère cheese or use your favourite vegan cheese.

Gluten-free: Use gluten-free stock concentrate and gluten-free buns.

Gnocchi with Pomodoro Sauce

Vegetarian • Nut-free • Freezer-friendly

Serves 4

Prep time: 2 hours, 15 minutes

Cook time: 10 minutes, plus
30 minutes resting

Pomodoro Sauce

2 tablespoons (30 mL) extra-virgin
olive oil

1 shallot, finely chopped

2 cloves garlic, minced

1 can (28 ounces/796 mL) San
Marzano tomatoes

½ red sweet pepper

¼ cup (60 mL) dry red wine

1 teaspoon (5 mL) salt

1 teaspoon (5 mL) sugar

½ cup (125 mL) chopped fresh
basil, plus more for garnish

Gnocchi

2 pounds (900 g) russet potatoes
(about 3 large potatoes),
scrubbed

2 eggs

½ cup (125 mL) finely grated
Parmesan cheese, plus more
for garnish

½ teaspoon (2 mL) salt

2 cups (500 mL) all-purpose flour,
plus more for dusting

Olive oil, for drizzling

Our friend Anthony was kind enough to share his Nonna's famous recipe for gnocchi—what a gift! Making gnocchi is a perfect example of how cooking a simple meal can bring friends and family together around the table. The passion of Italian cooking tends to leverage simple ingredients, including the most important—starch. Choose a dry and starchy potato variety for this recipe such as russet (older potatoes are preferred). If you don't have a potato ricer you can simply grate the cooked peeled potatoes. Anthony's Nonna's orders for this recipe: gather the family, pour some vino rosso, and crank up the Louis Prima. You don't have to tell us twice!

1. MAKE THE POMODORO SAUCE: Heat the olive oil in a heavy-bottomed pot over medium heat. Add the shallots and cook, stirring occasionally, until fragrant, about 2 minutes. Add the garlic and cook, stirring, for 30 seconds. Be careful not to brown the shallots or garlic. Stir in the tomatoes with their juice. Using an immersion blender, blend until smooth.

2. Stir in the sweet pepper, red wine, salt, and sugar. Reduce the heat to low, cover, and simmer, stirring occasionally, for 1½ to 2 hours to let the flavours meld.

3. Stir in the basil and simmer for another 15 minutes. Remove and discard the sweet pepper. Season with salt. Remove from the heat, cover, and keep warm. (The sauce can be cooled and stored in a resealable container in the fridge for up to 3 days or in the freezer for up to 1 month.)

4. MEANWHILE, MAKE THE GNOCCHI DOUGH: Bring a large pot of salted water to a boil. Add the potatoes and cook until fork-tender, about 35 minutes. Drain and set aside until cool enough to handle. Peel the potatoes while still warm.

5. Process the warm potatoes through a ricer into a large bowl. You should have 4 cups (1 L) of riced potato.

Recipe continues

6. In a small bowl, beat the eggs. Add the beaten eggs, Parmesan, and salt to the potatoes and mix together well. Add the flour and, using your hands, knead the ingredients together briefly just until combined. (Overhandling the dough will make it too sticky.) Shape the dough into a ball and dust with flour.

7. Transfer the dough to a lightly floured work surface. Using a sharp knife or dough scraper, divide the dough into 8 equal portions. Working with 1 piece at a time, use the palms of your hands to roll it out into a rope about ½ inch (1 cm) thick. Using a sharp knife or dough scraper, cut the dough crosswise into ¾-inch (2 cm) pieces. At this stage, you can either leave the gnocchi as smooth pillows (skip step 8) or indent the gnocchi to give it texture. (A textured surface captures more sauce and is recommended.)

8. INDENT THE GNOCCHI (OPTIONAL): Line a baking sheet with parchment paper and lightly flour the paper. Press each piece of dough against a gnocchi board or the back of a fork (even a bamboo placemat works) and use your index finger to lightly roll it toward you to create grooves in the dough. As you roll, place the gnocchi in a single layer on the prepared baking sheet, making sure they don't touch and keeping them covered with a kitchen towel to prevent them from drying out.

9. Let the gnocchi rest, covered with the towel, at room temperature for about 30 minutes. This helps prevent the gnocchi from sticking together when cooking. (At this stage, you can freeze the gnocchi if desired. Simply place the baking sheet in the freezer and, once the gnocchi are frozen, transfer them to a large resealable bag. Store in the freezer for up to 1 month.)

10. COOK THE GNOCCHI: Reheat the Pomodoro Sauce if needed. Bring a large pot of salted water to a boil. Working in batches so as not to overcrowd the pot, cook the gnocchi, without stirring, until they float to the surface, 3 to 5 minutes. Using a slotted spoon, transfer the gnocchi to a large bowl and drizzle with olive oil. Repeat with the remaining gnocchi.

11. Top the Gnocchi with the warm Pomodoro Sauce and gently stir. Garnish with more Parmesan and the basil.

Spanakopita

Dairy-free option • Gluten-free option • Nut-free

Serves 6

Prep time: 20 minutes

Cook time: 45 minutes

Spinach Filling

2 tablespoons (30 mL) extra-virgin
olive oil, plus more for brushing

2 cups (500 mL) finely chopped
yellow onion

3 cloves garlic, minced

2 green onions (white and light
green parts only), sliced

1 package (10.5 ounces/300 g)
frozen chopped spinach,
thawed and well drained

1 cup (250 mL) crumbled feta
cheese or vegan feta cheese

½ cup (125 mL) chopped fresh
flat-leaf parsley, plus more
for garnish

¼ cup (60 mL) chopped fresh dill

2 teaspoons (10 mL) dried oregano

2 eggs, well beaten

½ teaspoon (2 mL) salt

½ teaspoon (2 mL) pepper

Phyllo Crust

12 sheets phyllo pastry, thawed
(from a 16-ounce/454 g package;
you will not use all the phyllo)

⅓ cup (75 mL) extra-virgin olive oil,
for brushing

To say we love Greek food would be a big understatement. Spanakopita is a savoury Greek spinach pie, full of cheese, herbs, onions, and spinach (don't forget that one!) all wrapped in layers of flaky phyllo pastry. Typically, you see these in a small perfect triangle or roll, but we made it even simpler in this version! The more you crinkle and fold the phyllo pastry, the prettier it gets— rustic yet super impressive with a fresh, flavourful, filling packed with handfuls of herbs.

Serve it with a fresh Greek salad, Classic Chickpea Hummus (page 110), Pita-Style Flatbreads (page 71), and a drizzle of this epic Garlic Sauce for a little trip to the Mediterranean any day of the week.

1. Preheat the oven to 350°F (180°C) and brush a 9-inch (23 cm) pie plate with olive oil.

2. MAKE THE SPINACH FILLING: Heat the olive oil in a medium frying pan. Add the onions and cook, stirring occasionally, until soft and translucent, 3 to 4 minutes. Add the garlic and green onions and cook, stirring, 1 to 2 minutes. Remove from the heat.

3. Squeeze any excess liquid out of the spinach. Place the drained spinach in a medium bowl. Add the cooked onion mixture, feta, parsley, dill, oregano, eggs, salt, and pepper and mix together well.

4. ASSEMBLE THE PIE: Unwrap the phyllo and cover with plastic wrap and a slightly damp kitchen towel to keep it from drying out.

5. Place 1 sheet of phyllo on a work surface. Brush the pastry lightly with olive oil, then place it in the pie plate with the phyllo hanging over the edges. Repeat with the remaining 11 sheets of phyllo, layering each sheet brushed with olive oil on top. (The sheets of phyllo don't have to perfectly line up.) Brush the top sheet of phyllo with olive oil.

6. Transfer the spinach mixture to the phyllo-lined pie plate and spread it evenly. Using your hands, loosely and gently fold the overhanging phyllo toward the centre to make a ruffled crust (the phyllo won't completely cover the filling). You want the phyllo to look wavy with plenty of folds. Lightly brush the pastry with olive oil.

Recipe and ingredients continue

Garlic Sauce

1 cup (250 mL) plain full-fat Greek yogurt or non-dairy Greek yogurt

2 tablespoons (30 mL) mayonnaise or non-dairy mayonnaise

2 tablespoons (30 mL) fresh lemon juice

4 cloves garlic, minced

Salt

7. Loosely cover the pie with foil. Bake for 20 minutes, then remove the foil and continue baking the pie until golden brown, 20 to 25 minutes more.

8. MEANWHILE, MAKE THE GARLIC SAUCE: In a small bowl, stir together the yogurt, mayonnaise, lemon juice, and garlic. Season with salt. Cover and refrigerate until ready to use.

9. Garnish the spanakopita with parsley if desired. Serve with the Garlic Sauce on the side.

Dairy-free: Use vegan feta cheese, non-dairy phyllo, non-dairy yogurt, and vegan mayonnaise.

Gluten-free: Use a gluten-free pie crust instead of phyllo pastry.

Tortilla Pie

Vegan option • Gluten-free option • Nut-free • Freezer-friendly

Serves 6

Prep time: 15 minutes

Cook time: 45 minutes

1 tablespoon (15 mL) extra-virgin olive oil

1 pound (450 g) ground chicken or store-bought veggie ground

½ cup (125 mL) finely diced yellow onion

1 cup (250 mL) finely grated peeled carrots

1 cup (250 mL) finely grated zucchini

1¼ cups (300 mL) water, divided

1 cup (250 mL) frozen corn kernels

3 tablespoons (45 mL) taco seasoning

1 can (19 ounces/540 mL) black beans, drained and rinsed, divided

1 teaspoon (5 mL) ground cumin

5 large flour tortillas

2½ cups (625 mL) grated cheddar or Monterey Jack cheese or vegan cheese, divided

For serving

Pico de Gallo (page 329)

1 avocado, pitted, peeled, and diced

2 green onions (white and light green parts only), sliced

Chopped fresh cilantro

Sour cream or vegan sour cream

If you're looking for an easy, flavourful, crowd-pleasing dish, this is it! As busy moms, we love this make-ahead dinner that packs in all our favourite taco flavours without the fuss or mess. This tortilla pie is the perfect way to sneak in those extra veggies (the small holes of your box grater are your secret weapon here). Have fun with the toppings and serve with fresh guacamole or Pico de Gallo (page 329) for an effortless fiesta!

1. Preheat the oven to 350°F (180°C) and line a baking sheet with parchment paper.

2. Heat the olive oil in a large frying pan over medium heat. Once the oil is hot, add the ground and onion and cook, stirring occasionally, until the ground is lightly browned, about 5 minutes. Add the carrots, zucchini, and ¼ cup (60 mL) of the water and cook, stirring occasionally, until the vegetables are soft and have broken down, about 10 minutes. Add the corn, taco seasoning, and remaining 1 cup (250 mL) water, increase the heat to medium-high, and continue cooking, stirring occasionally, until the water has evaporated, about 8 minutes. Remove from the heat.

3. In a medium bowl, stir together the black beans and cumin.

4. Place 1 tortilla on the prepared baking sheet and sprinkle evenly with about ½ cup (125 mL) of the cheese. Spread half of the ground mixture on top of the cheese and layer on another tortilla. Sprinkle another ½ cup (125 mL) of the cheese on the tortilla, then spread a layer of half the beans on top. Layer on another tortilla and sprinkle evenly with about ½ cup (125 mL) of the cheese and spread with the remaining ground mixture. Layer on another tortilla with ½ cup (125 mL) of the cheese and spread with the remaining beans. Top with the last tortilla and the remaining ½ cup (125 mL) cheese. Bake until the cheese is melted and golden brown, about 15 minutes.

5. Serve with the Pico de Gallo, avocado, green onions, cilantro, and sour cream along with any other favourite taco toppings. Cover and store leftovers in the fridge for up to 3 days.

Vegan: Use veggie ground or tempeh, vegan cheese, and vegan sour cream.

Gluten-free: Use gluten-free tortillas.

Vegan Tourtière

Vegan • Gluten-free option • Nut-free option • Freezer-friendly

Serves 8

Prep time: 45 minutes (not including making the Pastry Dough)

Cook time: 55 minutes

2 batches Pastry Dough (page 51), made with vegan butter

Filling

¼ cup (60 mL) extra-virgin olive oil

1 cup (250 mL) finely chopped yellow onion

2 cloves garlic, minced

¼ cup (60 mL) dry red wine

1 tablespoon (15 mL) beef-flavoured vegetarian stock concentrate

2 pounds (900 g) cremini mushrooms or mixed mushrooms, finely chopped (about 10 cups/2.4 L)

1 cup (250 mL) finely diced peeled russet potatoes

1 cup (250 mL) finely diced celery

1 cup (250 mL) finely diced peeled carrot

¼ cup (60 mL) vegan butter

1 tablespoon (15 mL) soy sauce or tamari

1 tablespoon (15 mL) vegan Worcestershire sauce

2 cups (500 mL) panko crumbs

1½ teaspoons (7 mL) ground allspice

1 teaspoon (5 mL) dried thyme

½ teaspoon (2 mL) ground sage

1 cup (250 mL) finely ground walnuts

Salt and pepper

Tourtière is a French Canadian meat pie originating from Quebec, traditionally made with minced pork, veal, or beef and potatoes and often served during the holidays. This is one of the dishes Jillian missed most when she started eating more plant-based foods. This vegan version checks all the boxes, and bonus: it tastes even better the next day! This is a great dish to double to keep in the freezer for a food hug at your fingertips!

1. MAKE THE PASTRY DOUGH: Shape into 2 discs, wrap tightly in plastic wrap, and refrigerate for at least 1 hour before rolling it out.

2. Preheat the oven to 400°F (200°C).

3. MAKE THE FILLING: Heat the olive oil in a large frying pan over medium heat. Add the onions and cook, stirring occasionally, until soft and translucent, 3 to 4 minutes. Stir in the garlic and cook for 1 minute. Add the red wine and the stock concentrate and cook until slightly reduced, about 2 minutes.

4. Add the mushrooms and cook, stirring occasionally, until they are soft, 6 to 8 minutes. Add the potatoes, celery, carrots, and vegan butter and cook until the carrots and potato are fork-tender, about 8 minutes. Add the soy sauce and Worcestershire sauce and stir to combine. Remove from the heat. Stir in the panko crumbs, allspice, thyme, sage, and ground walnuts. Season with salt and pepper.

5. ASSEMBLE THE PIE: On a lightly floured work surface, use a floured rolling pin to roll out 1 disc of dough into a 12-inch (30 cm) round, about ⅛ inch (3 mm) thick. Carefully roll the dough around the rolling pin and unroll it over a 9-inch (23 cm) pie plate. Using your hands, gently press the dough into the bottom and up the sides to fit.

6. Scrape the filling mixture into the pastry shell and gently pat it down.

7. Roll out the second disc of dough into a circle slightly larger than the pie plate. Carefully roll the dough around the rolling pin and unroll it over the pie. Trim the excess dough and pinch the edges with your fingers to seal. Using a sharp knife, cut a few vent slits in the top of the pie.

8. Bake the pie until golden brown, about 35 minutes. Store the pie, covered, in the fridge for up to 3 days or in the freezer for up to 1 month.

Gluten-free: Use a gluten-free pie crust and gluten-free stock, soy sauce or tamari, Worcestershire sauce, and panko crumbs.

Nut-free: Skip the walnuts.

Vegan Mac and Cheeze

Vegan • Gluten-free option

Serves 4 to 6

Prep time: 15 minutes (not including making the Cheeze Sauce)

Cook time: 20 minutes

1 package (1 pound/454 g) Scoobi doo (cavatappi)

¼ cup (60 mL) extra-virgin olive oil or melted vegan butter

1½ cups (375 mL) panko crumbs or dry bread crumbs

½ teaspoon (2 mL) garlic powder

½ teaspoon (2 mL) salt

1 batch Cheeze Sauce (page 217)

As moms, we both know the importance of having a good mac and cheese recipe up your sleeve. When someone needs a real food hug, this is the type of dish we whip up. This simple plant-based version is an instant family favourite, with all the creamy cheezy flavour you expect and an extra-special crunchy garlic bread crumb topping. Be prepared for second (or third) helpings! Stir in steamed veggies like broccoli, cauliflower, or peas for extra goodness.

1. Position an oven rack 6 inches (15 cm) under the broiler and preheat the broiler.

2. COOK THE PASTA: Bring a large pot of salted water to a boil. Add the pasta and cook until just tender, 9 to 10 minutes. Reserve 1 cup (250 mL) of the pasta water and drain the pasta.

3. MEANWHILE, MAKE THE GARLIC BREAD CRUMBS: In a small bowl, stir together the olive oil, panko crumbs, garlic powder, and salt. Set aside.

4. ASSEMBLE AND FINISH: Pour the Cheeze Sauce over the pasta and stir to combine. (You might not use all the sauce, depending on how saucy you like your mac and cheese.) Thin with the pasta water to desired consistency if needed.

5. Transfer the mac and cheese to a 13 × 9-inch (3.5 L) baking dish. Sprinkle evenly with the garlic bread crumbs. Broil until the bread crumbs are golden brown, 2 to 3 minutes. Store, covered, in the fridge for up to 3 days.

Gluten-free: Use gluten-free pasta and gluten-free panko crumbs or bread crumbs.

Walnut Veggie "Ragu" with Rigatoni

Vegetarian • Vegan option • Gluten-free option

Serves 4 to 6

Prep time: 1 hour (includes making the Sheet-Pan Tomato Sauce and the Veggie Ground)

Cook time: 15 minutes

1 package (about 16 ounces/454 g) rigatoni

1 batch Sheet-Pan Tomato Sauce (page 314)

1 batch Veggie Ground (page 309)

Grated Parmesan cheese or vegan parm, for garnish

Chopped fresh basil, for garnish

Everyone in our family jokes about how much Jill loves pasta—she could eat it for breakfast, lunch, and dinner (this may or may not have happened). This vegetarian ragu was born out of her pasta love affair and is as hearty as a ragu should be. The best part? The Sheet-Pan Tomato Sauce (page 314) and the Veggie Ground (page 309) can both be made ahead and frozen, making this a perfect weeknight meal.

1. Bring a large pot of salted water to a boil. Add the pasta and cook until just tender, 10 to 14 minutes. Reserve 1 cup (250 mL) of the pasta water, drain the pasta, and return it to the pot.

2. Stir in the Sheet-Pan Tomato Sauce and Veggie Ground and heat the pasta if needed over medium heat for 1 to 2 minutes. Add reserved pasta water to loosen the sauce if needed.

3. Divide the pasta among bowls and garnish with the Parmesan and basil. Store, covered, in the fridge for up to 3 days.

Vegan: Use vegan parm.

Gluten-free: Use gluten-free rigatoni. Follow the gluten-free option to make the Veggie Ground.

One-Pot Mushroom Pappardelle

Vegan option • Vegetarian • Gluten-free option • Nut-free option

Serves 4 to 6

Prep time: 10 minutes

Cook time: 25 minutes

¼ cup (60 mL) butter or vegan butter

¼ cup (60 mL) extra-virgin olive oil

2 shallots, finely chopped

6 cloves garlic, minced

1 cup (250 mL) dry white wine

1½ pounds (675 g) mixed mushrooms, sliced (about 8 cups/2 L)

⅓ cup (75 mL) finely chopped fresh flat-leaf parsley, plus more for garnish

1 tablespoon (15 mL) chopped fresh thyme

1 package (16 ounces/454 g) pappardelle

5 cups (1.25 L) chicken-flavoured vegetarian stock or vegetable stock

½ cup (125 mL) table (18%) cream or Cashew Cream (page 324), optional

½ cup (125 mL) grated Parmesan cheese or vegan parm, plus more for garnish

Fresh lemon juice, to taste

Salt and pepper

For anyone who ever proclaimed that dinner isn't going to cook itself, this recipe is here to prove you wrong! Our granny was completely obsessed with mushrooms. This rustic and utterly unpretentious one-pot mushroom pasta was created in her honour. Granny collected mushroom art, books, and Christmas tree ornaments, and in her younger years she used to forage for wild mushrooms for days on end. It was literally her favourite thing to do.

We recommend wild mushrooms for this dish for ultimate flavour and presentation, but feel free to use white or cremini mushrooms should you wish. Add the cashew cream at the end to easily transform this pasta into a creamy version, and feel free to toss in a couple of generous handfuls of spinach at the end and stir until wilted to add some greens. Pour yourself a glass of red wine and crank up the Frank Sinatra while this pasta literally cooks itself.

1. Melt the butter with the olive oil in a large, heavy-bottomed pot with a lid over medium heat. Add the shallots and cook, stirring occasionally, until transparent and fragrant, 1 to 2 minutes. Add the garlic and cook for 30 seconds. Add the white wine and simmer until the wine has reduced by half, about 5 minutes.

2. Stir in the mushrooms, parsley, and thyme and cook, stirring occasionally, until the mushrooms are soft, 8 to 10 minutes. Add the pasta and vegetarian stock and stir to combine. Reduce the heat to medium-low, cover, and cook until the pasta is just tender, 13 to 15 minutes, stirring every 5 minutes. Remove from the heat.

3. Stir in the cream (if using), Parmesan, and a squeeze of lemon juice. Season with salt and pepper. Transfer to a serving platter or individual bowls and garnish with more Parmesan and parsley.

Vegan: Use vegan butter, vegetable stock, Cashew Cream, and vegan parm.

Gluten-free: Use gluten-free pasta.

Nut-free: If adding cream, use table (18%) cream or unsweetened soy creamer instead of Cashew Cream.

Deep Dish Sheet-Pan Pizza

Vegan option • Dairy-free option • Nut-free

Serves 4 to 6

Prep time: 15 minutes (not including making the Magic Dough)

Cook time: 12 minutes

½ batch Magic Dough (page 67)

Extra-virgin olive oil, for the pan and brushing the dough

All-purpose flour, for dusting

Vegan: Use vegan toppings and vegan cheese.

Dairy-free: Use vegan cheese.

There is something extra special about making your own pizza, from the sauce right down to the crust. This recipe makes a beautiful crust that is fluffier than a thin-crust pizza. Use our Sheet-Pan Tomato Sauce (page 314) and your favourite toppings for your next pizza night!

1. Preheat the oven to 500°F (260°C). Generously brush a 15 × 10-inch (38 × 25 cm) baking sheet with olive oil.

2. Gently deflate the Magic Dough by pushing it down with your hands. On a lightly floured work surface, use a rolling pin to roll out the Magic Dough to fit the baking sheet. Transfer the dough to the pan, pressing it into the corners of the pan.

3. Brush the top of the dough with olive oil. Add desired sauce and scatter toppings of choice on the pizza, being careful not to overload it and leaving a ½-inch (1 cm) border of dough around the outer edge. Bake until the crust is golden brown and the cheese (if using) bubbles, 10 to 12 minutes. Cut the pizza into squares and serve. Cooled pizza can be store in a resealable container in the fridge for up to 3 days.

FAVOURITE TOPPING COMBINATIONS

Margherita: Fresh tomatoes, mozzarella cheese, fresh basil leaves

Tropical: Pulled chicken or jackfruit tossed in barbecue sauce, sliced pineapple, red sweet peppers, sliced onions, fresh cilantro leaves

Pesto Shrimp: Sun-dried tomatoes, feta cheese, shrimp, pesto with an olive oil base, topped with fresh arugula

Hot Charles: Spicy capicola, feta cheese, sliced banana peppers, fresh tomatoes

Veggies and Sides

Steamed Cauliflower and Cheeze Sauce

Vegan • Gluten-free option

Serves 4 to 6

Prep time: 15 minutes

Cook time: 20 minutes

Cheeze Sauce

3 cups (750 mL) vegetable stock

2 cups (500 mL) raw cashews

1 carrot, peeled and cut into
½-inch (1 cm) coins

½ cup (125 mL) nutritional yeast

1 tablespoon (15 mL) apple cider
vinegar

2 teaspoons (10 mL) garlic powder

1 teaspoon (5 mL) salt, or to taste

¼ teaspoon (1 mL) pepper

Steamed Cauliflower

1 large head cauliflower

2 tablespoons (30 mL) olive oil
or melted vegan butter

Salt and pepper

If you were born in 1985 or earlier you probably remember eating steamed cauliflower mixed with Cheez Whiz. Dare we admit how much we loved it? We can still hear the Cheez Whiz jingle in our heads. We don't buy Cheez Whiz anymore, but we still crave this dish. Not ones to deprive our kids of our childhood classics, we created the next best thing, just healthier. Not to mention, it's a great way to sneak those extra veggies in at mealtime!

This sauce is also used in our Vegan Mac and Cheese (page 207). It was simply too good to keep it to one recipe! If you don't have a steamer, simply place the cauliflower in a large pot with an inch of water and proceed as directed below.

1. Position an oven rack about 6 inches (15 cm) under the broiler and preheat the broiler. Line a baking sheet with parchment paper.

2. START THE CHEEZE SAUCE: In a medium pot, combine the vegetable stock, cashews, and carrots and bring to a boil over medium-high heat. Cover and cook until the carrots are fork-tender, about 10 minutes. Set aside to cool.

3. MEANWHILE, STEAM THE CAULIFLOWER: Remove the leaves from the cauliflower and trim the end of the stalk. Set a steamer basket in a large pot with a lid. Add salted water to come to just below the basket. Bring to a boil over medium-high heat. Once the water is boiling, add the cauliflower stem side down to the basket, reduce the heat to low, cover, and steam until tender, 10 to 15 minutes.

4. MEANWHILE, FINISH THE CHEEZE SAUCE: Transfer the carrots and cashews along with the stock to a high-speed blender. Add the nutritional yeast, apple cider vinegar, garlic powder, salt, and pepper. Blend on medium speed until smooth, thinning with water or stock if needed. Season to taste with more salt and pepper. Return the sauce to the pot and keep warm over low heat if needed.

5. Transfer the cauliflower to the prepared baking sheet. Brush with the olive oil and season with salt and pepper. Broil until golden brown, about 3 minutes. Transfer the cauliflower to a serving platter. Pour the warm sauce over the cauliflower and serve.

Gluten-free: Use gluten-free vegetable stock.

Garlic Herb Button Mushrooms

Vegan • Gluten-free • Nut-free

Serves 4

Prep time: 5 minutes

Cook time: 15 minutes

2 tablespoons (30 mL) vegan butter

4 cloves garlic, minced

1 pound (450 g) whole button
mushrooms

¼ cup (60 mL) dry white wine

Salt and pepper

Finely chopped fresh flat-leaf
parsley, for garnish

Jill's dad Glen played a big role in the kitchen when she was growing up, and this was one of his specialties. He loved packing his dishes full of flavour (and garlic!) and he was never afraid to experiment. These vegan garlic herb mushrooms are a nod to Glen's affinity for garlic, and have the perfect ratio of butter, garlic, and herbs, making them a great side dish for just about any meal!

If you can't find button mushrooms, you can use cremini or white mushrooms cut in half.

1. Melt the vegan butter in a large frying pan over medium heat. Add the garlic and mushrooms and cook, stirring occasionally, until the mushrooms have browned and softened, 4 to 5 minutes.

2. Add the white wine and cook, stirring occasionally, until the liquid has mostly evaporated, about 5 minutes.

3. Reduce the heat to low, cover, and simmer for another 5 minutes. Season with salt and pepper. Serve garnished with the parsley.

Sweet and Spicy Green Beans

Vegan option • Vegetarian • Gluten-free option • Nut-free

Serves 4

Prep time: 10 minutes

Cook time: 10 minutes

2 tablespoons (30 mL) unseasoned
rice vinegar

2 tablespoons (30 mL) soy sauce

1 tablespoon (15 mL) pure liquid
honey or pure maple syrup

1 teaspoon (5 mL) sambal oelek

1 teaspoon (5 mL) sesame oil

2 tablespoons (30 mL) avocado oil
or canola oil

3 cloves garlic, minced

2 teaspoons (10 mL) grated peeled
fresh ginger

14 ounces (400 g) green beans,
trimmed

Sesame seeds, for garnish (optional)

These sweet and spicy crisp green beans might just be the perfect side dish. But be warned: it will take every ounce of your willpower to resist gobbling them down before you serve them! Prep all the ingredients ahead of time and this dish comes together quickly once you start cooking. We recommend serving these green beans as a side dish with the Ginger "Beef" (page 181).

1. In a small bowl, whisk together the rice vinegar, soy sauce, honey, sambal oelek, and sesame oil.

2. Heat the avocado oil in a large frying pan or wok over medium heat. Add the garlic and ginger and cook, stirring constantly, until fragrant, 2 to 3 minutes. Add the green beans and cook, stirring occasionally, until bright green and tender, 4 to 5 minutes. Pour in the sauce, stir to combine, and cook, stirring occasionally, for another 2 to 3 minutes. Transfer to a serving dish and garnish with the sesame seeds if desired.

Vegan: Use maple syrup instead of honey.

Gluten-free: Use gluten-free soy sauce or tamari.

Lazy Cabbage Rolls

Vegan option • Vegetarian • Gluten-free option • Nut-free option

Serves 6 to 8

Prep time: 20 minutes

Cook time: 1 hour

1 cup (250 mL) rice (we use jasmine)

¼ cup (60 mL) extra-virgin olive oil, plus more for the baking dish

2 cups (500 mL) finely chopped yellow onion

1½ pounds (675 g) sliced green or savoy cabbage (9 cups/2.1 L)

Salt and pepper

1 can (10 ounces/284 mL) condensed tomato soup

1 cup (250 mL) table (18%) cream or Cashew Cream (page 324)

Our granny made cabbage rolls for every single occasion, always perfectly rolled and neatly arranged in the same well-loved casserole dish. There are many ways to make cabbage rolls, but our Ukrainian granny always made hers with a mix of rice, sautéed onions, and bacon, topped with a creamy tomato sauce and baked to perfection. Always short on time, we took her recipe and created a *lazy* casserole out of the dish with all the same flavours (without the bacon—sorry, Granny!) minus the hours of rolling.

1. Preheat the oven to 375°F (190°C).

2. Cook the rice until tender according to the package directions.

3. Meanwhile, heat the olive oil in a large frying pan over medium heat. Add the onions and cook, stirring occasionally, until soft and translucent, 3 to 4 minutes. Add the cabbage and cook, stirring occasionally, until it has softened and just starts to turn golden brown, 10 to 12 minutes. Remove from the heat.

4. Stir in the cooked rice to combine. Season with salt and pepper. Transfer the mixture to a lightly oiled 13 × 9-inch (3.5 L) baking dish.

5. In a medium bowl, whisk together the tomato soup and cream. Pour the creamy tomato soup evenly over the rice mixture.

6. Bake until the mixture bubbles and is golden brown on top, 35 to 40 minutes.

Vegan: Use Cashew Cream.

Gluten-free: Use 2 cups (500 mL) of prepared gluten-free tomato soup (we use Pacific brand) instead of condensed tomato soup.

Nut-free: Use table (18%) cream or unsweetened soy creamer instead of Cashew Cream.

Cilantro Lime Rice

Vegan • Gluten-free • Nut-free

Serves 4

Prep time: 10 minutes

Cook time: 20 minutes

2 tablespoons (30 mL) coconut oil

1½ cups (375 mL) long-grain white basmati rice

1 clove garlic, minced

2¼ cups (550 mL) water

1 teaspoon (5 mL) salt

Zest of 1 lime

3 tablespoons (45 mL) fresh lime juice

¼ cup (60 mL) roughly chopped fresh cilantro, plus more for garnish

This recipe came from our friends at 19 Okanagan Grill + Bar in West Kelowna, along with the Fish Tacos recipe (page 163). We begged Neil, the owner, for three years for both recipes, and it was worth every moment of grovelling. This fragrant cilantro- and lime-scented rice has an extra depth of flavour thanks to toasting the rice before steaming.

1. Melt the coconut oil in a medium saucepan with a lid over medium-high heat. Add the rice and cook, stirring occasionally, until the rice begins to brown, 2 to 3 minutes.

2. Add the garlic and cook, stirring constantly, for 1 minute until fragrant. Add the water, salt, and lime zest and bring to a boil. Once the water is boiling, reduce the heat to low, cover, and simmer until the rice is tender, 18 to 20 minutes. Remove from the heat and let the rice sit, covered, for 10 minutes.

3. Fluff the rice with a fork and stir in the lime juice and cilantro. Transfer to a medium serving dish and garnish with more cilantro if desired.

Pineapple Fried Rice

Vegan • Gluten-free option • Nut-free

Serves 6 to 8

Prep time: 15 minutes

Cook time: 30 minutes

2 cups (500 mL) jasmine rice
(or 4 to 5 cups/1 to 1.125 L
cooked and cooled rice)

2 tablespoons (30 mL) avocado oil
or canola oil

1 cup (250 mL) finely chopped yellow
onion

1 cup (250 mL) diced red sweet
pepper

1 cup (250 mL) cooked shelled
edamame

4 cloves garlic, minced

¼ cup (60 mL) soy sauce

1 tablespoon (15 mL) sesame oil

2 teaspoons (10 mL) grated peeled
fresh ginger

2 cups (500 mL) diced fresh
pineapple

¼ cup (60 mL) chopped fresh
cilantro, plus more for garnish

2 green onions (white and light
green parts only), sliced, for
garnish

There's pure magic in a sweet/salty combination of flavours, and this pineapple fried rice ticks both boxes. Loaded with vegetables, ginger, cilantro, and (of course) garlic, it can be served as a meal (add sautéed tofu or chicken if you wish) or as a side (try it with our Coconut-Crusted Halibut, page 176). Fried rice traditionally starts with leftover rice—a fabulous way to use up extra rice in the fridge! While you don't *need* to serve this in a pineapple bowl, it sure does make it extra impressive.

To create a pineapple bowl, simply cut a pineapple in half lengthwise, keeping the stem intact. Using a sharp knife, cut around the centre, leaving a ½-inch (1 cm) border of fruit. Score the fruit and scoop it out with a serving spoon.

1. Cook the rice until tender according to the package directions. Fluff the cooked rice with a fork, cover with the lid, and set aside.

2. Heat the avocado oil in a large frying pan or wok over medium heat. Add the onions and cook, stirring occasionally, until soft and translucent, 3 to 4 minutes. Add the sweet peppers, edamame, and garlic and cook, stirring occasionally, 2 to 3 minutes.

3. Add the steamed rice and cook until it is golden brown and slightly crispy. Add the soy sauce, sesame oil, and ginger and cook, stirring constantly, about 2 minutes. Stir in the pineapple and cilantro, then transfer to a serving dish or hollowed-out pineapple bowl for serving. Garnish with the green onions and more cilantro if desired.

Gluten-free: Use gluten-free soy sauce or tamari.

Maple Acorn Squash

Vegan option • Vegetarian • Gluten-free • Nut-free option

Serves 4

Prep time: 10 minutes

Cook time: 30 minutes

1½-pound (675 g) acorn squash

2 tablespoons (30 mL) butter or vegan butter, melted

1 tablespoon (15 mL) pure maple syrup

1 tablespoon (15 mL) brown sugar

½ teaspoon (2 mL) salt, plus more for serving

¼ teaspoon (1 mL) cinnamon, plus more for serving

⅛ to ¼ teaspoon (0.5 to 1 mL) cayenne pepper (optional)

¼ cup (60 mL) finely chopped raw pecans

If ever there was an underrated vegetable, it would be the humble acorn squash. It is sweet, inexpensive, healthy, showy, and versatile. Oh, and it lasts a long time in the pantry. The best part is that you can eat the skin once roasted, which means that this dish works as both a side dish and a snack. We'll bet that it doesn't make it to the dinner table, it's that good!

1. Preheat the oven to 400°F (200°C) and line a baking sheet with parchment paper.

2. Cut the squash in half lengthwise. Scoop out the seeds and discard or save them to roast. Cut the squash halves crosswise into ½-inch (1 cm) slices.

3. In a large bowl, whisk together the melted butter, maple syrup, brown sugar, salt, cinnamon, and cayenne, if using. Add the sliced squash and using your hands, toss to combine. Arrange the squash slices in a single layer on the prepared baking sheet.

4. Bake for 15 minutes. Turn the squash slices and sprinkle with the pecans. Continue baking until tender and slightly crisp, about 15 minutes more.

5. Transfer to a serving platter. Add a sprinkle of salt or cinnamon if desired before serving.

Vegan: Use vegan butter.

Nut-free: Skip the pecans.

Pizza Zucchini Gratin

Vegan option · Vegetarian · Gluten-free option · Nut-free

Serves 4 to 6

Prep time: 10 minutes

Cook time: 15 minutes

2 tablespoons (30 mL) extra-virgin olive oil, divided

1½ pounds (675 g) small zucchini, cut crosswise into ¼-inch (5 mm) thick slices

2 cloves garlic, minced

½ teaspoon (2 mL) salt

½ teaspoon (2 mL) pepper

1 cup (250 mL) pizza sauce

¾ cup (175 mL) grated mozzarella cheese or vegan mozzarella cheese

¼ cup (60 mL) grated Parmesan cheese or vegan parm

⅓ cup (75 mL) panko crumbs

½ teaspoon (2 mL) dried oregano

We each plant zucchini in our gardens every year, and at some point find ourselves completely overwhelmed trying to keep up with the garden, which seems to grow basketball-sized zucchini overnight. It's the very best kind of problem to have! Since our families ask for pizza every other night, we felt inspired to create a veggie-based side dish with all of those delicious pizza flavours. This is a low-maintenance dish (and lower carb, if that interests you) that is bound to become part of your dinner rotation.

Be sure to use smaller zucchini for this dish, as they are more tender than their older, larger counterparts. Feel free to use store-bought pizza sauce or make our Sheet-Pan Tomato Sauce (page 314), adding a pinch more dried oregano.

1. Position an oven rack about 6 inches (15 cm) under the broiler and preheat the broiler.

2. Heat 1 tablespoon (15 mL) of the olive oil in a large frying pan over medium heat. Add the zucchini, garlic, salt, and pepper and cook, stirring occasionally, until the zucchini is light golden brown, 4 to 5 minutes. Remove from the heat.

3. Spread the pizza sauce in an 11 × 7-inch (2 L) or 9-inch (2.5 L) square or round baking dish. Layer the zucchini over the pizza sauce. Top with the mozzarella, Parmesan, and panko crumbs. Drizzle with the remaining 1 tablespoon (15 mL) olive oil. Sprinkle with the oregano. Broil until golden brown, about 2 minutes.

Vegan: Use vegan cheese.

Gluten-free: Use gluten-free panko crumbs.

Peaches and Creamed Corn

Vegan option • Vegetarian • Gluten-free option • Nut-free option

Serves 4 to 6

Prep time: 15 minutes

Cook time: 20 minutes

¼ cup (60 mL) butter or vegan butter

½ cup (125 mL) finely chopped yellow onion

2 cloves garlic, minced

2 tablespoons (30 mL) all-purpose flour

4 cups (1 L) fresh corn kernels (from about 5 cobs)

1½ cups (375 mL) chicken-flavoured vegetarian stock or vegetable stock

¼ cup (60 mL) table (18%) cream or Cashew Cream (page 324)

Salt and pepper

Chopped fresh flat-leaf parsley, for garnish

We're still a bit shocked that we survived the '80s. Between the processed food and no seatbelts rule in Alberta (to name a few), it's a miracle we're alive. All that said, most of our favourite things come from that era, and this more wholesome version of canned creamed corn is one of them. It's pretty awesome, if you ask us. Make this side dish at the height of summer when local corn is bursting with flavour and readily available.

To remove the corn kernels from the cob, simply stand the husked cob on end and, using a sharp chef's knife, run the blade down the kernels where they meet the cob. To transform this dish into a corn soup, simply add a generous splash of stock to reheated leftovers.

1. Melt the butter in a large frying pan with a lid over medium heat. Add the onion and cook, stirring occasionally, until soft and translucent, 3 to 4 minutes. Add the garlic and cook, stirring, until fragrant, about 1 minute. Add the flour and cook, stirring constantly, until the flour is lightly browned, about 2 minutes. Stir in the corn.

2. Pour in the vegetarian stock and bring to a simmer. Reduce the heat to low, cover, and simmer, stirring occasionally, until the corn is tender, about 10 minutes.

3. Remove from the heat. Transfer half the corn mixture to a medium bowl with high sides. Using an immersion blender, blend the corn to slightly purée it.

4. Return the puréed corn to the frying pan. Pour in the cream and season with salt and pepper. Stir to combine. Transfer to a serving dish and garnish with the parsley if desired.

Vegan: Use vegan butter and Cashew Cream.

Gluten-free: Use a 1:1 gluten-free flour blend instead of all-purpose flour.

Nut-free: Use table (18%) cream or unsweetened soy milk instead of Cashew Cream.

Pierogi Mashed Potatoes

Vegan option • Vegetarian • Gluten-free • Nut-free option

Serves 6

Prep time: 15 minutes

Cook time: 25 minutes

3 pounds (1.4 kg) russet potatoes, peeled

¼ cup (60 mL) extra-virgin olive oil

4 tablespoons (60 mL) butter or vegan butter, divided

2 cups (500 mL) finely chopped yellow onion

3 cloves garlic, minced

¾ cup (175 mL) table (18%) cream or Cashew Cream (page 324), plus more if needed

¼ cup (60 mL) nutritional yeast

¼ cup (60 mL) finely chopped fresh chives, plus more for garnish

¼ cup (60 mL) roughly chopped fresh dill, plus more for garnish

Salt and pepper

We love a good dish of mashed potatoes, and this Ukrainian-inspired version of a classic is beyond delicious—a generous portion of sweet caramelized onions mashed with fluffy boiled potatoes, cream or cashew cream, nutritional yeast (for that cheesy flavour), and fresh herbs. Leftovers make unbelievable savoury Pierogi Waffles (page 44)!

1. Cut the peeled potatoes in half and place them in a large pot of salted water. Bring to a boil over high heat and cook the potatoes until fork-tender 15 to 20 minutes. Drain the potatoes and mash with a potato masher or ricer until smooth.

2. Meanwhile, heat the olive oil and 2 tablespoons (30 mL) of the butter in a medium frying pan over low heat. Add the onions and cook, stirring occasionally, until they have caramelized, about 20 minutes. Add the garlic and cook, stirring occasionally, until the garlic is fragrant, 2 to 3 minutes.

3. Stir the onion mixture into the mashed potatoes. Add the remaining 2 tablespoons (30 mL) butter, cream, nutritional yeast, chives, and dill. Stir well. Season with salt and pepper. Add more cream if needed. Transfer to a serving dish and serve with dill and chives to garnish if desired.

Vegan: Use vegan butter and Cashew Cream.

Nut-free: Use table (18%) cream or unsweetened soy creamer instead of Cashew Cream.

Salt and Vinegar Potatoes

Vegan • Gluten-free • Nut-free

Serves 4 to 6

Prep time: 5 minutes

Cook time: 40 minutes

1½ pounds (675 g) baby or fingerling potatoes, cut in half

2 cups (500 mL) water

2 cups (500 mL) white vinegar

1 teaspoon (5 mL) salt

1 tablespoon (15 mL) avocado oil or canola oil

Flaky sea salt, for sprinkling

If you're a fan of salt and vinegar potato chips, you will *love* these potatoes. What's the trick? Adding vinegar to the water when boiling the potatoes to infuse them with flavour. For a little extra wow factor, gently smash the potatoes before baking them. White or yellow baby potatoes work best, but the red variety will work too.

Serve these potatoes with Patsy's Fried Fish (page 190) and our Okanagan Coleslaw (page 131).

1. Preheat the oven to 425°F (220°C) and line a baking sheet with parchment paper.

2. Put the potatoes in a large pot and cover with the water, vinegar, and salt. Bring to a boil and cook, uncovered, until the potatoes are fork-tender, about 10 minutes. Drain the potatoes.

3. Transfer the potatoes to the prepared baking sheet and arrange them in an even layer. Drizzle with the avocado oil, sprinkle lightly with flaky sea salt, and bake until golden and crispy, about 25 minutes, tossing halfway through. Transfer to a serving dish and serve hot.

Desserts

Coco Loco Cookies

Vegan • Gluten-free option • Nut-free option • Freezer-friendly

Makes about 24 cookies

Prep time: 20 minutes

Cook time: 15 minutes

⅓ cup (75 mL) water

2 tablespoons (30 mL) ground flaxseed

1 cup (250 mL) vegan butter, softened, or coconut oil

1 cup (250 mL) lightly packed brown sugar

2 teaspoons (10 mL) pure vanilla extract

1¾ cups (425 mL) all-purpose flour

1½ cups (375 mL) old-fashioned rolled oats

1½ cups (375 mL) unsweetened shredded coconut, toasted

1 cup (250 mL) chopped toasted pecans

½ teaspoon (2 mL) baking soda

½ teaspoon (2 mL) cinnamon

½ teaspoon (2 mL) salt

7 ounces (200 g/1¼ cups/300 mL) dairy-free dark chocolate chunks or chips

½ cup (125 mL) dried cherries, raisins, or cranberries (optional)

2 tablespoons (30 mL) instant espresso powder (optional)

Who doesn't love a good nubby chocolate oatmeal cookie? Nobody we know! These vegan cookies mean business and have earned a special place in our cookie jar since we created them.

Feel free to replace the flax mixture with 2 eggs, should you wish. These freeze beautifully, so consider baking extras. And trust us, you should.

1. Position the oven racks in the upper and lower thirds of the oven and preheat the oven to 350°F (180°C). Line 2 baking sheets with parchment paper.

2. In a small bowl, stir together the water and flaxseed. Let sit for 5 minutes.

3. In a large bowl using an electric mixer, or in the bowl of a stand mixer fitted with the paddle attachment, cream the butter with the sugar on high speed. Add the flax mixture and vanilla and beat until light and fluffy.

4. Add the flour, oats, coconut, pecans, baking soda, cinnamon, and salt and mix on medium speed to combine. Fold in the chocolate chunks, dried fruit (if using), and espresso powder, if using.

5. Scoop 3-tablespoon (45 mL) portions of dough and shape into 1-inch (2.5 cm) balls. Place the balls on the prepared baking sheet 2 inches (5 cm) apart. Lightly press down on the balls to slightly flatten. Bake until golden brown on the bottom, 13 to 15 minutes, rotating the pans halfway through. Transfer the cookies to a rack to cool. Store in a resealable container at room temperature for up to 1 week or in the freezer for up to 3 months.

Gluten-free: Use a 1:1 gluten-free flour blend instead of all-purpose flour. Use certified gluten-free rolled oats.

Nut-free: Skip the pecans.

Grandma Laurin's Ginger Snaps

Vegan option • Vegetarian • Gluten-free option • Nut-free • Freezer-friendly

Makes 24 cookies

Prep time: 10 minutes

Cook time: 10 minutes

1 cup (250 mL) sugar, plus more
  for rolling

¾ cup (175 mL) coconut oil, solid
  at room temperature (we use
  Nutiva)

1 egg

¼ cup (60 mL) fancy molasses

1¾ cups (425 mL) all-purpose flour

1 tablespoon (15 mL) ground ginger

2 teaspoons (10 mL) baking soda,
  sifted

1 teaspoon (5 mL) cinnamon

½ teaspoon (2 mL) salt

Tori's grandma Laurin had a few recipes that were seriously the best. Among them are these famous ginger snaps. Tori will forever remember the large cookie tin her grandma kept on her counter, always full of fresh ginger snaps. These beauties are crunchy on the outside and chewy on the inside and perfectly spiced, just how Grandma Laurin intended.

1. Position the oven racks in the upper and lower thirds of the oven and preheat to 350°F (180°C). Line 2 baking sheets with parchment paper.

2. In a medium bowl using a hand-held electric mixer, or in the bowl of a stand mixer fitted with the whisk attachment, cream together the sugar and coconut oil. Add the egg and beat until light and fluffy. Add the molasses and beat until incorporated.

3. Add the flour, ginger, baking soda, cinnamon and salt and beat until combined.

4. Set out a small bowl of sugar for rolling. Using your hands, roll the dough into 1-inch (2.5 cm) balls and roll in the sugar. Place the cookies on the prepared baking sheets 2 inches (5 cm) apart (do not flatten them). Bake until golden on the bottom, 8 to 10 minutes, rotating the pans halfway through. Transfer the cookies to a rack to cool. Store the cookies in a resealable container at room temperature for up to 1 week or in the freezer for up to 2 months.

Vegan: Use a Flax Egg (page 330) instead of an egg.

Gluten-free: Use 2¼ cups (550 mL) of a gluten-free 1:1 flour blend instead of all-purpose flour, add an extra 1 tablespoon (15 mL) of molasses, and use 2 eggs.

Haystack Cookies

Vegan • Gluten-free option • Nut-free option • Freezer-friendly

Makes 36 small cookies

Prep time: 10 minutes

Cook time: 5 minutes, plus 30 minutes to 2 hours chilling

3 cups (750 mL) unsweetened shredded coconut

2 cups (500 mL) old-fashioned rolled oats

Pinch of salt

¾ cup (175 mL) pure maple syrup

½ cup (125 mL) cocoa powder (we use Dutch-processed)

½ cup (125 mL) coconut oil, solid at room temperature

½ cup (125 mL) unsweetened non-dairy milk

1 teaspoon (5 mL) pure vanilla extract

These cookies held a spot on our holiday cookie platter every single year when we were growing up. Young Jillian liked to call these cookies "Puppy Poos," for reasons we don't need to explain! Tori took a stab at giving Jillian's mom Peggy's old-fashioned recipe a healthy makeover. The result was a softer, even more delicious vegan version of our childhood favourite with less sugar.

Dutch-processed cocoa powder gives these no-bake cookies a richer brown colour, but any cocoa powder will work.

1. Line 2 baking sheets with parchment paper.

2. In a large bowl, combine the coconut, oats, and salt.

3. In a medium saucepan, combine the maple syrup, cocoa powder, coconut oil, and milk and bring to a simmer over medium heat, stirring constantly with a whisk. Reduce the heat to medium-low and simmer for 1 minute, stirring constantly with a whisk. Remove from the heat and stir in the vanilla.

4. Pour the liquid mixture over the coconut mixture and stir well to combine.

5. Drop 1-tablespoon (15 mL) portions of the mixture onto the prepared baking sheets, gently pressing them together with your fingers to form mounds.

6. Refrigerate the cookies on the baking sheets for about 2 hours or freeze for at least 30 minutes until firm. Store in a resealable container in the fridge for up to 1 week or in the freezer for up to 2 months.

Gluten-free: Use certified gluten-free rolled oats.

Nut-free: Use a nut-free non-dairy milk.

Cornflake Chews

Vegetarian • Nut-free option • Freezer-friendly

Makes 24 cookies

Prep Time: 15 minutes

Cook Time: 10 minutes

5 (1½ ounces/45 g each) Mackintosh's Toffee candy bars, roughly chopped

3 tablespoons (45 mL) heavy (35%) cream or coconut cream

½ cup (125 mL) sliced almonds

½ cup (125 mL) unsweetened ribbon coconut

2½ cups (625 mL) cornflakes cereal

Out of all the treats that Tori makes over the winter holidays, these Cornflake Chews are always the first to disappear. They also hold a special place in Jillian's heart: they are the only cookie that Jillian has ever requested from Tori. Chewy toffee is melted down and mixed with nuts, coconut, and cornflakes to make clusters that almost can't be described.

These are perfect for making with little ones. Feel free to double or triple the recipe! You can find ribbon coconut in most health food stores.

1. Heat the toffee and cream in a large, heavy-bottomed pot over low heat, stirring occasionally, until the toffee is melted, about 8 minutes.

2. Meanwhile, in a small frying pan, lightly toast the almonds over medium heat. Transfer the almonds to a medium bowl.

3. In the same pan, lightly toast the coconut over medium heat. Add the coconut to the almonds and stir together.

4. Add the almond and coconut mixture and the cornflakes to the warm toffee mixture. Stir together until combined.

5. Drop heaping tablespoons of the warm mixture (leaving space in between each) onto a large piece of parchment paper or waxed paper. Lightly wet your fingers (to prevent sticking) and gently press each portion into a little mound. Cool completely before serving. Store in a resealable container at room temperature for up to 1 week or in the freezer for up to 1 month.

Nut-free: Skip the almonds and use ½ cup (125 mL) more ribbon coconut or cornflakes.

Puffed Wheat Squares

Vegan option • Vegetarian • Nut-free

Makes 12 to 18 squares

Prep time: 5 minutes

Cook time: 5 minutes

½ cup (125 mL) butter or vegan butter

½ cup (125 mL) corn syrup or brown rice syrup

½ cup (125 mL) lightly packed brown sugar

3 tablespoons (45 mL) cocoa powder

2 teaspoons (10 mL) pure vanilla extract

10 large marshmallows (don't use jumbo size)

7 cups (1.75 L) natural puffed wheat cereal

Our Aunty Jackie makes the best puffed wheat squares. These chewy, chocolatey no-bake squares have been served at every single gathering in northern Alberta that we can remember, and her recipe is the best that we have eaten—and we've had a lot. We took Aunty Jackie's recipe, cut the sugar in half, and still found them plenty sweet enough! During recipe testing we handed these out to every person from northern Alberta that we could find and got two thumbs up from everyone.

You can find natural puffed wheat cereal, the kind without any added sugar, next to the oats in the cereal aisle.

1. Lightly grease an 8-inch (2 L) square pan and line it with parchment paper, leaving extra to overhang on the sides to make it easier to remove the squares.

2. In a large, heavy-bottomed pot, combine the butter, corn syrup, brown sugar, and cocoa powder. Bring to a boil over medium heat and cook, stirring constantly, for 2 minutes. Remove from the heat and stir in the vanilla and marshmallows. Cover and let the mixture sit for 5 minutes. Uncover and stir until the marshmallows have completely melted.

3. Add the puffed wheat cereal and stir until well combined. Scrape the mixture into the prepared pan. Using wet hands or the flat bottom of a glass, press the mixture evenly into the bottom of the pan.

4. Cool completely before cutting into squares. Store in a resealable container at room temperature for up to 1 week.

Vegan: Use vegan butter and vegan marshmallows.

Blender Blondies

Vegan • Gluten-free option • Nut-free option • Freezer-friendly

Serves 6 to 8

Prep time: 10 minutes

Cook time: 35 minutes

1 cup (250 mL) old-fashioned rolled oats

½ cup (125 mL) natural smooth peanut butter

½ cup (125 mL) pure maple syrup

½ cup (125 mL) vegan butter, melted

½ cup (125 mL) unsweetened non-dairy milk

¼ cup (60 mL) ground flaxseed

2 teaspoons (10 mL) pure vanilla extract

1 teaspoon (5 mL) baking powder

Pinch of salt

½ cup (125 mL) dairy-free dark or white chocolate chips or chunks

Flaky sea salt, for finishing (optional)

Dairy-free vanilla ice cream, for serving (optional)

After a gazillion attempts at tweaking these blondies, we finally arrived at this perfect recipe that we're rather proud of. These healthier blondies are naturally gluten-free (simply use certified gluten-free rolled oats), vegan, and perfectly sweet with a soft, chewy centre. The best part is that they are whipped up in a blender (we wish all recipes were this easy), which means zero fuss and practically no mess to clean up—minus those chocolate fingerprints if you have little ones. We can't help you there!

1. Preheat the oven to 350°F (180°C) and grease a 9-inch (2.5 L) cast-iron frying pan or round or square baking dish.

2. In a high-speed blender, combine the oats, peanut butter, maple syrup, melted butter, milk, flaxseed, vanilla, baking powder, and salt. Blend on high speed until smooth, 1 to 2 minutes.

3. Scrape the batter into the prepared pan and spread evenly with a rubber spatula. Sprinkle the chocolate and flaky sea salt (if using) on top. Bake until the edges are light golden brown, 30 to 35 minutes. Let the blondie cool slightly in the pan before cutting.

4. Serve with a scoop of dairy-free ice cream if desired. Store in a resealable container at room temperature for up to 3 days or in the freezer for up to 1 month.

Gluten-free: Use certified gluten-free rolled oats.

Nut-free: Use a seed butter instead of peanut butter and a nut-free non-dairy milk.

Nanaimo Bars

Vegetarian • Gluten-free option • Nut-free • Freezer-friendly

Makes 24 bars

Prep time: 30 minutes, plus 3 hours setting

Base

¾ cup (175 mL) butter or vegan butter, softened

½ cup (125 mL) cocoa powder

½ cup (125 mL) sugar

3 eggs, whisked

1 teaspoon (5 mL) pure vanilla extract

3 cups (750 mL) graham cracker crumbs

1½ cups (375 mL) unsweetened shredded coconut

Filling

½ cup (125 mL) butter or vegan butter, softened

½ cup (125 mL) whipping (35%) cream

½ cup (125 mL) vanilla custard powder (we use Bird's)

4 cups (2 L) icing sugar, sifted

Ganache

8 ounces (255 g) semi-sweet chocolate

⅓ cup (75 mL) whipping (35%) cream

Our Aunty Becky is famous for her magic in the kitchen, and at the top of the list of family favourites are her Nanaimo Bars. Tori's dad Bob would request these for every single camping trip (and there were many back in the day), and Becky would always make them for him without fail. These no-bake bars originated in Nanaimo, British Columbia, and have a chocolate coconut base, a custard icing filling, and a topping of rich chocolate ganache. They are very decadent, and almost as sweet as our childhood memories.

1. MAKE THE BASE: Grease a 13 × 9-inch (3.5 L) baking dish and line with parchment paper, leaving extra to overhang on the sides to make it easier to remove the bars.

2. In a large microwave-safe bowl, mix together the butter, cocoa powder, sugar, eggs, and vanilla. Heat the mixture in the microwave in 1-minute intervals, stirring after each interval, until the mixture is the consistency of pudding, 3 to 5 minutes total. Do not overcook. Stir in the graham cracker crumbs and coconut until well combined.

3. Press the mixture firmly and evenly into the bottom of the prepared pan using your fingers or the flat bottom of a glass.

4. MAKE THE FILLING: In a medium bowl, combine the butter, whipping cream, custard powder, and icing sugar. Using an electric mixer, beat on high speed until smooth. Spread the filling evenly over the base.

5. MAKE THE GANACHE AND FINISH: In a medium microwave-safe bowl, combine the chocolate and whipping cream. Heat in the microwave in 30-second intervals, stirring after each interval, until the chocolate is melted. Spread the ganache evenly over the filling.

6. Chill in the fridge until firm, at least 3 hours or overnight, before cutting into 24 squares. Store the bars in a resealable container in the fridge for up to 1 week or in the freezer for up to 2 months.

Gluten-free: Use gluten-free graham cracker crumbs and gluten-free custard powder.

Baked Apples with Oat Crumble

Vegan option • Vegetarian • Gluten-free option • Nut-free

Baked Apples with Oat Crumble

6 medium apples (we use Gala)

1 cup (250 mL) old-fashioned rolled oats

¼ cup (60 mL) all-purpose flour

¼ cup (60 mL) lightly packed brown sugar

½ teaspoon (2 mL) cinnamon

⅓ cup (75 mL) butter or vegan butter, melted

Pinch of salt

Caramel Apple Sauce

¼ cup (60 mL) butter or vegan butter

1 tablespoon (15 mL) all-purpose flour

½ cup (125 mL) lightly packed brown sugar

¼ cup (60 mL) pure apple juice

¼ cup (60 mL) whipping (35%) cream or coconut cream

1 teaspoon (5 mL) pure vanilla extract

Pinch of salt

Vanilla ice cream or dairy-free vanilla ice cream, for serving

Vegan: Use vegan butter, coconut cream, and dairy-free ice cream.

Gluten-free: Use a 1:1 gluten-free flour blend instead of all-purpose flour. Use certified gluten-free rolled oats.

This recipe is straight from the kitchen of Jillian's mom Peggy. Growing up in Peace River, Alberta, we didn't have much to choose from when it came to fresh produce, but we do remember there always being a supply of apples. As a treat, Jillian's mom would prepare a baked apple for her, which she absolutely loved. Fast-forward to today, and Jillian makes baked apples with oat crumble for her own children, Leo and Annie, and they love them just as much as she did!

Assemble them ahead of time if desired and pop in the oven about an hour before serving. To give the caramel apple sauce an adult twist, replace half the apple juice with bourbon.

1. MAKE THE BAKED APPLES WITH OAT CRUMBLE: Preheat the oven to 350°F (180°C) and pour ½ inch (1 cm) of water into a 13 × 9-inch (3.5 L) baking dish.

2. If needed, shave the bottoms of the apples with a paring knife so they stand upright. Using an apple corer, paring knife, or melon baller, core the apples, creating a well about 2 inches (5 cm) wide, making sure not to go all the way to the bottom.

3. In a medium bowl, stir together the oats, flour, brown sugar, cinnamon, melted butter, and salt. Fill the apples with the oat mixture, packing it down. Place the filled apples in the prepared baking dish. Bake until you can poke the apples with the tip of a paring knife and not meet with much resistance, about 50 minutes.

4. MEANWHILE, MAKE THE CARAMEL APPLE SAUCE: In a small saucepan over medium-low heat, melt the butter. Whisk in the flour and cook, whisking constantly, until smooth, 1 to 2 minutes. Add the brown sugar and apple juice and simmer, whisking constantly, until the sugar is dissolved and the sauce has slightly thickened, 2 to 3 minutes. Add the cream and continue to simmer, stirring, until the sauce thickens and coats the back of a spoon. Remove from the heat and whisk in the vanilla and salt.

5. Serve the baked apples warm with a scoop of ice cream and a drizzle of Caramel Apple Sauce. The baked apples are best served warm from the oven, but they can be stored in a resealable container in the fridge for up to 3 days and reheated in the microwave.

Tip: Have leftover Baked Apples? Simply blend each apple with 1 cup (250 mL) of ice and 1 cup (250 mL) of milk or non-dairy milk to make a delicious smoothie. Garnish with extra cinnamon and an apple slice if desired.

Rustic Fruit Galette

Vegan option • Vegetarian • Gluten-free option • Nut-free option

Serves 6 to 8

Prep time: 15 minutes

Cook time: 40 minutes

4 cups (1 L) sliced pitted stone fruit (nectarines, peeled peaches, apricots, plums)

¼ to ½ cup (60 to 125 mL) sugar

2 tablespoons (30 mL) cornstarch

1 tablespoon (15 mL) fresh lemon juice

1 teaspoon (5 mL) pure vanilla extract

1 sheet or block (8 ounces/225 g) puff pastry, thawed

1 tablespoon (15 mL) cold butter or vegan butter, diced

2 tablespoons (30 mL) 2% milk or unsweetened non-dairy milk (optional)

1 tablespoon (15 mL) coarse sugar (optional)

Vanilla ice cream or dairy-free vanilla ice cream, for serving (optional)

Make this galette toward the end of summer when the fruit is ripe, and the days are long. You can adjust the amount of sugar depending on how sweet you like your desserts and use whatever type of stone fruit you wish. Our vote is a mix of fruit, which looks so stunning. Served warm with a scoop of your favourite vanilla ice cream or dairy-free ice cream, this rustic fruit tart is our idea of a perfectly imperfect dessert.

1. Preheat the oven to 400°F (200°C).

2. In a large bowl, combine the fruit, sugar, cornstarch, lemon juice, and vanilla. Toss to coat.

3. Place the puff pastry on a lightly floured sheet of parchment paper. Using a lightly floured rolling pin, roll out the pastry into about a 12-inch (30 cm) square (it doesn't have to be perfect). Slide the parchment paper with the pastry onto a baking sheet.

4. Pile the fruit into the centre of the pastry, leaving a 3-inch (8 cm) border. Scatter the diced butter over top. Gently fold the sides of the pastry up and over the filling, overlapping slightly and lightly pressing the edges together to seal, leaving the centre of the galette exposed with fruit.

5. Brush the pastry lightly with the milk and sprinkle with the coarse sugar, if using. Bake until the pastry is golden brown and the fruit is soft and bubbling, 30 to 40 minutes. Transfer to a serving plate and cool for about 5 minutes before serving. Serve warm with a scoop of ice cream if desired. Store the galette in a resealable container in the fridge for up to 3 days.

Vegan: Use vegan puff pastry, vegan butter, and non-dairy milk. Use dairy-free vanilla ice cream.

Gluten-free: Use gluten-free puff pastry or pie crust.

Nut-free: If using non-dairy milk, use a nut-free option.

Strawberry Vanilla Crisp

Vegan option • Vegetarian • Gluten-free option • Nut-free

Serves 6

Prep time: 10 minutes

Cook time: 60 minutes

Oat Layer

1 cup (250 mL) old-fashioned rolled oats

½ cup (125 mL) all-purpose flour

½ cup (125 mL) lightly packed brown sugar

½ cup (125 mL) butter or vegan butter, melted

1 teaspoon (5 mL) pure vanilla extract

¼ teaspoon (1 mL) salt

Strawberry Layer

4 cups (1 L) sliced fresh or unthawed frozen sliced strawberries

¼ cup (60 mL) sugar

2 tablespoons (30 mL) cornstarch

2 teaspoons (10 mL) lemon zest

1 tablespoon (15 mL) fresh lemon juice

1 teaspoon (5 mL) pure vanilla extract

Vanilla ice cream or dairy-free vanilla ice cream, for serving (optional)

For those summer days when you're craving something cozy or those fall days when you want something summery, this Strawberry Vanilla Crisp fits the bill. This lighter take on a traditional crisp combines sweet strawberries with a touch of lemon and vanilla to make a perfectly sweet base for the crumbly vanilla oat crust. Use fresh strawberries only if they are local and in season; otherwise, we find that frozen sliced strawberries work best (with less effort!).

1. Preheat the oven to 350°F (180°C) and grease a 9-inch square (2.5 L) or round (1.5 L) baking dish.

2. MAKE THE OAT LAYER: In a medium bowl, combine the oats, flour, brown sugar, melted butter, vanilla, and salt. Stir to combine.

3. MAKE THE STRAWBERRY LAYER: In a large bowl, combine the sliced strawberries, sugar, cornstarch, lemon zest, lemon juice, and vanilla. Stir to combine.

4. ASSEMBLE AND BAKE: Scrape the strawberry mixture into the prepared baking dish. Sprinkle evenly with the oat mixture. Bake until the topping is golden brown and the strawberry mixture bubbles, 50 to 60 minutes. Let the crisp cool for about 5 minutes before serving. Serve warm with a scoop of ice cream if desired. Store the crisp, covered, in the fridge for up to 3 days.

Vegan: Use vegan butter and dairy-free ice cream.

Gluten-free: Use certified gluten-free rolled oats and use oat flour instead of all-purpose flour.

Rhubarb Yogurt Coffee Cake

Vegan option · Vegetarian · Gluten-free option · Nut-free option

Serves 12

Prep time: 15 minutes

Cook time: 40 minutes

Streusel

½ cup (125 mL) finely chopped pecans

¼ cup (60 mL) whole wheat flour

¼ cup (60 mL) lightly packed brown sugar

¼ cup (60 mL) butter or vegan butter, melted

1 teaspoon (5 mL) cinnamon

¼ teaspoon (1 mL) salt

Cake

2 cups (500 mL) all-purpose flour

1 teaspoon (5 mL) baking soda

1 teaspoon (5 mL) baking powder

¼ teaspoon (1 mL) salt

4 cups (1 L) sliced fresh or unthawed frozen rhubarb

1 cup (250 mL) sugar, divided

¼ cup (60 mL) butter or vegan butter, softened

2 eggs

1½ cups (375 mL) plain or vanilla yogurt or non-dairy yogurt

2 teaspoons (10 mL) pure vanilla extract

Glaze (optional)

1 cup (250 mL) icing sugar, sifted

½ teaspoon (2 mL) pure vanilla extract

2 to 3 tablespoons (30 to 45 mL) 2% milk or non-dairy milk, divided

Rhubarb brings us both back to our northern Alberta roots. It's one of those vegetables (yes, a vegetable) that grows so well in the northern climate, and at the right time of year we were blessed with everything rhubarb. From cakes to relish, it made its way into our little bellies as kids, and now our hearts as adults. This moist, slightly tart, and not-too-sweet classic cake is best enjoyed with friends over coffee where no invitation is required and the door is always open.

1. Preheat the oven to 350°F (180°C) and grease a 13 × 9-inch (3.5 L) baking dish.

2. MAKE THE STREUSEL: In a medium bowl, stir together the pecans, flour, brown sugar, melted butter, cinnamon, and salt. Set aside.

3. MAKE THE CAKE: In a large bowl, whisk together the flour, baking soda, baking powder, and salt.

4. In a medium bowl, combine the rhubarb with ¼ cup (60 mL) of the sugar and toss together.

5. In a large bowl using an electric mixer, or in the bowl of a stand mixer fitted with the paddle attachment, beat the butter with the remaining ¾ cup (175 mL) sugar on high speed until light and fluffy. Add the eggs, 1 at a time, beating well after each addition. While mixing on low speed, add the flour mixture, yogurt, and vanilla until just combined, stopping to scrape down the sides of the bowl as needed. Fold in the rhubarb.

6. Scrape the batter into the prepared baking dish and spread evenly. Sprinkle the streusel evenly over the batter. Bake until the cake is golden brown and a toothpick inserted into the centre comes out clean, about 40 minutes. Let the cake cool in the pan.

7. MEANWHILE, MAKE THE GLAZE (IF USING): In a small bowl, whisk together the icing sugar, vanilla, and 2 tablespoons (30 mL) of the milk. Add a bit more of the remaining milk to thin if needed. The glaze should be thick but drizzle off the tip of a spoon. Drizzle the glaze over the cooled cake before serving.

Vegan: Use a store-bought egg replacer or Flax Eggs (page 330) instead of eggs. Use vegan butter, non-dairy yogurt, and non-dairy milk.

Gluten-free: Use a 1:1 gluten-free flour blend instead of all-purpose flour and whole wheat flour.

Nut-free: Skip the pecans. If using non-dairy milk, use a nut-free option.

Lazy Daisy Cake

Vegetarian • Vegan option • Gluten-free option • Nut-free • Freezer-friendly

Serves 12

Prep time: 15 minutes

Cook time: 20 minutes

Cake

1 cup (250 mL) sugar

3 eggs

1½ cups (375 mL) all-purpose flour

2 teaspoons (10 mL) baking powder

1 teaspoon (5 mL) pure vanilla extract

½ teaspoon (2 mL) salt

¾ cup (175 mL) 2% milk or unsweetened non-dairy milk

2 tablespoons (30 mL) butter or vegan butter

Coconut Topping

1 cup (250 mL) lightly packed brown sugar

¾ cup (175 mL) whipping (35%) cream or coconut cream

⅓ cup (75 mL) butter or vegan butter

2 tablespoons (30 mL) corn syrup or brown rice syrup

1 teaspoon (5 mL) pure vanilla extract

1½ cups (375 mL) unsweetened flaked or shredded coconut, toasted

Tori's mom Patsy brings this one-bowl classic to every single picnic and it's literally attacked. Spongy and moist, with the most heavenly chewy coconut brown sugar topping, there's pure joy in every single (indulgent) bite! We asked Patsy where the name came from, expecting a great story. She just shrugged and said, "Who knows? Certainly nobody was lazy back in the day!" We've since learned that some people know this as hot milk cake.

1. Preheat the oven to 350°F (180°C) and grease a 13 × 9-inch (3.5 L) baking dish.

2. MAKE THE CAKE: In a large bowl, beat the sugar and eggs using an electric mixer on high speed until thick and frothy, about 3 minutes. Add the flour, baking powder, vanilla, and salt and beat until incorporated.

3. Heat the milk and butter in a small saucepan over medium heat, whisking until the butter is melted and the mixture reaches a simmer, about 4 minutes. Add the milk mixture to the flour mixture and beat just until combined. Do not overmix.

4. Scrape the batter into the prepared baking dish. Bake until the cake springs back when touched and a toothpick inserted into the centre comes out clean, 18 to 20 minutes.

5. MAKE THE COCONUT TOPPING: Position an oven rack 6 inches (15 cm) under the broiler and preheat the broiler.

6. In a medium saucepan, combine the brown sugar, cream, butter, and corn syrup. Bring to a boil over medium-high heat, stirring constantly, and boil for 2 minutes, stirring constantly. Remove from the heat and stir in the vanilla.

7. Evenly spread half of the glaze over the baked cake. Sprinkle the toasted coconut evenly over the cake. Starting at the edges and working inwards, pour the remaining glaze over the cake and use the back of a large spoon to evenly spread the glaze, ensuring that the coconut is covered in glaze. Broil the cake until the topping bubbles, about 1 minute. Serve slightly warm if desired. Store the cake in a resealable container in the fridge for up to 5 days or in the freezer for up to 1 month.

Vegan: Use a store-bought egg replacer or Flax Eggs (page 330) instead of eggs. Use non-dairy milk, vegan butter, and coconut cream.

Gluten-free: Use a 1:1 gluten-free flour blend instead of all-purpose flour.

Peaches and Cream Layer Cake

Vegetarian • Dairy-free option • Nut-free

Makes one 2-layer round cake,
serves 12 to 14

Prep time: 30 minutes

Cook time: 40 minutes

Peach Cake

1 pound (450 g) ripe peaches,
peeled, pitted, and roughly
chopped

3 cups (750 mL) all-purpose flour

4 teaspoons (20 mL) baking powder

2 cups (500 mL) sugar

½ teaspoon (2 mL) salt

4 eggs

¾ cup (175 mL) vegetable oil or
avocado oil

2 teaspoons (10 mL) pure vanilla
extract

Vanilla Bourbon Cream

2 cups (500 mL) whipping (35%)
cream

¼ cup (60 mL) sugar

1 tablespoon (15 mL) bourbon
(optional)

1 teaspoon (5 mL) pure vanilla
extract

2 packages (0.35 ounces/10 g each)
whipping cream stabilizer
(optional)

For assembly

3 to 4 ripe peaches, peeled, pitted,
and sliced

Imagine a sweet, fluffy Okanagan cloud in the form of a dessert, and this cake is what will appear. Moist layers of peach cake are separated by a delicate Vanilla Bourbon Cream and piles of juicy sliced ripe peaches. It's a showy but old-fashioned dessert that's a guaranteed crowd-pleaser.

When peaches aren't in season, you can use drained canned peaches, which is rather convenient as it means you can enjoy this cake all year round! Of course, omit the bourbon if desired.

We love decorating the cake with sliced ripe peaches and a few flowers for extra wow factor. Simply wrap the flower stems in plastic wrap or place them in a floral tube before arranging on the cake. The cake layers can be baked ahead, wrapped tightly in plastic wrap, and frozen for up to 1 week (thaw before assembling). This cake is best if assembled close to the time of serving.

1. Preheat the oven to 325°F (160°C) and grease and lightly flour two 8-inch (1.2 L) round cake pans.

2. MAKE THE PEACH CAKE: In a high-speed blender, blend the peaches on low speed until puréed, about 20 seconds. You will need 1¾ cups (425 mL) purée.

3. In a large bowl, sift together the flour and baking powder. Whisk in the sugar and salt.

4. In a medium bowl, whisk the eggs. Add the peach purée, vegetable oil, and vanilla, and whisk to combine.

5. Add the peach mixture to the flour mixture and stir with a rubber spatula to combine.

6. Divide the batter evenly between the prepared cake pans. Bake until the cake springs back when touched and a toothpick inserted into the centre comes out clean, about 40 minutes. Cool the cakes in the pans for 5 minutes before carefully turning out onto racks. Cool completely before making the Vanilla Bourbon Cream.

Recipe continues

7. MAKE THE VANILLA BOURBON CREAM: In a large bowl if using a hand-held electric mixer, or in the bowl of a stand mixer fitted with the paddle attachment, combine the whipping cream, sugar, bourbon (if using), and vanilla. If you are assembling the cake more than 1 hour in advance, add the whipping cream stabilizer. Whip the cream until stiff peaks form.

8. ASSEMBLE THE CAKE: Once the cakes are completely cool, level off the tops, if needed, with a serrated knife, holding the knife as straight as possible horizontally to create even cake layers.

9. Place the bottom layer, cut side up, on a cake pedestal or cake plate. Spoon half of the Vanilla Bourbon Cream onto the cake and spread in an even layer. Arrange a layer of sliced peaches on top of the cream. Top with the other cake layer, cut side down. Spoon the remaining whipped cream on top of the cake and use a large spoon or offset spatula to spread it in an even layer. (We like a rustic look; the whipped cream layer doesn't need to be smooth.) Garnish with peach slices and chill in the fridge until ready to serve. Store, covered, in the fridge for up to 2 days.

Dairy-free: Use 4 cups (2 L) of coconut whip instead of whipped cream.

Chocolate "Nice" Cream

Vegan • Gluten-free • Nut-free option • Freezer-friendly

Serves 10

Prep time: 15 minutes, plus 4 hours chilling

2 cans (14 ounces/400 mL each) coconut cream

1 cup (250 mL) pitted, peeled, and chopped ripe avocado

½ cup (125 mL) pure maple syrup

⅓ cup (75 mL) cocoa powder

¼ cup (60 mL) sugar or coconut sugar

2 teaspoons (10 mL) pure vanilla extract

1 teaspoon (5 mL) instant espresso powder (optional)

¼ teaspoon (1 mL) almond extract

1 cup (250 mL) dairy-free dark chocolate chips or chunks, melted

This "nice" cream is so rich and creamy that you would never guess that it is dairy-free! The secret ingredient? Avocado. There is something about this ice cream that time-warps us back to our childhood. One scoop and you'll see what we mean.

The ice-cream maker yields a softer and easier to scoop dessert, but if you don't have one, simply freeze in a parchment-lined loaf pan. Leave out the espresso powder to make this more kid-friendly.

1. In a high-speed blender, combine the coconut cream, avocado, maple syrup, cocoa powder, sugar, vanilla, espresso powder (if using), and almond extract. Blend on high speed until smooth. With the blender running, drizzle the melted chocolate through the vent cap and blend until combined. Place in the fridge to chill for at least 2 hours. You want the mixture to be ice cold before churning.

2. Pour the cold mixture into an ice-cream maker and process according to the manufacturer's instructions until the "nice" cream looks like thick soft serve. Scrape into a resealable container or a 9 × 5-inch (2 L) loaf pan lined with parchment paper and freeze until firm, about 2 hours. The "nice" cream is best enjoyed on the day it is made but can be stored in a resealable container in the freezer for up to 1 week.

Nut-free: Skip the almond extract.

Boozy Peach Creamsicles

Vegan • Gluten-free • Nut-free • Freezer-friendly

Makes 8 to 10 ice-pops

Prep time: 15 minutes, plus 4 hours chilling

1 cup (250 mL) coconut cream, divided

2 ounces (60 mL) coconut rum

2 tablespoons (30 mL) sugar, divided

2 cups (500 mL) frozen peach slices

3 ounces (90 mL) peach schnapps

8 to 10 fresh peach slices (optional)

This Okanagan-inspired adult creamsicle is the perfect treat on a hot summer day. Serve the creamsicles on top of a bowl of ice to keep them cold. We freeze extra peaches at the height of peach season just for these—of course the store-bought work as well. Layering the peach and coconut mixtures adds a touch of extra work, but the result is beautiful and worth the little bit of effort.

Make these non-alcoholic by omitting the coconut rum and peach schnapps and adding more sugar to taste.

1. In a medium bowl, whisk together ½ cup (125 mL) of the coconut cream, rum, and 1 tablespoon (15 mL) of the sugar. Set aside.

2. In a high-speed blender, combine the frozen peaches, peach schnapps, the remaining ½ cup (125 mL) coconut cream, and the remaining 1 tablespoon (15 mL) sugar. Blend until smooth.

3. Divide the coconut cream mixture among 8 to 10 ice-pop moulds. Insert a fresh peach slice (if using) into each mould.

4. Pour the peach mixture evenly over the coconut cream mixture in each ice-pop mould.

5. Insert the ice-pop sticks into the moulds and freeze for at least 4 hours or overnight. Store the ice-pops in the freezer for up to 2 months.

Coconut Key Lime Pie

Vegetarian • Vegan option • Gluten-free option • Freezer-friendly

Serves 10 to 12

Prep time: 20 minutes

Cook time: 7 minutes, plus 3 hours chilling

Filling

2 cups (500 mL) raw cashews

⅔ cup (150 mL) pure maple syrup

½ cup (125 mL) canned full-fat coconut milk or coconut cream

1 tablespoon (15 mL) lime zest, plus more for garnish

½ cup (125 mL) fresh lime juice

Crust

1 cup (250 mL) graham cracker crumbs

½ cup (125 mL) sweetened shredded coconut

½ cup (125 mL) vegan butter or coconut oil, melted

¼ cup (60 mL) quick-cooking rolled oats

2 tablespoons (30 mL) sugar

Pinch of salt

Garnishes

Coconut whip

Lime slices (optional)

Jillian's mom Peggy is a key lime pie connoisseur. Our mission was to create a healthier key lime pie that she would give two thumbs up, and this, our friends, was the winner! A sweet coconut and crunchy oat crust, reminiscent of a childhood cookie, gets filled with a satisfying creamy, zesty coconut filling and topped with mounds of fluffy coconut whip.

Make sure to use fresh lime juice—it makes a world of difference! You will need 3 to 4 limes for this recipe.

1. START THE FILLING: Put the cashews in a medium bowl. Cover the cashews with boiling water and let them sit for at least 20 minutes.

2. MEANWHILE, MAKE THE CRUST: Preheat the oven to 350°F (180°C) and spray a deep 9-inch (23 cm) or 10-inch (25 cm) pie plate with cooking spray.

3. In a medium bowl, combine the graham cracker crumbs, coconut, melted butter, oats, sugar, and salt. Stir together. Press the crumb mixture evenly into the bottom and up the sides of the prepared pie plate. Using even pressure, flatten the mixture with the flat bottom of a glass.

4. Bake for 7 minutes or until lightly golden brown. Set aside to cool. If the crust has fallen down the sides, simply press it back up in the pan with the glass while it is warm.

5. FINISH MAKING THE FILLING: Drain the cashews. In a high-speed blender, combine the cashews, maple syrup, coconut milk, lime zest, and lime juice. Blend on high speed until smooth, about 2 minutes. Pour the filling into the prepared pie crust and smooth the top. Place the pie in the freezer to chill until set, about 3 hours, then transfer to the fridge for about 20 minutes to make it easier to cut.

6. Garnish with the coconut whip and more lime zest, and lime slices if desired before slicing and serving. If the crust sticks to the dish, simply immerse the bottom of the pan in hot water for 1 to 2 minutes to loosen the crust. Store the pie, covered, in the freezer for up to 1 week.

Vegan: Use vegan graham crackers.

Gluten-free: Use gluten-free graham cracker crumbs and certified gluten-free rolled oats.

Kona Mud Pie

Vegan option • Vegetarian • Gluten-free option • Nut-free option • Freezer-friendly

Serves 8 to 10

Prep time: 40 minutes, plus 2 hours chilling

Crust

1⅓ cups (325 mL) chocolate cookie crumbs

⅓ cup (75 mL) butter or vegan butter, melted

Filling

2⅔ cups (650 mL) coconut cream

10 Medjool dates, pitted

1 tablespoon (15 mL) instant espresso powder (optional)

1 teaspoon (5 mL) pure vanilla extract

1 cup (250 mL) dark chocolate chips, divided

⅓ cup (75 mL) chocolate cookie crumbs

For serving

1 cup (250 mL) coconut whip

¼ cup (60 mL) crushed macadamia nuts

Coffee and chocolate were meant for each other, just like us! A match made in heaven, this healthier ice cream pie reminds us of the black sand beaches of Hawaii and is naturally sweetened with dates and a handful of dark chocolate. A creamy coconut chocolate base is topped with mounds of coconut whip, drizzled with melted chocolate, and sprinkled with macadamia nuts.

Kona coffee is grown in the Kona district on Hawaii's Big Island and is known for its high quality. You can order Kona espresso powder online or just use regular espresso powder. Alternatively, you can omit the coffee to make it kid-friendly. An ice-cream maker will give you the very best texture, but this pie can be made without one. Simply pour the blended filling mixture into the prepared crust.

1. MAKE THE CRUST: Spray a 9-inch (23 cm) pie plate with cooking spray.

2. In a medium bowl, mix together the chocolate cookie crumbs and melted butter. Press the crumb mixture evenly into the bottom and up the sides of the prepared pie plate. Using even pressure, flatten the mixture with the flat bottom of a glass. Set aside.

3. MAKE THE FILLING: In a high-speed blender, combine the coconut cream, dates, espresso powder (if using), vanilla, and ⅓ cup (75 mL) of the chocolate chips. Blend on high speed until smooth.

4. Pour the mixture into an ice-cream maker and process according to the manufacturer's instructions until the mixture looks like soft serve ice cream. Add the chocolate cookie crumbs and ⅓ cup (75 mL) of the chocolate chips and process again until the crumbs and chocolate chips are evenly distributed, 1 to 2 minutes. Scrape the filling into the prepared crust. Place the pie in the freezer to chill until set, at least 2 hours.

5. Top with a layer of the coconut whip. Melt the remaining ⅓ cup (75 mL) chocolate chips in the microwave and drizzle over the pie. Immediately sprinkle with the crushed macadamia nuts and serve. Store, covered, in the freezer for up to 1 month.

Vegan: Use vegan butter, dairy-free dark chocolate, and vegan chocolate cookie crumbs.

Gluten-free: Use gluten-free chocolate cookie crumbs.

Nut-free: Skip the macadamia nuts.

Drinks

Blender Paloma

Vegan • Gluten-free • Nut-free

Serves 2

Prep time: 5 minutes

Rimmer

1 teaspoon (5 mL) Himalayan pink
   salt

1 teaspoon (5 mL) sugar

1 lime wedge

Paloma

2 cups (500 mL) ice cubes

1 large (or 2 small) pink grapefruit,
   peeled and white pith removed

2 ounces triple sec

2 ounces tequila

1 ounce fresh lime juice

1 ounce agave nectar or Simple
   Syrup (page 331)

Grapefruit slices, for garnish

Sweet, sour, a little bitter, and salty: what's not to love about this Mexican classic? There are few things more refreshing than grapefruit, and this blender Paloma is the answer to all your summer patio prayers. It lands somewhere between a slushy and a regular drink, with a frothy, beautiful blush colour thanks to a whole pink grapefruit. Make a batch for your besties for the ultimate treat.

Adjust the amount of simple syrup depending on how sweet you like your drink. While Palomas are traditionally served in highball glasses, we like to serve ours in stemmed glasses to feel extra fancy. Feel free to use whatever you have on hand!

1. RIM THE GLASSES: Combine the pink salt and sugar on a small plate. Stir together. Wet the rim of 2 highball glasses or stemmed glasses with the lime wedge, then dip in the rimmer to coat.

2. MAKE THE PALOMA: In a high-speed blender, combine the ice, grapefruit, triple sec, tequila, lime juice, and agave nectar. Blend on high speed until smooth and frothy. Pour into the rimmed glasses and garnish with the grapefruit slices.

Espresso Martini

Vegetarian • Gluten-free • Nut-free

Serves 2

Prep time: 10 minutes

Rimmer

2 tablespoons (30 mL) sugar

1 teaspoon (5 mL) vanilla sugar (optional)

1 tablespoon (15 mL) crushed or ground coffee beans

½ teaspoon (2 mL) cinnamon

RumChata

Martini

4 ounces cold espresso

4 ounces RumChata

2 ounces espresso-flavoured vodka

Ice cubes

Is it a pick-me-up? Is it a cocktail? It's both, people, *let's wake up and party!* Nothing close to a true martini (and we're okay with it), this creamy, sweet, and lightly spiced coffee cocktail is just the drink to serve at the start of a dinner party or girls' night out.

You can find vanilla sugar in the baking section of most grocery stores.

1. MAKE THE RIMMER: Combine the sugar, vanilla sugar, coffee, and cinnamon on a small plate. Stir together. Place a splash of RumChata in a small wide bowl. Wet the rim of 2 coupe glasses in the RumChata, then dip in the rimmer to coat.

2. MAKE THE MARTINI: In a cocktail shaker, combine the espresso, RumChata, vodka, and a handful of ice. Shake well.

3. Fill the rimmed glasses with ice and pour in the martini.

Granny's Caesar

Dairy-free • Nut-free

Serves 2

Prep time: 5 minutes

Caesar rimmer or celery salt

2 lemon or lime wedges

Ice cubes

2 cups (500 mL) tomato-clam juice
(we use Clamato)

2 ounces vodka or gin

2 teaspoons (10 mL) Worcestershire
sauce

2 to 4 teaspoons (10 to 20 mL) dill
pickle juice

½ to 1 teaspoon (2 to 5 mL) Tabasco
sauce

Squeeze of lemon or lime juice

2 stalks celery, for garnish

There were few things in life that our granny enjoyed more than a good Caesar. We pour a round of tall ones for the family every year on her birthday to celebrate her and her beautiful legacy. This classic cocktail is the Canadian version of a Bloody Mary and was invented in Calgary in 1969 by food and beverage worker Walter Chell. While you can use either gin or vodka, Granny was Team Vodka, always Smirnoff.

1. Pour the Caesar rimmer onto a small plate. Moisten the rim of 2 high-ball glasses (or glasses of choice) with the lemon wedge, then dip in the rimmer to coat.

2. Add the ice to the rimmed glasses. Divide the tomato-clam juice, vodka, Worcestershire sauce, dill pickle juice to taste, and Tabasco to taste between the glasses. Stir to combine and add a squeeze of lemon juice to taste. Garnish with the celery stalks.

Hugo Cocktail

Vegan • Gluten-free • Nut-free

Serves 2

Prep time: 5 minutes

2 sprigs fresh mint, plus more for garnish

1 ounce fresh lime juice, or to taste

Ice cubes

4 slices or ribbons of cucumber

2 ounces elderflower syrup

4 ounces soda water

Prosecco

Lime wheels, for garnish

Tori and Charles were introduced to this cocktail on a European vacation, and it was love at first sip. This refreshing spritzer is originally from northern Italy and is filled with fresh mint, lime, elderflower syrup, Prosecco, and sparkling water.

You can find elderflower syrup (also known as elderflower cordial) online or at specialty food stores. It is worth the extra effort to get it and it lasts a long time (assuming you don't overindulge in Hugos!). You can use elderflower liqueur (St-Germain) instead of syrup, should you wish.

1. Divide the mint and lime juice between 2 large wine glasses and muddle until fragrant.

2. Fill the glasses three-quarters full with ice. Divide the cucumber between the glasses.

3. Pour in the elderflower syrup and soda water, then top with prosecco and give it a gentle stir. Garnish with a mint sprig and a lime wheel.

Maui Mai Tai

Vegan • Gluten-free • Nut-free option

Serves 4

Prep time: 10 minutes

Vegan Whipped Topping

½ cup (125 mL) aquafaba (canned chickpea liquid)

1 pinch cream of tartar

2 ounces pineapple juice

2 ounces Simple Syrup (page 331) (or 2 tablespoons/30 mL sugar)

Mai Tai

4 ounces white rum

2 ounces orange liqueur (such as Curaçao or triple sec)

2 ounces almond syrup or macadamia nut syrup

3 ounces fresh lime juice

3 ounces pineapple juice

Ice cubes

Crushed ice

4 ounces dark rum

Pineapple wedges, for garnish

A tribute to the countless mai tais Jill and Tori have enjoyed during their trips to Hawaii. These are best served over crushed ice if you have it!

Aquafaba is the liquid from canned chickpeas, and it whips up beautifully for a vegan drink topper in this recipe. Should you wish to dial up the Hawaiian flavours, you can substitute passionfruit syrup (look for it online among syrups often used for coffees) for the simple syrup in the topping.

1. MAKE THE VEGAN WHIPPED TOPPING: In a medium bowl using an electric mixer, whip the chickpea liquid with the cream of tartar on high speed until foamy, 3 to 5 minutes. Pour in the pineapple juice and Simple Syrup and whip to combine.

2. MAKE THE MAI TAI: In a cocktail shaker, combine the white rum, orange liqueur, almond syrup, lime juice, and pineapple juice. Add the ice cubes and shake for 10 to 15 seconds.

3. Fill 4 highball glasses with crushed ice and strain the cocktail into them. Gently float the dark rum by slowly pouring it on top of the cocktail over the back of a spoon.

4. Spoon the Vegan Whipped Topping on top and garnish with a pineapple wedge.

Nut-free: Use almond or macadamia nut syrup instead of Simple Syrup.

Virgin Chi Chi

Vegan • Gluten-free • Nut-free

Makes 2 drinks

Prep time: 5 minutes

1 cup (250 mL) fresh or frozen pineapple chunks (see headnote)

1 cup (250 mL) ice cubes

¾ cup (175 mL) pineapple juice

½ cup (125 mL) coconut cream

2 tablespoons (30 mL) Simple Syrup (page 331)

Pineapple wedges, for garnish

Maraschino cherries, for garnish

We grew up having virgin chi chis at the Golden Palace Chinese restaurant in Peace River, Alberta. Frank and Sam would bring them to the table in fancy glasses complete with a bright maraschino cherry and a pretty paper umbrella. We felt so special! Nowadays, we make these for our own sweet kids.

Feel free to add an ounce of vodka for a grown-up version (or turn it into a piña colada with a splash of rum). If using fresh pineapple instead of frozen, simply add more ice.

1. In a high-speed blender, combine the pineapple, ice cubes, pineapple juice, coconut cream, and Simple Syrup. Blend on high speed until smooth. Add more ice if you want them slushier.

2. Pour into highball glasses. Garnish with a fresh pineapple wedge and a maraschino cherry. Don't forget the cocktail umbrella!

Okanagan Sangria

Vegan • Gluten-free • Nut-free

Serves 6

Prep time: 5 minutes

½ cup (125 mL) hulled and halved strawberries

½ cup (125 mL) pitted cherries

½ cup (125 mL) sliced pitted peaches

1 (26-ounce/750 mL) bottle rosé wine

½ cup (125 mL) peach schnapps

1 cup (250 mL) unsweetened peach juice or peach nectar

Simple Syrup (page 331), to taste (optional)

1 (12-ounce/355 mL) can soda water

Ice cubes

When the summer sun is shining here in Kelowna you can find us poolside with a pitcher of this Okanagan sangria. Wine and fruit have put the valley on the map, making this drink completely on point!

You can use any fruit you wish. Fresh or frozen work equally well—just keep the ratios the same.

1. In a large pitcher, combine the strawberries, cherries, peaches, rosé wine, peach schnapps, and peach juice. Stir to combine. Add the Simple Syrup to taste if desired. Store in the fridge until ready to serve.

2. Add the soda water and ice to the pitcher just before serving in large wine glasses filled with ice.

Spicy Coconut Margarita

Vegan • Gluten-free • Nut-free

Serves 2

Prep time: 5 minutes

3 tablespoons (45 mL) agave syrup, divided

¼ cup (60 mL) sweetened shredded coconut, toasted

4 thin slices fresh jalapeño pepper, or to taste, plus more for garnish

½ ounce fresh lime juice

⅓ cup (75 mL) canned full-fat coconut milk

2 ounces tequila

1 ounce triple sec

Handful of ice cubes, plus more for serving

2 lime wheels, for garnish

One sip and you'll be mentally transported to a sandy beach. The margarita is a classic cocktail made traditionally from tequila, lime juice, and triple sec. We've enjoyed our share of coconut margaritas, and this recipe really is something else! Adjust the number of jalapeños based on your spice tolerance.

1. Set out 2 small plates. Put 2 tablespoons (30 mL) of the agave syrup in the first plate. Put the coconut in the second plate. Dip the rim of the margarita glasses in the agave syrup, then dip in the coconut to coat.

2. In a cocktail shaker, gently muddle the jalapeño slices with the lime juice. Add the coconut milk, tequila, triple sec, and remaining 1 tablespoon (15 mL) agave syrup and half fill with ice. Shake well to combine.

3. Fill the glasses with ice and strain the cocktail into the glasses. Garnish with a lime wheel and jalapeño slice.

Pink Polar Bear Hot Chocolate

Vegetarian • Vegan option • Gluten-free • Nut-free option

Serves 4

Prep time: 5 minutes

Cook time: 5 minutes

Hot Chocolate

3 cups (750 mL) unsweetened non-dairy milk

1 can (14 ounces/400 mL) full-fat coconut milk

¼ cup (60 mL) maple syrup

1 teaspoon (5 mL) pure vanilla extract

2 ounces (57 g) white chocolate, roughly chopped

3 full-size (½ ounce/14 g each) red-and-white-striped candy canes, crushed

Coconut whip, whipped cream, or mini marshmallows, for serving

Candy Cane Rimmer

2 tablespoons (30 mL) unsweetened non-dairy milk

2 tablespoons (30 mL) finely crushed candy canes

The only thing that beats hot chocolate in the winter is *pink* hot chocolate. We are swooning over this blush winter treat and love making these for the kids as a special treat after a day playing in the snow.

Feel free to add a splash of peppermint schnapps to the mugs for the adults. Just be sure to reduce or omit the maple syrup so the drink isn't too sweet.

1. MAKE THE HOT CHOCOLATE: In a medium saucepan, combine the non-dairy milk, coconut milk, maple syrup, vanilla, white chocolate, and crushed candy canes. Bring to a simmer over low heat, stirring constantly, until the chocolate melts and the candy canes dissolve.

2. RIM THE MUGS: Set out 2 small plates. Add the non-dairy milk to one plate and the crushed candy canes to the other plate. Dip the rim of the mugs first in the milk and then in the candy canes.

3. Pour the hot chocolate into the rimmed mugs and top with coconut whip, whipped cream, or mini marshmallows.

Vegan: Use dairy-free white chocolate and coconut whip or vegan mini marshmallows.

Nut-free: Use a nut-free non-dairy milk.

Canadian Hot Apple Cider

Vegan • Gluten-free • Nut-free

Serves 2

Prep time: 5 minutes

Cook time: 5 minutes

---

2 cups (500 mL) fresh apple cider

1 tablespoon (15 mL) pure maple
syrup

2 ounces bourbon whiskey

Garnishes

Cinnamon sticks

Dried apple rings

Canadian winters are cold, requiring every possible effort to stay cozy and warm. Like sipping on this Canadian Hot Apple Cider, for instance. Steaming mugs of fresh apple cider (unfiltered fresh apple juice) are lightly sweetened with Canadian maple syrup and given a little kick thanks to a splash of bourbon. Top with a dollop of whipped cream to make them taste like a boozy apple pie! Come to think of it, winter doesn't sound so bad after all!

1. In a small saucepan, combine the apple cider and maple syrup and heat over medium heat, stirring occasionally, until hot. Stir in the whiskey and pour into mugs.

2. Garnish with a cinnamon stick and a dried apple ring. Serve steaming hot.

Banana Coconut Latte

Vegan • Gluten-free • Nut-free option

Serves 4

Prep time: 5 minutes

Cook time: 5 minutes

Banana Coconut Purée

1 can (14 ounces/400 mL) full-fat
    coconut milk

1 ripe banana

2½ tablespoons (37 mL) sugar

Lattes

4 shots espresso

3 to 4 cups (750 mL to 1 L) steamed
    unsweetened non-dairy milk

Sweetened shredded coconut,
    toasted, for garnish (optional)

This is the viral banana coconut latte! That's right. While Jillian was filming *Love It or List It Vancouver*, her second home was the Fairmont Pacific Rim, and every morning without fail she would head down to their café and order herself one of their delicious banana coconut lattes. She can honestly say that she has *never* tasted a latte as delicious as this one. It was her go-to. Sadly, the hotel discontinued them. But after some trial and error, we think we have dialled in this doppelgänger. If you're looking to spoil yourself with a drool-worthy weekend treat, let this be it!

1. MAKE THE BANANA COCONUT PURÉE: In a high-speed blender, combine the coconut milk, banana, and sugar. Blend on high speed until completely smooth and creamy, about 3 minutes. Transfer the coconut mixture to a small saucepan and whisk over medium-low heat until hot. Remove from the heat and cover to keep warm. The purée can be stored in a resealable container in the fridge for up to 1 week. Reheat before using.

2. MAKE THE LATTES: Pour an espresso shot into each mug. Divide the Banana Coconut Purée among the mugs. Top with steamed milk and garnish with toasted coconut if desired.

Nut-free: Use a nut-free non-dairy milk.

Staples

Carrot-Top Pesto

Vegetarian • Vegan option • Gluten-free • Nut-free option • Freezer-friendly

Makes ¾ cup (175 mL)

Prep time: 10 minutes

2 cups (500 mL) lightly packed chopped carrot tops

¼ cup (60 mL) grated Parmesan cheese or vegan parm

¼ cup (60 mL) unsalted roasted cashews or pine nuts

1 teaspoon (5 mL) fresh lemon juice

2 cloves garlic

½ teaspoon (2 mL) salt, or more to taste

¼ cup (60 mL) extra-virgin olive oil

This is a brilliant way to use up those carrot tops from those garden-fresh carrots! Carrot tops taste absolutely delicious blended up into a pesto. Toss it into pasta, use as a base for Pita-Style Flatbreads (page 71), or spread on a veggie sandwich.

1. In a food processor, combine the carrot tops, Parmesan, cashews, lemon juice, garlic, and salt. Blend until smooth. With the motor running, slowly drizzle in the olive oil and blend until smooth. Transfer to a resealable container and store in the fridge for up to 1 week or in the freezer for up to 3 months.

Vegan: Use vegan parm.

Nut-free: Use pumpkin seeds or sunflower seeds instead of cashews or pine nuts.

Garlic Croutons

Vegan • Gluten-free option • Nut-free

Makes 4 cups (1 L)

Prep time: 5 minutes

Cook time: 10 minutes

½ loaf (8 ounces/225 g) day-old artisanal bread, cut into ½-inch (1 cm) cubes

¼ cup (60 mL) extra-virgin olive oil

2 cloves garlic, minced

½ teaspoon (2 mL) salt

Like most things, once you go homemade, you can't go back. These garlic croutons are no exception! Your soups and salads will be changed forever. Tori always has a big jar of these on hand in her pantry. It is such a great way to use up leftover or stale bread that might otherwise go to waste. Feel free to add a tablespoon of chopped fresh herbs such as rosemary or thyme for a flavour boost.

1. Preheat the oven to 350°F (180°C) and line a baking sheet with parchment paper.

2. Place the cubed bread on the prepared baking sheet and drizzle with the olive oil. Add the garlic and salt and mix together with your hands to coat the bread. Spread the bread in a single layer and bake until golden brown, about 10 minutes, stirring halfway through. Cool the croutons on the baking sheet. Store in a resealable container at room temperature for up to 1 month.

Gluten-free: Use gluten-free bread.

Veggie Ground

Vegan • Gluten-free option • Freezer-friendly

Makes 3 to 3½ cups (750 to 875 mL)

Prep time: 15 minutes

Cook time: 20 minutes

3 tablespoons (45 mL) butter or vegan butter, divided

½ cup (125 mL) finely chopped yellow onion

2 cloves garlic, minced

8 ounces (225 g) finely chopped white or cremini mushrooms (3 cups/750 mL)

2 teaspoons (10 mL) beef-flavoured vegetarian stock concentrate

1 teaspoon (5 mL) ground fennel seeds

½ teaspoon (2 mL) ground sage

½ teaspoon (2 mL) pepper

1 cup (250 mL) walnuts, coarsely ground

1 cup (250 mL) panko crumbs

¼ cup (60 mL) all-purpose flour

1 tablespoon (15 mL) pure maple syrup

1 tablespoon (15 mL) soy sauce

If making patties

1 tablespoon (15 mL) ground flaxseed

3 tablespoons (45 mL) water

Jill has been perfecting her plant-based ground for years, and this recipe is the delicious result! Whether you eat plant-based or not, this veggie ground is a simple, versatile, and healthier staple to add to your repertoire. Use it in Breakfast Burritos (page 25), form the mixture into patties for Breakfast Sandwiches (page 39), or use it in our hearty Walnut Veggie "Ragu" (page 208).

1. MAKE THE VEGGIE GROUND: Melt 2 tablespoons (30 mL) of the butter in a large frying pan over medium heat. Add the onion and cook, stirring occasionally, until soft and translucent, 3 to 4 minutes. Add the garlic and mushrooms and cook, stirring occasionally, until the mushrooms have slightly softened, 3 to 4 minutes. Add the concentrated stock, fennel, sage, and pepper. Reduce the heat to low and cook until the mushrooms are soft and the liquid has mostly absorbed.

2. In a medium bowl, mix together the walnuts, panko crumbs, flour, maple syrup, and soy sauce. Add the nut mixture to the mushroom mixture, stir in the remaining 1 tablespoon (15 mL) butter, and mix until combined and hot.

3. Serve as is as a ground replacer or as instructed in your recipe. Store in a resealable container in the fridge for up to 5 days or in the freezer for up to 1 month.

4. IF MAKING PATTIES: Let the Veggie Ground cool completely. Preheat the oven to 400°F (200°C) and line a baking sheet with parchment paper.

5. Stir together the flaxseed and water in a small bowl and set aside for 5 to 10 minutes. Stir into the Veggie Ground mixture to combine.

6. Using your hands, scoop 2-tablespoon (30 mL) portions of the Veggie Ground (about the size of a golf ball) and using your hands, roll into a tight ball. (If the mixture doesn't stick together well, add a drizzle of water and try again.) You should have about 24 balls. Arrange them on the prepared baking sheet with ample space between. Using the palm of your hand, press down lightly to flatten the balls. Bake the patties until golden brown on the bottom, about 15 minutes, flipping halfway through. Serve immediately or let cool before storing in a resealable container in the fridge for up to 5 days or in the freezer for up to 1 month.

Gluten-free: Use gluten-free stock concentrate, gluten-free panko crumbs, a 1:1 gluten-free flour blend instead of all-purpose flour, and gluten-free soy sauce.

Chia Jam

Vegan • Gluten-free • Nut-free

Makes 1 to 1½ cups (250 to 375 mL)

Prep time: 5 minutes, plus 6 hours setting

2 cups (500 mL) fresh or frozen berries, thawed

2 to 4 tablespoons (30 to 60 mL) pure maple syrup or sugar, to taste

2 tablespoons (30 mL) chia seeds

This is a quick, simple, and wholesome chia jam that is sweetened with a touch of maple syrup and whipped up in under 5 minutes with zero canning! Make this chia jam when local berries are bursting out of the farmers' markets. Strawberries, blackberries, or raspberries work best in this recipe. Our kids love this jam spread over homemade pancakes or hot buttered biscuits.

Frozen berries can be used in place of fresh. Just be sure to measure the fruit while it's frozen for accuracy.

1. Put the fruit in a medium bowl. Using the back of a fork or a potato masher, mash the fruit until broken down.

2. Stir in the maple syrup and chia seeds until well incorporated. Cover and refrigerate for 4 to 6 hours or overnight before serving. Store in a resealable container in the fridge for up to 1 week.

Applesauce

Vegan • Gluten-free • Nut-free • Freezer-friendly

Makes 4 cups (1 L)

Prep time: 15 minutes

Cook time: 40 minutes

---

3 pounds (1.4 kg) apples, peeled, cored, and cut into ½-inch (1 cm) chunks (10 cups/2.4 L)

1 teaspoon (5 mL) cinnamon

¼ cup (60 mL) water, more if needed

¼ cup (60 mL) lightly packed brown sugar (optional)

Tori's mom Patsy made applesauce nearly every week when we were growing up. The scent of the apples and cinnamon alone made it all worthwhile. This applesauce can be used in baking (mashed), spooned over ice cream, stirred into oatmeal—and that's just for starters! We prefer to use either McIntosh or Spartan varieties, as they soften best.

1. In a large, heavy-bottomed pot, combine the apples, cinnamon, water, and brown sugar (if using) over medium-low heat. Simmer, stirring occasionally, until the apples are soft and cooked through, about 40 minutes. If you don't like your applesauce chunky, simply mash with a potato masher. Let cool. Store in a resealable container in the fridge for up to 1 week or in the freezer for up to 3 months.

Sheet-Pan Tomato Sauce

Vegan • Gluten-free • Nut-free • Freezer-friendly

Makes 4 cups (1 L)

Prep time: 10 minutes

Cook time: 45 minutes

3 pounds (1.4 kg) ripe tomatoes
(8 to 10 tomatoes)

1 pound (450 g) yellow onions
(1 large or 2 small onions)

¼ cup (60 mL) extra-virgin olive oil

1 teaspoon (5 mL) salt, more to taste

½ teaspoon (2 mL) pepper, more
to taste

4 cloves garlic, peeled

Pinch of sugar

Handful of fresh basil leaves

1 teaspoon (5 mL) dried oregano

For those days where you want something homemade but don't feel like tying yourself to the stove (isn't that every day?), this one's for you. The oven does all the heavy lifting by coaxing out the sweet flavours of the tomatoes and onions, leaving you with a rich, flavourful, incredibly versatile tomato sauce. This sauce freezes beautifully; simply reheat and toss with your favourite pasta and a handful of fresh Parmesan cheese.

Garden-fresh tomatoes yield the best-tasting sauce, and you can use any variety. You can thin the sauce with a touch of stock, heavy cream, or cashew cream if desired.

1. Preheat the oven to 400°F (200°C) and line a baking sheet with parchment paper.

2. Cut any large tomatoes in half. Cut the onions into quarters. Place the tomatoes and onions on the prepared baking sheet. Drizzle with the olive oil, sprinkle with salt and pepper, and toss to combine. Evenly spread on the pan and roast until the vegetables are golden, about 30 minutes. Add the garlic to the pan and roast for another 10 to 15 minutes, until the tomatoes are blistered and the garlic is golden.

3. Carefully scrape the mixture into a large bowl with tall sides. Add the sugar, basil, and oregano. Using an immersion blender, purée until smooth. Season with salt and pepper. Store the sauce in an airtight container in the fridge for up to 5 days or in the freezer for up to 2 months.

Cowboy Candy

Vegan • Gluten-free • Nut-free

Makes about four 2-cup (500 mL) mason jars

Prep time: 1 hour

Resting time: 24+ hours

3 pounds (1.4 kg) jalapeño peppers

1½ cups (375 mL) apple cider vinegar

3 cups (750 mL) sugar

1 teaspoon (5 mL) garlic powder

¼ teaspoon (1 mL) ground turmeric

¼ teaspoon (1 mL) celery seeds

This recipe for candied jalapeños is an iconic Justin Pasutto creation, born out of his love for creating recipes from plants he and Jill grow in their garden. Justin never thought he would have such a green thumb, which he owes to his strong Italian roots. There is something truly special and rewarding about growing something from seed, picking it, processing it, and storing it. The first time Justin made this recipe, he almost lit the house on fire with how spicy his first batch was! With some tweaking, the second batch came out with the perfect balance of sweet and spicy.

Add these to margaritas, to a cheese board, or as a sweet addition to your next veggie sandwich. Cowboy candy has become a hugely popular staple in all our families' homes, and we hope it becomes one in yours too! We highly recommend wearing food prep gloves when cutting the jalapeño peppers.

1. Cut off the stems from the peppers, then thinly slice the peppers crosswise. If you want to reduce the spice level, rinse the slices under cool running water, then drain.

2. In a large pot, combine the apple cider vinegar, sugar, garlic powder, turmeric, and celery seeds. Bring to a boil over medium-high heat, then reduce the heat to low. Add the jalapeño slices, stir, cover, and simmer for 20 to 30 minutes. The longer you simmer, the milder the jalapeños will be.

3. MEANWHILE, STERILIZE THE MASON JARS AND LIDS: Place 4 clean 2-cup (500 mL) mason jars on a rack in a boiling water canning pot. Add 4 sealing discs (but not screw bands). Cover the jars with water, bring to a simmer, and simmer for 10 minutes. Turn off the heat and keep the jars and sealing discs in the water until ready to use.

4. FILL AND SEAL THE JARS: Using a slotted spoon, fill the sterilized jars with the jalapeños, leaving ½-inch (1 cm) headspace. Pour the syrup into the jars to cover the jalapeños. Make sure the jalapeños are covered in syrup. Remove any air bubbles in the syrup by passing a clean thin wooden or plastic utensil around the contents.

5. Wipe the jar rims with a clean cloth. Centre a hot sealing disc on a rim and twist on a screw band just until fingertip tight. Unprocessed jars can be stored in the refrigerator for up to 1 month.

6. **TO PROCESS THE COWBOY CANDY:** Return the sealed jars to the rack in the canning pot and add enough water to cover them by 1 to 2 inches (2.5 to 5 cm). Return the water to a boil, cover, and boil for 15 minutes. Remove the jars from the bath (canning tongs will help for this) and place them on a kitchen towel on the counter. Cool, undisturbed, at room temperature for 24 hours.

7. Once the jars have cooled, check the jar seals. If sealed properly, the centre of the lid will be concave and not pop up when pressed. Store any jars that have not sealed properly in the fridge for up to 1 month. Label and date the well-sealed jars and store in a cool, dark place for up to 2 years.

Overnight Pickled Beets

Vegan • Gluten-free • Nut-free

Makes 2 quarts (2 L)

Prep time: 20 minutes

Cook time: 20 minutes, plus 8 hours for setting

2 pounds (900 g) red beets

2 cups (500 mL) water

2 cups (500 mL) white vinegar

1½ cups (375 mL) sugar

1 tablespoon (15 mL) salt

1 tablespoon (15 mL) whole cloves

1 teaspoon (5 mL) ground allspice

We grew up on pickled beets—a jar was always on the table at special occasions. Sweet, vinegary, and with a hint of cloves, these beets are full-stop addictive.

1. Bring a large pot of water to a boil over high heat.

2. Wash the beets and cut off the leaves, keeping the stem end intact.

3. Place the beets in the boiling water and cook, covered, until fork-tender, about 20 minutes. Drain the beets and rinse under cool running water. Once the beets are cool enough to handle, use your hands to peel the beets. (You might want to wear food prep gloves so you don't stain your hands.)

4. MEANWHILE, MAKE THE BRINE: In a medium pot, combine the water, vinegar, sugar, salt, cloves, and allspice. Bring to a boil over medium-high heat, then reduce the heat to low and simmer for 5 minutes.

5. Cut the peeled beets into quarters. Divide the beets between two 1-quart (1 L) mason jars. Pour the brine into the jars to cover the beets. (If you want a more subtle taste of cloves, simply strain them out and discard before pouring the brine into the jars as the clove flavour will intensify the longer you leave them in.) Seal the jars and refrigerate for at least 8 hours before serving. The pickled beets can be stored in the fridge for up to 1 month.

Quick Pickled Red Onions

Vegan • Gluten-free • Nut-free

Makes 1 cup (250 mL)

Prep time: 5 minutes, plus
30 minutes setting

⅓ cup (75 mL) unseasoned rice
vinegar

1 tablespoon (15 mL) sugar

1½ teaspoons (7 mL) salt

2 cups (500 mL) thinly sliced
red onion

You are guaranteed to always find a jar of these in Tori's fridge! If you are looking for the perfect tangy, crunchy, flavourful addition to just about any dish, this is it. This simple staple is the best addition to tacos, burritos, burgers, salads, or truly anything your heart desires. Enjoy them in recipes like Fish Tacos (page 163), Butternut Squash Gyros (page 167), or Loaded Hummus (page 113).

1. In a medium non-reactive bowl (stainless steel, plastic, or glass), combine the vinegar, sugar, and salt. Whisk until the sugar and salt are dissolved.

2. Add the red onions, stir to combine, and let sit at room temperature for 30 minutes, tossing occasionally.

3. Transfer the red onions and the pickling juice to a mason jar. Seal with the lid and store in the fridge for up to 3 weeks.

Fred's Dill Pickles

Vegan • Gluten-free • Nut-free

Makes 4 quarts (4 L)

Prep time: 45 minutes

Resting time: 24 hours

4 pounds (1.8 g) small pickling cucumbers

12 small fresh dill heads

4 cloves garlic, peeled

9 cups (2.25 L) water

3 cups (750 mL) distilled white vinegar

¾ cup (175 mL) pickling salt

8 bay leaves

We love a good dill pickle as much as the next person, and this crunchy, garlicky classic is a keeper. This recipe is based on one given to Justin by his friend Matty's dad, Fred Bulloch. We are thrilled that Fred allowed us to include it in our cookbook! You can either process the pickles to keep them for longer or skip the processing for a quick refrigerator pickle. Either way, they're sure to disappear quickly!

1. STERILIZE THE MASON JARS AND LIDS: Place 4 clean 1-quart (1 L) mason jars on a rack in a boiling water canning pot. Add 4 sealing discs (but not screw bands). Cover the jars with water, bring to a simmer, and simmer for 10 minutes. Turn off the heat and keep the jars and sealing discs in the water until ready to use.

2. Divide the cucumbers, dill heads, and garlic among the sterilized jars, squeezing the cucumbers in tightly.

3. In a large pot, combine the water, vinegar, and pickling salt. Bring to a boil over medium-high heat, stirring to dissolve the salt. Pour the hot brine into the jars to cover the cucumbers, leaving ½-inch (1 cm) headspace. Add 2 bay leaves to each jar. Remove any air bubbles by passing a clean thin wooden or plastic utensil between the cucumbers and the sides of the jars.

4. Wipe the jar rims with a clean cloth. Centre a hot sealing disc on a rim and twist on a screw band just until fingertip tight. Unprocessed jars can be stored in the refrigerator for up to 1 month.

5. TO PROCESS THE PICKLES: Return the sealed jars to the rack in the canning pot and add enough water to cover them by 1 to 2 inches (2.5 to 5 cm). Return the water to a boil, cover, and boil for 15 minutes. Remove the jars from the bath (canning tongs will help for this) and place them on a kitchen towel on the counter. Cool, undisturbed, at room temperature for 24 hours.

6. Once the jars have cooled, check the seals. If sealed properly, the centre of the lid will be concave and not pop up when pressed. Store any jars that have not sealed properly in the fridge for up to 1 month. Label and date the well-sealed jars and store in a cool, dark place for up to 2 years.

Homemade Buttermilk

Vegetarian • Vegan option • Gluten-free • Nut-free option

Makes 1 cup (250 mL)

Prep time: 10 minutes

1 cup (250 mL) 2% milk or unsweetened non-dairy milk

1 tablespoon (15 mL) white vinegar
or fresh lemon juice

You can make your own buttermilk out of any milk, including non-dairy milks. While traditional buttermilk is superior, our homemade version works well and is handy for when you don't have buttermilk on hand.

1. In a small bowl, stir together the milk and vinegar. Let sit for 10 minutes before using.

Vegan: Use non-dairy milk.

Nut-free: If using non-dairy milk, use a nut-free option.

Cashew Cream

Vegan • Gluten-free

Makes 1⅓ cups (325 mL)

Prep time: 20 minutes

1 cup (250 mL) raw cashews

Boiling water, for soaking

1 cup (250 mL) water, more if
needed

This cashew cream recipe requires no straining and zero hassle with only two steps! It works well as a substitute for cream in most recipes (baking is an exception).

1. In a medium bowl, cover the cashews with enough boiling water to cover them completely. Let soak for 15 minutes (or for up to 12 hours in the fridge). Drain the cashews.

2. Combine the drained cashews and 1 cup (250 mL) water in a high-speed blender and blend until very smooth, 3 to 4 minutes. Add more water if needed to achieve the desired consistency. Store in a resealable container in the fridge for up to 3 days.

Vegan Ranch Dressing

Vegan • Gluten-free • Nut-free

Makes ½ cup (125 mL)

Prep time: 5 minutes

½ cup (125 mL) vegan mayonnaise

Juice of ½ lemon

1½ teaspoons (7 mL) apple cider vinegar

1 teaspoon (5 mL) finely chopped fresh parsley

1 teaspoon (5 mL) finely chopped fresh chives

¼ teaspoon (1 mL) dried dill

¼ teaspoon (1 mL) onion powder

¼ teaspoon (1 mL) garlic powder

⅛ teaspoon (0.5 mL) sweet paprika

⅛ teaspoon (0.5 mL) pepper

Salt

Once you make your own ranch dressing, you'll never go back to store-bought. This zippy dressing can be used as a dip or a salad dressing and is a terrific one to keep on hand. We suggest cutting up veggies at the beginning of the week to have on hand for easy snacking. If you have young kids, put out a veggie platter after school to let them graze as they wish. You'll be surprised how many vegetables they eat, especially when they are served with this dip!

1. In a small bowl, whisk together the mayonnaise, lemon juice, apple cider vinegar, parsley, chives, dill, onion powder, garlic powder, paprika, and pepper. Season with salt. Store in a resealable container in the fridge for up to 5 days.

Creamy French Dressing

Vegan option • Vegetarian • Gluten-free • Nut-free

Makes ¾ cup (175 mL)

Prep time: 5 minutes

1 clove garlic, minced

2 tablespoons (30 mL) fresh lemon juice

2 teaspoons (10 mL) Dijon mustard

2 tablespoons (30 mL) mayonnaise or vegan mayonnaise

1 tablespoon (15 mL) sugar or pure liquid honey

1 tablespoon (15 mL) white wine vinegar

¼ cup (60 mL) avocado oil or extra-virgin olive oil

Salt, to taste

Everyone needs a quick classic salad dressing recipe, and this one is ours. Using just a few common pantry and fridge ingredients, a homemade salad dressing makes a world of difference to a salad. To switch up the flavour, add a spoonful of finely chopped fresh herbs or use a different type of vinegar (such as balsamic).

1. In a small bowl or mason jar, combine all the ingredients. Whisk together, or seal the jar and shake, until emulsified. Store in the fridge in a sealed container for up to 1 week.

Vegan: Use vegan mayonnaise and use sugar instead of honey.

Spicy Mayo

Vegan • Gluten-free • Nut-free

Makes ½ cup (125 mL)

Prep time: 5 minutes

½ cup (125 mL) vegan mayonnaise

2 tablespoons (30 mL) Sriracha sauce or chipotle hot sauce

1 teaspoon (5 mL) lime juice

This zesty spicy mayonnaise is our favourite condiment. It is so versatile and always adds the perfect amount of heat and a burst of flavour. Make it with either Sriracha sauce or chipotle hot sauce, depending on what you're adding it to. We purchase clear squeeze bottles at the restaurant supply shop and always keep this mayo on hand.

1. Whisk together all the ingredients in a small bowl until combined. Store in a resealable container in the fridge for up to 2 weeks.

Dill Tartar Sauce

Vegan option • Gluten-free • Nut-free

Makes 1¼ cups (300 mL)

Prep time: 10 minutes

¾ cup (175 mL) mayonnaise or vegan mayonnaise

¼ cup (60 mL) finely diced dill pickles

¼ cup (60 mL) finely diced red onion

¼ cup (60 mL) chopped fresh dill, plus more for garnish

1 teaspoon (5 mL) chopped drained capers

Juice of 1 lemon

This tartar sauce is leagues above any store-bought version you'll ever find and is one of our claims to fame. Serve it alongside Patsy's Fried Fish (page 190), grilled salmon, or crab cakes.

1. In a small bowl, combine all the ingredients. Stir until well combined. Cover and store in the fridge until ready to serve or for up to 3 days. Garnish with more dill before serving.

Pico de Gallo

Vegan • Gluten-free • Nut-free

Serves 6 to 8

Prep time: 10 minutes

2½ cups (625 mL) finely diced tomatoes, drained in a sieve

1 cup (250 mL) chopped fresh cilantro leaves

½ cup (125 mL) finely diced red onion

½ to 1 jalapeño pepper (depending on how spicy you like it), seeds and membranes removed, finely diced

2 cloves garlic, minced

Juice of 2 limes

2 tablespoons (30 mL) extra-virgin olive oil

1 teaspoon (5 mL) sugar

Salt

Fresh is always best! This fresh salsa is whipped up in minutes and tastes unbelievable with your favourite tortilla chips or served with Breakfast Burritos (page 25) or Tortilla Pie (page 203)—or with anything you want!

1. In a medium bowl, combine the tomatoes, cilantro, red onion, jalapeño, garlic, lime juice, olive oil, sugar, and salt to taste. Stir together. Cover and store in the fridge until ready to serve. This is best served the day it's made but can be made up to 1 day in advance.

Everything Bagel Seasoning

Vegan • Gluten-free • Nut-free

Makes ½ cup (125 mL)

Prep time: 5 minutes

2 tablespoons (30 mL) poppy seeds

1 tablespoon (15 mL) white sesame seeds

1 tablespoon (15 mL) black sesame seeds

1 tablespoon (15 mL) dried minced garlic

1 tablespoon (15 mL) dried minced onion

2 teaspoons (10 mL) flaky sea salt

Shayna from Team Fraîche whipped up this mixture for the team one day and it was a game changer. We were putting it on, well, everything! Try our Everything Bagel Sheet-Pan Hash Browns (page 40) or sprinkle this on your next avocado toast or bagel with cream cheese.

1. Combine all the ingredients in a resealable container and store at room temperature for up to 6 months.

Flax Egg

Vegan • Gluten-free • Nut-free

Makes 1 egg replacer

Prep time: 10 minutes

1 tablespoon (15 mL) ground flax-seed or ground chia seeds

3 tablespoons (45 mL) water

You can use this recipe to replace eggs in most baking recipes. The baked product is usually denser, but it typically works out and doesn't change the flavour. While chia seeds and ground flaxseed both work well, we prefer the flax option as we find it yields a slightly better texture. Both chia and flax seeds are a good source of plant-based protein.

1. Stir together the ground flaxseed or chia seeds and water in a small bowl. Let sit for 5 to 10 minutes before using.

Simple Syrup

Vegan • Gluten-free • Nut-free

Makes 1½ cups (375 mL)

Prep time: 5 minutes

Cook time: 10 minutes

1 cup (250 mL) water

1 cup (250 mL) sugar

We use this liquid sweetener in many of our cocktail recipes. It truly is the easiest way to add a bit of sweetness to a beverage without the grainy texture of sugar. Make a big batch and keep it in a jar for your next round of drinks. Add a sprig of rosemary or thyme, or some orange zest, or other flavouring while cooking to put a twist on it should you wish.

1. Combine the water and sugar (and any flavouring you desire) in a small saucepan and bring to a simmer over medium-low heat. Simmer, stirring occasionally, until the sugar has completely dissolved, about 5 minutes. Cool completely, strain out solid flavourings (if used), and store in a resealable container in the fridge for up to 1 month. (If flavoured, store for up to 2 weeks.)

Meal Plans

MEAL	MONDAY	TUESDAY	WEDNESDAY	THURSDAY	FRIDAY	SATURDAY	SUNDAY
BREAKFAST	Fruit Crumble Muffins* (page 57)	Breakfast Burritos* (page 25)	Good Morning Smoothies (page 27)	Fruit Crumble Muffins** (page 57)	Breakfast Burritos** (page 25)	Big Breakfast Bake (page 32) + toasted No-Knead Bread (page 79)	French Toast Sticks (page 43) (from leftover bread)
LUNCH	Soba Noodle Salad* (page 144)	Sweet and Spicy Vegan Lettuce Wraps (page 125)	Soba Noodle Salad* (page 144)	Sweet and Spicy Vegan Lettuce Wraps (page 125)	Prawn Chopped Salad (page 143)	Tex-Mex Loaded Hummus (page 114) + Pita Crisps (page 117)	Grilled Halloumi Watermelon Salad (page 147)
DINNER	One-Pot Mushroom Pappardelle (page 211) + Spring Garden Salad (page 140)	Chip-Crusted Baked Tenders (page 175) + Pizza Zucchini Gratin (page 230) + Salt and Vinegar Potatoes (page 237)	Spanakopita (page 199) + Pita-Style Flatbreads* (page 71)	Tropical Tofu Bowls (page 186)	Baked Crispy Cauliflower Sandwiches (page 165) + Okanagan Coleslaw (page 131)	Prawn Potstickers (page 123) + Chow Mein (page 179)	Coconut-Crusted Halibut (page 176) + Fraiche Fruit Salsa (page 120) + Cilantro Lime Rice (page 225)

FALL/WINTER

MEAL	MONDAY	TUESDAY	WEDNESDAY	THURSDAY	FRIDAY	SATURDAY	SUNDAY
BREAKFAST	Carrot Cake Breakfast Cookies* (page 35)	Jilly's Breakfast Sandwiches* (page 39)	Top Secret Granola* parfaits (page 54)	Carrot Cake Breakfast Cookies* (page 35)	Jilly's Breakfast Sandwiches** (page 39)	Piña Colada Sheet-Pan Pancakes (page 47)	Sheet-Pan Breakfast Pizza (page 36)
LUNCH	Lentil Soup* (page 151)	Tortilla Pie (page 203) (leftover)	Lentil Soup* (page 151)	Mediterranean Loaded Hummus (page 113) + Pita-Style Flatbreads* (page 71)	Vegan Mac and Cheeze (page 207)	Coconut Seafood Chowder (page 156) + Pull-Apart Garlic Bread Biscuits (page 87)	Autumn Beet Salad with Honey Mustard Dressing (page 139) + Goat Cheese Croquettes (page 135)
DINNER	Tortilla Pie (page 203)	Ginger "Beef" (page 181) + Sweet and Spicy Green Beans (page 221)	Butternut Squash Gyros (page 167)	Coconut Curry (page 185) + Cilantro Lime Rice (page 225) + Pita-Style Flatbreads* (page 71)	Mushroom French Dip Sandwiches (page 192)	Walnut Veggie "Ragu" with Rigatoni (page 208)	Fish Tacos (page 163)

*Make ahead on prep day

**Make ahead on prep day and freeze

A-to-Z Fruit and Veggie Freezer Guide

A lot of produce can be frozen to reduce food waste when you have extra on hand. Generally, the higher the water content, the more shape the veggie or fruit will lose when it is thawed. Some vegetables require a brief heat treatment, called blanching, to destroy the enzymes before freezing. Blanching vegetables by briefly submerging them in boiling water followed by an ice bath, helps keep them vibrant in colour and yields a superior texture for freezing and including in your favourite dishes. Here are our tried-and-true freezing tips for commonly used fruits and vegetables.

Note: A lot of leftovers freeze beautifully. Extra pasta sauce, smoothies (put them in ice-pop moulds for a fun and healthy treat), soups, and casseroles all freeze well and make for a convenient "fast food" when you're looking for a quick meal.

Apples: Either grate them and freeze in a resealable container for future baking or turn them into Applesauce (page 313) before freezing in individual containers.

Avocados: If you have avocados that are about to turn, simply pit, peel, chop, and freeze them on a baking sheet and store in the freezer in a resealable container to use in smoothies.

Bananas: Freeze bananas by peeling them and placing them whole or chopped on a baking sheet before storing them in a resealable container. You can also freeze bananas in their peel; just squeeze out the banana once thawed for use in muffins and quick breads (you will want to drain most of the liquid that comes out).

Berries: Frozen berries are easy to add to pancakes, waffles, and baking recipes. If that's not your jam, they are amazing when added to smoothies or made into a fruit pie or a crisp such as our Strawberry Vanilla Crisp (page 258). Speaking of jam, try using frozen berries to make your own no-fuss Chia Jam (page 310).

Broccoli: Frozen broccoli is simple to pull out of the freezer and steam. Simply cut broccoli into florets and blanch for 1 to 2 minutes before freezing on a baking sheet and storing in a resealable container.

Carrots: Sliced or diced frozen carrots can be used in many cooked recipes such as chili, soups, and stews. You can also grate them before freezing in a resealable container to use in baked goods like our Carrot Cake Breakfast Cookies (page 35).

Cauliflower: Cauliflower is great to have on hand to pull out of the freezer to steam for a quick and healthy side dish. You can also add it to smoothies! Just cut it into chunks and blanch before freezing on a baking sheet and storing in a resealable container. Frozen cauliflower can also be roasted with olive oil, salt, and pepper and puréed to add to soups or mashed potatoes.

Celery: Frozen sliced celery is great to use in soups. Since it is high in moisture, it will lose its shape when thawed and is best used in puréed or broth-based soups like our Lentil Soup (page 151).

Cherries: Pit cherries and spread them out on a baking sheet to freeze before placing in a resealable container in the freezer. Use them in smoothies, fruit crisps and crumbles, or our Okanagan Sangria (page 292).

Grapes: Freeze grapes whole for an instant summertime snack. You can also add them to smoothies.

Herbs: Our Ukrainian grandma never wasted fresh dill. Just chop it up and freeze it in a small resealable container to use when you need it. For other herbs such as basil, chop it up and mix with olive oil before freezing in ice cube trays. Store the cubes in a resealable bag to add to soups and pastas in a snap.

Kale: We love a good green smoothie in our house (see page 27), and keeping frozen kale on hand makes mornings so much easier! Simply wash and dry your kale and tear into smaller pieces before freezing on a baking sheet. Store in a resealable bag or make smoothie packs out of them with other frozen fruits and veggies. You can also add frozen kale to soups and pasta dishes for some extra greens.

Kiwi: Peel the kiwi fruit if desired (the skin is edible), cut it into chunks, and freeze in a resealable container for a quick addition to smoothies. Note that it will get mushy when thawed.

Lemons and Limes: You can freeze these whole, but they will get mushy when thawed (which is fine if you just want the juice!). We recommend zesting and juicing citrus first and freezing each separately. Freeze the juice in ice cube trays, and freeze the zest in a small resealable container for baking.

Lettuce: Don't freeze lettuce—it contains too much water. Same goes for cucumbers and other water-packed veggies.

Mushrooms: Clean and slice your mushrooms before freezing to make them easier to use in dishes like mushroom soup. Alternatively, you can blanch them first, which may extend their life. Mushrooms are very high in water so they will lose their texture once thawed but still make good additions to many cooked dishes.

Onions: You can simply chop up onions (any kind) and freeze them in a resealable container. Note that they will lose their shape and some texture once thawed, so you will want to use them in cooking rather than in recipes that use them raw. Though it's not a frozen option, try our Quick Pickled Red Onions (page 320) for another great way to use up extra onions.

Oranges: Peel and cut them up or keep in segments and freeze on a baking sheet to use in smoothies. Freeze zest separately in a small resealable container for baking.

Peaches, Nectarines, Apricots, and Plums: Simply remove the pits, cut the stone fruit into wedges, and freeze on a baking sheet before transferring to a resealable container or bag. Use them to make a fruit crisp or crumble or a pie such as our Rustic Fruit Galette (page 257) or add them to smoothies or Okanagan Sangria (page 292).

Peppers (Sweet): Frozen seeded and chopped sweet peppers make a great addition to sauces, pastas, and soups. Cut into halves or slices, blanch, freeze on a baking sheet, and store in a resealable container—or roast them with olive oil before freezing to increase the flavour. Since they are high in water, use them in cooked dishes such as soups, stews, and casseroles where it won't matter that they break down.

Pineapple: Cut off the skin and trim the ends, remove the eyes and core, cut it up, and freeze on a baking sheet before transferring to a resealable container. What a perfect addition to a smoothie or a Virgin Chi Chi (page 290)!

Potatoes: Waxy potatoes like yellow potatoes or even red potatoes freeze better than starchy varieties like russets. Peel, cut, and freeze on a baking sheet before transferring to a resealable container. Leftover roasted, boiled, and mashed potatoes tend to freeze well. *See also* Sweet Potatoes.

Spinach: You can either freeze raw spinach to add to smoothies or soups, or sauté or blanch it to freeze as cooked. Squeeze as much water as possible out of it once cooked or blanched, then freeze in a resealable container.

Squash: Winter squash such as butternut, acorn, and buttercup freeze well. Simply peel them, remove the seeds, and cut them into about 1-inch (2.5 cm) pieces to be used in soups and stews. Freeze on a baking sheet before transferring to a resealable container. *See also* Zucchini.

Sweet Potatoes: Peel, cube, and blanch for 2 to 3 minutes before freezing on a baking sheet and storing in a resealable container. You can also freeze cooked mashed sweet potatoes.

Tomatoes: Freeze whole or chopped tomatoes on a baking sheet and store in a resealable container for making pasta sauce or pizza sauce, or roast them from frozen for Sheet-Pan Tomato Sauce (page 314).

Zucchini: When it comes to freezing zucchini, it's best to grate it first if using it in baking. Just be sure to squeeze out most of the excess moisture once thawed. Frozen grated zucchini is amazing in baked goods like our incredible Double Chocolate Zucchini Bread (page 63). *See also* Squash.

Thank You

A giant thank you is owed to our incredible team for the hours and hours of tireless work that has gone into bringing this cookbook to life. To say that this was a group effort is an understatement, and what an incredible group it is. Each person brought a special gift to the very long process of creating this book. Our hearts are so full.

Thank you, Rachelle, for your beautiful photography and for being such a joy to work with. Your professional eye and magic touch for capturing the perfect moment and a great food shot was pivotal to the success of this cookbook.

To our editor, Andrea Magyar, and our agents, Tyler Evans and Meg Delaney: thank you for once again believing in us. Your support, kindness, and guidance throughout this process of publishing our second book has been so appreciated.

Shayna Lawrie, what can we say? You were there at every step of the way, keeping us all in line, working all kinds of extra hours, and going above and beyond to make sure that no detail was missed. We appreciate you and every minute you have put into this project. You pour so much of your heart into your work, and it really shows.

Shay Merritt, we are forever grateful for your talented eye and creative vision. Thank you for caring so much about every little detail and for the hours spent getting it all perfect. Your beautiful touch turns everything to gold.

To Brea, who has been with us now for both cookbooks, a huge thank you! You are a gem, and we couldn't imagine pulling it off without your help in the kitchen. Your willingness to get the job done, no matter how big or small, always smiling, means the world to us.

To Victoria Bannerman, who helped us get to the finish line with the countless hours of testing, editing, and eating her way through the recipes with such a valuable critical lens, thank you from the bottom of our hearts!

Victoria Heppell, thank you for your assistance on those busy shoot days; your laughter and talent in the kitchen were such a gift.

To each of our many recipe testers: we are so appreciative of the time you took to test our recipes and provide us with your honest feedback. We are so grateful!

To Sabrina Meherally from Pause and Effect, thank you for your honest and thoughtful insights and reflections in helping us create a cookbook with a respectful and inclusive lens, helping us honour our planet and the beautiful cultures within.

Of course, we can't forget our amazing families for letting us take over our kitchens during the shoot days and for taste-testing every single recipe flop and hit on repeat. That's one big task!

And last but certainly not least: Sandhill Winery, thank you for yet again supplying us with (much-needed) wine to pair with many of our dishes and to get us through those long photo-shoot days!

Index